TH
STREETS

Confessions of an undercover cop

LACHLAN McCULLOCH

SLY
Ink..

The Streets

Published in Australia by
Floradale Productions Pty Ltd and Sly Ink Pty Ltd
June 2006
Reprinted August 2006

Distributed wholesale by
Gary Allen Pty Ltd
9 Cooper Street
Smithfield, NSW
Telephone 02-9725 2933

The Streets
Confessions of an undercover cop
Lachlan McCulloch

ISBN 0 9775440 2 8

Cover design: R.T.J. Klinkhamer
Cover photograph by James Braund
jamesbraund@bigpond.com

The Street

Confessions of an
undercover cop

by Lachlan McCulloch

Dedication

To my father, Rob, who taught me
right from wrong and to my wife,
Bernadette, who made sure I
remembered the difference.

Foreword

I was a member of the Victoria Police for almost sixteen
years, working undercover and in the drug squad.
I loved (almost) every minute of it, but the most exciting
time for me was working around Fitzroy Street, St Kilda
– known as 'The Street'. It was never-ending, full-on
policing – every day was filled with drama, tragedy and
black humour.
This is a composite picture of my experiences and those of
my colleagues. Angus is a policeman who could have
worked in any major city in Australia. His partner,
Darren, is a mixture of every policeman and woman
I ever worked with.
These are the stories police tell each other when they think
no-one else is listening.
All the names and addresses used in this book are
fictitious, so don't bother sueing or I will deny it all.

Contents

the road to the street

'Never expect people to react
the way you think they will'

COPPERS see a lot of unhappy endings. Ambos, doctors
and nurses see bad shit, too, but mostly it's the cops who get
there first. Some have their own way of dealing with the
really bad stuff. Some never do.

I'll never forget the afternoon I was driving down Fitzroy
Street, St Kilda, with my partner Sandy, when a radio call
came over saying 'Shots fired in the vicinity of the St Kilda
Cafe.' We were close by. I screamed the car to a halt and
double-parked in front of the cafe. I walked towards the
front door, gun drawn.

As I got near the door I saw a small-time junkie crim
called Terry crawling along on his elbows inside the cafe
toward the doorway. Behind him were two trails of blood,
like tram tracks. The blood led back to where two slip-on
shoes were in front of the counter. They marked the spot
where Terry had been kneecapped a few seconds before.
Trouble was, it had been done with a shotgun at close range,
and it had almost blown his legs off.

Kneecapping is normally done with a pistol as a
gangster's payback. It's not meant to kill people. Only a

maniac would use a shotgun. Terry was blown out of his shoes, poor bastard.

Sandy grabbed the radio and called for an ambulance. The area was safe, as the offender had gone. I stopped Terry as he crawled through the tassels at the doorway and knelt down. He crawled onto my lap. He was becoming weaker by the second. He looked up into my face and whispered, 'Tank said I owed him eighty bucks, but that's shit. I paid him. I'm not a dog, but Tank's killed me.'

I squeezed his shoulder and said, 'You'll be right, I've got you, it's okay.'

He squeezed me back weakly and then he just seemed to tune out. There was less and less, then there was nothing. I held his lifeless head and looked at our reflection in the window. He had bled to death. There was nothing I could do. I hated him and all crooks like him, but in this brief moment we were brothers in the same senseless world.

Ambulance men took him from me. I put out an urgent 'Keep a look out for' and an 'Approach with caution' warning to all members about Tank, a local lunatic who had supposedly fought in Vietnam although no-one knew, or cared, if it was true.

I automatically 'crime scened' the area and looked for witnesses. I noticed someone look at the front of my shirt. It had Terry's bloody hand prints all over it. I immediately ripped it off and threw it in a rubbish bin, exposing my shoulder holster with speed loader and cuffs attached.

As I walked away from the bin I stopped and looked back at it. Suddenly, I realised what a cold-hearted, rotten thing I'd done. For a split-second I had actually been pissed off at the poor dead bastard for bleeding on me.

I wanted to reach back in the bin and get the shirt, as if that would somehow make it better. Then I thought: I'm a cop. I'm supposed to be a hard son-of-a-bitch. I walked a couple of shops away to a clothes store and bought another shirt. Why? Because I thought that's what a tough copper should do.

That night on the way home I stopped and ate a pizza with the lot and double anchovies. And I told myself, not for the first time, that if you can eat a pizza afterwards, everything must be all right. That it's just another day working The Street.

To this day whenever I see slip-on shoes I think of how peculiar Terry's pair looked that day on the floor in the cafe.

Anyway …

AS a young boy I cried during every episode of *Lassie* and *Kimba the White Lion*.

I get emotional about most things. I never had the makings of a hard-boiled copper, but being a round peg that didn't fit in the police department's square hole would prove to be a great advantage.

I went to a boys' private grammar school and left at the end of year eleven to do a variety of jobs, mostly selling one thing or another.

I sold cars, fishing tackle and even pine tree plantations. It turned out to be great training for a job I didn't know I even wanted.

I later sold myself, undercover. I found it easier than pine tree plantations. When you're undercover, first you have to sell yourself to the crooks and then sell them a story they'll believe.

If you're believed and accepted, you're in. The thing is, it's not acting. The minute you act, you're not real. When a crook asks you a question, looking for a real person, he must reach out and touch you, if there is nothing there, you're 'blown', but if he finds a real person, you're in. Cops are like school teachers. Nobody thinks they're real people. If you go undercover and give a bad act most crooks will see right through it. We can all pick a fake, but give them a real person and they are stuffed.

EACH year in my late teens my father bought me a plane ticket to anywhere I wanted to go. I mostly chose exotic fishing locations in Northern Australia.

I went fishing for two weeks at a fishing lodge in the Gulf of Carpentaria on my eighteenth birthday. For my nineteenth birthday I got a return ticket to London – originally for three months. At my going away party, I overheard my father tell my uncle that I wouldn't last ten minutes over there because I couldn't look after myself.

I stayed in Europe for twelve months. I travelled around; I coached tennis for a few months in England at the Harpendon Lawn Tennis Club, worked in hotels, drove around Europe for more than seven months and worked the rest to pay for it.

I bought a vehicle with another Aussie and a Kiwi – it cost us five hundred pounds – and after driving it for a year I paid a bloke twelve quid to tow it away.

I was never exposed to criminals in all my upbringing and had never met a police officer on duty until I was pulled up for speeding when I was about nineteen.

My opinion of policemen, back then, was they were basically arrogant arseholes … and now I'm sitting here after sixteen years in the job knowing that first impressions aren't always wrong.

With some great exceptions, I still think some of them can still be arrogant and, at times, arseholes. But now I think I know why they end up like that.

MY parents had a close friend they had known for many years. His name was Phil Watson and they'd met him in Queensland fifty years ago. He was a big Queensland policeman who would visit Victoria every few years and when he did, he came to our home. He didn't inspire me to join the job and I don't even remember him telling me old cop stories.

He died about twelve years ago. My parents told me he always thought that he was the reason I joined the job and I saw no reason to spoil his illusion.

He was a very large, very nice man, but I was never very close to him. I remember he came to my graduation at the Victoria Police Academy. That was the last time I ever remember speaking to him.

He said something like, 'Angus, just remember, always do the right thing.' I remember thinking that it was a ridiculous thing to say to a policeman. Now, I know exactly why he said it. It is always so easy in 'The Job' to do the wrong thing. But let's not get ahead of the story ...

The fact is, I never dreamt of being a policeman until I was about twenty-one when I met a guy at a party – a fancy dress turn in North Carlton. He was dressed as Clint Eastwood in some spaghetti western, wearing a heavy-knitted wool poncho, a cowboy hat and a beard.

He was the first cop I had ever really spoken to in a social way. He was a homicide cop and I asked him what it was

5

like. He said it was just fantastic. He drove fast cars, caught crooks and just generally had a ball.

I was hooked.

I made the decision and did a course on how to pass the entrance exam and ended up getting in. I walked into the Victoria Police Academy on the fourth of January, 1984. I did my five months there and I came just about last in my squad, thirty-ninth out of forty-one. Not a brilliant start – and a sign that as a copper, I was a bit different from most of the others.

At my thirtieth birthday I had about sixty guests, and only one was a copper. His name was Darren. We forged our friendship during the St Kilda days.

BEING an undercover operative throughout most of my career meant that I spent the whole time trying not to be a cop.

This meant that my whole demeanour was not one of a typical cop. The consequence was that for a lot of cops, I didn't really fit in. Many typical arrogant cops had no idea where I was coming from. I didn't play football and go to the pub after work with them. In many ways, I was a bit of an outsider.

What really fucked them was that I caught heaps of crooks. That's because I understood crooks. Real crooks could see through the 'Would be if they could be – I'm a legend' type of cop. Crooks knew they could buy them a few drinks – or, better still, get them a 'drink card' at a night club – and those cops would be in their pocket without them even knowing.

What crooks didn't like was cops who paid for their own drinks, or even bought them some. Cops that couldn't be given a head job by a prostitute while waiting for a bust to go down, couldn't be given a diamond ring for their girlfriend, or a stereo, a TV set or a new watch. Crooks hated not knowing where they stood – or, worse, knowing they stood as nothing but a crook, pure and simple. Maintaining the boundaries made the cop dangerous and totally unpredictable to them.

The typical arrogant 'cockheaded' detective got his information from crooks by befriending them, or trying to. For a lot of them it's cool to have crooks as friends and associates, and most crooks like the idea of knowing detectives, too. These cops can be heard to say, 'You don't find crooks sitting in church.' Whereas I say, crooks are crooks and cops are cops. There should be a difference. Too often there wasn't.

When a cop meets a crook, the crook must instantly know the difference. The difference between right and wrong and good and evil.

If the cop befriends the crook, the difference is lost, or at least blurred. Wrong becomes acceptable. The cop then finds that wrong can become valuable. Mostly the crook pays with information.

I preferred to get my information by fear. Not fear of personal violence, but fear of the professional detective, fear of me 'working' on them.

I found that crooks respected cops who would catch them lawfully, thus liking or respecting them for just doing the job. Deep down, most crooks would like to be detectives, or undercover cops. Crooks feared me 'setting them up' – not with fake evidence, but by organising a prostitute or another criminal to do a drug deal at a certain location, at a certain time with a certain crook, thus obtaining real evidence by arresting them in the middle of the deal. I would organise a straight-up pinch and that assured respect and assured fear – thus assuring good current information regarding current criminal activity.

Some cops would obtain information from crooks by threatening to set them up. Some cops might just pick up the crook in The Street, (after warnings to give them information or else) put them in the car and start singing 'Happy Birthday to you', then giving the crook a 'birthday present,' such as a quantity of drugs, drug-associated equipment such as scales or bags, then charging them with trafficking. This was commonly called 'loading up'.

IN my early days in the job I was directing traffic at the intersection of Swanston Street and Flinders Street outside the clocks. It's the biggest intersection in Melbourne. We had to turn the lights off during each peak hour period and control it by hand.

I was being abused by motorists all the time and it didn't take me long to get jack of it. The first time you do traffic duty it is terrifying – you are frightened, then you put your hand up to order people to stop and they do just that. You quickly learn you are The Man.

I remember waiting for certain motorists to indicate to me where they wanted to go, if they wanted to go straight ahead I would stop them and make them turn left or right. If they wanted to turn, I would make them go straight ahead.

I only did it because I could.

You would see some bloke in a suit looking at you like you were a pain in the neck and slowing them from getting where they wanted to go. They were the type I would make go the wrong way. I recall looking at my open hand (the palm with all fingers together) and thinking 'Christ, that's powerful.'

To a young policeman, the uniform is very powerful. I don't know why I have included this little story because it doesn't really make me look good. But it's the truth, and most cops know it in their hearts. I included it because it's part of a learning curve. When you get a fast car, you want to see how fast you can drive it; when you get a new golf driver, you want to see how far you can hit with it. When you leave the Police Academy you are given a uniform and power and you want to push against the limits to see how far you can go. In the end most police grow out of it.

But some don't.

VERY early on, about a week out of the Police Academy, I was working with an old senior constable when we got a radio message, 'We have been notified by the morgue that they have just identified a body, being one Stanley John Davis. He suicided off the Westgate Bridge last night. Please attend 15 Smith Street, Richmond, and notify next of kin, Ruth Davis.'

The senior constable said, 'Will this be your first death message?'

I went into vapour lock. My mouth went all dry and I could hardly breathe, I was so shocked at the thought of delivering a death message. We practised at the academy, but this was for real. I knew I would have to do it one day, but not in my worst nightmare did I think it would happen after only just one week on the road. My experienced partner gave me all the advice. Most of it was things like, 'Slowly lead up to it. First introduce yourself, then say you have bad news and slowly lead up to the fact that he has died. Take a deep breath – you'll be right.' I secretly hoped he would take pity on me and do it himself, but I knew it was going to be up to me.

We both walked up to the door. I knocked. A well-presented, middle aged women answered.

I said, 'Hello, I'm Constable Angus and ...'

She interrupted, saying 'What's the matter?'

She was full-on, right on top of me, and cut me off in the middle of my hastily-prepared speech.

I tried to gather my thoughts. 'Well,' she snapped, stopping me in my tracks again. 'Well, what is it?'

I said, 'Well, we um, got a message from the morgue.'

She said, 'The morgue?'

I thought, 'Shit, morgue is a bad word.'

She screamed, 'Morgue! You get a message from the morgue and you come here to my front door. Why?'

I said, 'Well, your husband is at the morgue.'

She said, 'My husband is at the morgue sending you a message to come here. What message?'

I was out of my depth and sinking faster than a Russian sub.

I looked at my partner and so did she. 'What is this bloke on about?' she asked.

The experienced senior connie was a picture or calmness and compassion. 'I'm sorry to inform you that your husband has passed away,' he said gently. 'He died last night.'

She didn't even draw breath. 'He didn't wreck the car, did he?' she said. 'It's a Subaru Liberty station wagon. Where is it?' It had never gone like that out at the academy. I stood there with my mouth open. I was in greater shock than she was, and definitely more emotional. It turned out that her husband had left her several months earlier and she had been trying to get the car from him ever since. I learnt a valuable lesson that day. Never use the word 'morgue' in a prepared speech leading up to a death message – and never expect people to react the way you think they will.

I WAS keen from the word go to become a detective. That's all I wanted to do – to be a detective and catch real crooks.

I became the first one in my squad to become a detective, three years and four months into The Job.

After leaving the academy I wanted to go to the busiest station I could. In those days trainees weren't allowed to go to St Kilda, so I transferred to the nearest place to St Kilda that would take me, which was Richmond. At that time the talk of the town was Dennis Allen, Peter Allen, Kath Pettingill, in fact the whole Pettingill family. They were probably the worst criminal family in Australia and later implicated in the murders of two young cops, Senior Constable Steven Tynan and Constable Damian Eyre, in Walsh Street.

Dennis was reporting twice a day for trafficking heroin and heaps of serious assault charges.

Kath was reporting daily for possessing a machine gun and heroin trafficking. Every shift you just drove around looking for taxis and movement in the Stephenson Street and Chestnut Street area where the Pettingills and Allens were selling drugs. We just had to pull over anybody driving in those streets that looked suspicious. Nearly every time they either had $90 to buy heroin or they had heroin in their possession that they had just bought.

They'd also take heaps of stolen goods and jewellery to

11

various places. They'd be in stolen cars at times. The fact is, the area around the Pettingills was just full of shit. Every shift you just caught crook after crook and the only thing that held you back was the time it took to process them. You could either lock them up and remand them or, if they gave you information, they got bail. It was like going to your favourite fishing spot: you rarely came home disappointed.

I RECALL as a trainee opening the front door to the Richmond Police Station for Kath Pettingill. I didn't know it was the woman who gave birth to most of the biggest crime family in Melbourne; I'd only been in the job a couple of days and as she walked up to the door, I just thought, 'Here's a lovely old lady'.

She was about fifty at the time, but she looked older. As I saw her coming, I'd just walked out of the station, so I stopped and held the door open for her.

She looked at me and said, 'What the fuck do you think you're doing?' Then she knocked on the window which is right next to the door (the station's still the same now) and a policeman in the watchhouse area opened it.

Kath then called to the police inside, 'have a look at this fuck'n bloke.' And I'll never forget, there were about three or four coppers peeping out of the window looking at me holding the door open, and I was just in shock.

I couldn't believe this old lady was swearing her head off and I couldn't understand why it was so interesting for everyone to come and look at me holding the door open.

She finished up by saying, 'Anyway, thanks love' and walked in to sign the bail book for heroin trafficking and possessing a machine gun.

I turned to my partner and said, 'What the fuck was that all about?' He just laughed and laughed and said to me, 'That's Kath Pettingill, mate – hop in the car and I'll tell you all about her.'

That was my very first meeting with Kath.

It's funny, you know. Nine years later I worked undercover and Kath introduced me to her son Trevor Pettingill and his associates. I sent sixteen of them to jail for a total of forty-two years, including Kath herself for nine months.

In the end I opened another door for her … a prison door. Thanks, love.

AFTER about two weeks at Richmond I was driving past a park and there was an old undercoat grey panel van pulled over on the side of the road with two people in it, so we pulled up behind them.

My partner asked me to check them while he ran the registration through D24.

I looked in the driver's door window. There was a young bloke, about twenty odd, with his back to me.

He was leaning over to the passenger side and in the passenger seat was a young girl of about fifteen, leaning back in the seat looking at the roof. The guy in the driver's seat was leaning over her and injecting a blood and heroin filled syringe into her eye.

Obviously he'd already sucked up blood into the syringe and then mixed the heroin with the blood as they do, prior to injecting it. That's why I was confronted with this blood-filled syringe being slowly plunged into the base of her eye.

I couldn't believe it and just froze – it felt like ages. I couldn't grab him because he had the needle in her eye and I was scared that I would cause her more damage and I was torn between grabbing him and not grabbing him.

Anyway, it felt like ages but it was probably only a few seconds. He finished plunging this bloody liquid into the base of her eye.

I reached in and grabbed the hand holding the syringe, knocking the syringe onto the floor of the vehicle. I put my left arm around his throat, my elbow under his chin and dragged him backwards out the driver's window onto the road.

I knelt on the back of his head, pushing his face into the roadway, and handcuffed him. I dragged him over to the grass by his hair; I couldn't hear him screaming. By this time my partner jumped out to see what was going on.

As for the girl in the passenger seat, the heroin had basically gone straight into her brain and she was unconscious. We carried her limp body onto the verge next to the park. Next thing two girls in a passing car pulled up, jumped out and asked if they could help. I said, 'No, no. Please get in your car and leave.' They explained to me that they were nurses and could actually help, so I asked them to check the girl.

A few minutes later the ambulance arrived and injected her with Narcan, which instantly reverses the effects of the heroin. Meanwhile, I wanted to kill the bloke who had done the injecting. I dragged him over to the back of the divisional van, but my partner grabbed me by the arm and said, 'hang on a second', so I let him go. I put him on the ground again and walked back to the car to talk to my partner.

He said, 'Listen, have a look' and he held up his watch. It was 2.50pm and our shift ended at 3pm. It was a Sunday,

7am to 3pm shift. He said, 'Come on, we've got ten minutes 'til we knock off – it's Sunday, for fuck's sake'. I said, 'What, after what he did?' Even in those days the charge was 'Introduce a Drug into the Body of Another.'

He directed me to uncuff the guy and let him go. I did what I was told, walked back to the car and sat there in total disbelief.

Letting him go was against everything I believed in. I lost track of what I was all about. I was there to fight crime, not finish work on time.

Fighting real crime was far more important than anyone's private life. I was there to protect the community. This was not a job, it was The Job. I was not there for the pay and to clock on and clock off. If I wanted that I would have worked in a factory.

I had been selected to protect and preserve life and property. To me, then, one of the perks of The Job was receiving a wage.

I truly believed. Letting him go was condoning everything I was against. To a young cop like me it was devastating.

I left my girlfriend and I didn't feel anything for anyone for a while. Of course, there were no psychologists to see back then. That would be a sign of weakness.

At around this time I remember saying to my girlfriend 'I don't love you – I don't love anything or anyone.' I was left with just me. You saw so much shit and grief it just left you numb.

Eventually, I must have got my act together and carried on. I truly believed that I could actually make a difference. It sounds corny, but I did. Now, more than sixteen years later, I feel like an angry little ant. If I hadn't investigated and charged crooks, they wouldn't have wanted to kill me. Then the barristers wouldn't have abused me in open court and my superiors wouldn't have hassled me for paperwork.

Maybe I should have been a time server. Maybe I should have looked at my watch more often and realised it was ten to three and nearly knock-off time. Now it's quarter to midnight. It's always later than you think.

I WAS driving down a side street in the divisional van in broad daylight in the back streets of Richmond. I stopped the van in the middle of a small street because to my right was a pathetic drug-fucked, twenty-four-year-old female, stuck half way through a window, her legs and arse sticking out, wiggling, feebly struggling to extricate herself.

I parked, stepped out of the police car in the tiny side street and walked through the front gate up to the legs.

I said: 'It's okay, it's the police. You can come with us, we'll look after you.' I had to look at the badge on my shoulder to make sure I was a cop and not a social worker.

We removed her backwards out of the window. You could see the lock had been forced. I left my business card under the front door for the owner to ring me.

The druggie in our custody was a sorry sight. Dirty, smelly, I reckon she would have been a real looker in her day. She was twenty-four, but looked a rough forty. She was slim, with pert breasts, but had the heroin look – a haggard face, old before its time. I remember thinking that the face reflects the truth: You can hide it in the body, but the face shows the sorrow and the damage of drugs.

She had the sallow, gaunt, pitiful face of impending death. I recall thinking if I lock her up, I can help her live a little bit longer. She didn't appreciate that though. She was on a one-way trip and no well-meaning young copper was going to stop it.

My partner and I laughed as we helped her out of her predicament. But it wasn't funny at all, it was desperately sad.

To me, we were all in the same game, all working together. It starts with the crooks. Back then cops always gave them a few extra charges so the solicitor would look good when a few charges had to be dropped, thus allowing the crook to plead guilty without losing face. Every child wins a prize.

They were all stupid crooks with no credibility whatsoever – heroin-addicted, low-life, petty shitheads.

But sometimes we would have fun with them. The black humour was the only thing that kept you sane. I was known to say: 'You are not obliged to say anything, anything you say will be grossly exaggerated and used in evidence against you. Do you understand that?'

Or 'You're not obliged to say nothing, and anything you don't say will be grossly exaggerated and used in evidence against you. Do you understand that?'

They would say, 'That's not fair.'

I'd say, 'It's not meant to be, it's the law.'

I'd say, 'You're nothing but a criminamle.'

They'd say, 'I'm not a criminamle.'

I'd say, 'You can't even say it properly.'

When you're bored, processing crooks for petty offences, you say and do silly things. I always tried to make being arrested by me a funny and memorable experience. Some crooks catch on and know that being arrested is all part of being a crook. Others remained shitty, and dreamed of meeting you off-duty in a dark lane.

I HAD been in The Job for about two days when I was given the important task of picking up dinner from the Chinese takeaway in Chinatown. It was night shift and dinner was about 3am.

I picked it up and found myself in the city driving a real police car. I was all by myself when I stopped the marked police car in the middle of the road at the very top of Bourke Street.

I looked down the hill towards The Mall. I turned the blue lights and both sirens on, then planted the foot and roared down Bourke Street. It was fantastic, as the shop windows reflected the blue lights back towards me and the sound was amplified by the concrete arcades. It felt good. Now I was a cop.

Around this time, a month or so out of the academy, I was on night shift when I drove down to the local 7/11 store. As I drove the marked police sedan into the car park, I noticed three hotted-up old Holden hot rods.

A dozen or so young bucks were milling around. They all looked at me as I quietly parked the cop car next to them. I walked in to the store and did the toughest thing I could think of. I purchased a large multi-coloured, multi-flavoured 'Slurpie', walked outside and stepped back into the car.

I put it in reverse, and did a burnout, completing what is commonly called a 'reverse donut' so that a black cloud of smoke engulfed the bucks. I paused long enough to smile at them.

I only did it because I could. The 'Superman Suit' (the blue uniform) sometimes does that to kids out of the academy. I didn't think I represented the law in the early days. I tended to think I was the law.

I HAVE always enjoyed the odd Slurpie. I was buying heroin as an undercover (as Lenny Rogers) for about four months from several criminals. The worst of them was called 'Stacker' because they said he used to stack up dead bodies.

Anyway, I had bought about $50,000 worth of heroin and speed from him, and he finally had to be arrested by the Special Operations Group after I bought him a Slurpie at a 7/11 store in Preston. We were both arrested at the time as part of the cunning plan.

Stacker had to be held in custody for several hours before he was interviewed, as I had to complete five 'buy busts' that day. (Buy busts are when you buy drugs or similar, then arrest all involved).

When Stacker was finally interviewed, he just said 'no comment' when questioned at length. Finally, the investigator played his ace, when he said, 'I now must inform you that Lenny Rogers is, in fact, an undercover policeman'.

Stacker thought about that for a moment and said, 'Well, he's fucked then isn't he?' To him I was a drug trafficker first and foremost. He could not even contemplate the fact that I was a police officer acting undercover to collect evidence against him. I have found that undercover operatives tend to totally embarrass the hell out of crooks, who think they are so smart. Can you imagine how embarrassing being caught by an undercover operative actually is? It could get them drummed out of the union.

Most crooks think they can pick an undercover a mile away. When someone is caught, everyone thinks they are idiots, so some crooks get very pissed off. In my experience it is then that the undercover operative could be in danger, as the crook has lost 'face'. The only way to get 'face' back is to get back at the undercover. The undercover operative can then become a target. This is amplified if Asian targets are involved, as they seem to relish revenge. Maybe it's part of their criminal culture or maybe they are just bad losers.

It is as if some crooks think that undercover work is unfair. They get their wires crossed. They think that because the undercover has got close to them that they have been betrayed. They react as if the undercover is one of them who has turned into an informer and not a policeman who has gathered evidence against them. They sell smack and kill people and yet they think an undercover has broken the rules.

Give me a break.

fair weather friends

'You'll have to harden up if you're
gonna stay in this job, mate'

WHEN I finally got the chance to transfer to St Kilda I felt right at home. My life as a private schoolboy was a distant memory until I ran into a childhood friend. Greg had gone to my primary school and we hadn't seen each other for about fourteen years. His father owned the Silver Q pool parlour in the main shopping centre of Oakleigh. My father had recently retired as the managing director of a large car manufacturing company.

We often played games together in the playground and Greg accidentally broke one of my front teeth playing British Bulldog. I couldn't clean my teeth without thinking of him.

We used to race small sticks down a creek at the back of my house. He was tough; when I got picked on by the older kids in school I remember Greg protecting me, because we were mates. Even at that stage we were from different worlds.

Anyway, Greg was now a chronic junkie. One day while I was working the divisional van, he decided to rob the Commonwealth Bank in Fitzroy Street, St Kilda.

He was now a short, angry little man covered in tattoos, with a nose that looked like it had been regularly punched over the years. Greg enlisted his prostitute girlfriend Leanne, who had blonde hair with a bright red streak through it; she came along to be 'lookout'.

Greg didn't have a gun or a knife, but he did have a paint spatula, which sort of looked like a knife if you were short sighted. I don't know if he wanted to rob the bank or paint it.

He made sure there were no cops about and walked into the bank. The branch was packed with customers, as it was lunch time. Greg had never worked a day in his life so he didn't realise that this was the bank's busiest time.

He needed money that minute so he didn't let the crowds worry him. He saw there were large queues in front of each teller, so he paused at the rear of one of them, then strode forward to commit his armed robbery. He shoved an old lady out of the way and pushed his paint spatula forward under his jacket, but he was so short the young teller couldn't see the bulge.

He said, 'Listen, I want …'

At that moment a large male (straight off a building site) standing in the queue decided that a little shitty-looking short arse wasn't going to push in and get served before him, so he leant forward, grabbed Greg by the back of the neck and said, 'I don't care what you want, you worm, wait your turn.'

This bloke then physically placed Greg at the back of the queue. The would-be-bandit was extremely embarrassed, he bent forward and looked out the glass door of the bank to make sure his 'lookout', not to mention girlfriend, hadn't seen what happened.

Reassured by the fact that she was still madly looking up and down the street, he changed his plans. He took a deep breath then tapped the shoulder of the guy standing in front of him and, while pushing the spatula forward under his jacket, quietly said, 'Give me all your money.'

The guy said, 'That's what I'm waiting for.' Greg hadn't worked out that if you wanted to rob a bank customer it would be better to wait until they had withdrawn their money.

The guy then produced $3.70 from his pocket and Greg grabbed it and ran out of the bank.

The bandit and his accomplice then ran off together, thus disclosing to all that Leanne was his lookout. The plan was for Leanne to just walk off, but the sight of Greg running was too much. She ran with him. You may have worked out by now that this couple were no Bonnie and Clyde.

I heard the 'Armed Robbery In Progress' call come over the radio. Their description followed. We knew immediately it was Leanne. Even in the freak show that was St Kilda there weren't too many blonde 'crows' with a red streak through their hair.

It was well-known to all St Kilda police that she would put out for the latest 'hot' crook in St Kilda for nothing.

We all knew she had been pounding Greg for about a week. People like Greg only lasted about a week because she earned $1000 a night. This often upset young crooks; being a pimp wasn't macho enough, and so they'd pull stupid armed robberies.

My partner and I arrested them within ten minutes, but I didn't want to interview him because we had grown up together. Greg kept on pleading with me to let him go; I just ignored him.

About a month later he was on remand, being held at the Prahran police station lock-up when I had about the tenth police officer come up to me and tell me that Greg was bragging to all the crooks and every copper he met that he grew up with me and we were the best of friends.

As I was a police officer and he was a heroin-addicted armed robber, albeit with a paint spatula, I thought it was time to have a chat.

One Sunday when it was very quiet and no other crooks could see me talking to him (for his sake) I arranged with the sergeant in charge at the time for me to go into his cell for a private chat.

I walked into his cell and he was really happy to see me. We shook hands.

His handshake was strong and firm; it was the sort of handshake that meant true mateship. My handshake was soft and sad, it made me feel guilty. I don't know why, because I hadn't done anything wrong. I was the law and he was well out of order.

I talked to him about how we grew up together and had been really good friends. Greg started recalling some old stories. Together we laughed and I fed him smokes.

I chewed a piece of toilet paper and threw it; it stuck on the lens of the video camera installed on the roof. The sergeant must have seen me throw it because no-one came into the cell.

I removed a small hip flask of Southern Comfort from my inside jacket pocket and handed it to Greg. Then came the hard part, as I tried to explain that we had taken different paths and that we were always from different worlds. I told him how I would always remember our friendship and I also explained that our friendship was over from that moment.

We shook hands overhand style. I shook it firmly and I squeezed his shoulder with my left hand. I truly meant it this time. I felt my lower lip quiver.

I started to walk out of the cell, opened the door and turned back to Greg. In a low, serious tone I said, 'Now don't ever mention my name again.'

He looked at me. That look made me feel like his last friend had just deserted him, but the truth was that he deserted himself when he got on the gear. Greg was already low on friends and he didn't need this. As I walked away from the cell I felt like I had just taken my dog to the vet and had it put down.

I have never seen or heard of Greg again. Leanne died of a heroin overdose about six months later.

A PARTICULAR cafe in St Kilda is the most well-known cafe in Victoria, if not Australia – not for cappuccinos but for for selling heroin. The cafe owners charged heroin traffickers $20 (pre-GST) an hour to sell heroin from their tables.

The owner of the cafe was losing so many spoons to heroin addicts – who used them to mix and inject heroin – that he drilled a small hole in the middle of each one. Not one of those spoons has ever been stolen since.

The cafe closed its doors for business for one minute as a sign of respect in remembrance of Leanne. This meant a lot to all the street kids and heroin-addicted prostitutes. It meant that you had been a somebody in a world of nobodies.

At Leanne's inquest it was discovered the caretaker in her hostel accommodation had made a statement disclosing the fact that he had sexual intercourse with her around 8am the morning she died.

Unfortunately, the State Coroner made a statement disclosing the fact that she had died of a heroin overdose about 10pm the night before.

Her dubious chastity was not safe, even in death. Her twin sister Simone, also a prostitute, had a very bad attitude towards police. She was foul mouthed, and could never come to terms with the fact that coppers charge people who commit crime because that's their job.

In the years afterwards, some officers were heard to say to Simone that her sister was a 'dead root.' This was not in the best taste, I thought.

In the St Kilda days, I can't recall meeting any criminals who weren't junkies. Armed robberies would go off at the end of most shifts during our changeover; especially later in the week when the banks had more money. Real armed robberies were happening all the time in the early 1980s – now they're a bit of a rarity.

I spent most of my time buying half-gram deals of heroin in Fitzroy Street, St Kilda. I would buy the heroin with one hand and put them in a headlock with the other. Literally. I loved those days. They moulded me as a copper and as a man. As Frank Sinatra said, 'If you can make it there you can make it anywhere.'

ONE Sunday morning, I was the watchhouse keeper. This means that you're in charge of the whole reception area and all the prisoners. You have to maintain the security, health and well-being of all prisoners as well as attend the watchhouse counter area.

At the time we had had a bit of a crackdown on the local street walkers, commonly known as 'crows'. So we had seven female prostitutes, three male drunks and a bloke on parking warrants in the cells.

The seven women were allowed to walk up and down the

whole walkway area, out of their cells. All the blokes were locked up in two cells. I started at 7am. At 7.05am I could hear the crows screaming out for cigarettes.

I opened the back door of the station and screamed at them to shut up. On doing this I noticed that one of them was holding up her t-shirt, exposing her rather large breasts.

This caused me to realise that smoking is not all that bad. I grabbed a packet of cigarettes from the prisoners' drawer and took the packet outside.

I found that after I handed the exposed breasts a cigarette, there were lots of other exposed breasts to give cigarettes to. Within an hour or so I would hear several girls screaming out 'watchhouse keeper, can I have a cigarette?' I looked outside and found all seven girls holding up their tops, pushing their breasts between the bars, screaming out for a smoke.

A short time later, Inspector Blaire walked into the watch house. Unfortunately, he was a deeply religious man. I was busy on the phone and he walked past me saying he was going to check the prisoners. I thought 'fine'. Then I realised too late that it wasn't fine at all.

I rushed out the back door to try to stop what was going to happen. It was too late.

He opened the door and walked towards the cells. Yep, you don't have to be told. They all lifted their tops, pushed their breasts through the bars and asked for a smoke.

Inspector Blair turned and looked at me. I looked at him, raising my eyebrows and smiling just a little in a desperate attempt to get him to see the funny side.

I truly believe he would have demoted me except for one thing – I was only a constable. It was in the days before you had to be politically correct. It was the crazy eighties; if that happened now you would be instantly dismissed and probably go to jail for extortion. I still think it was funny. On second thoughts, no, I don't.

WHILE working in undercover in St Kilda I found a new working girl, Sheree. She was a very large Maori with huge breasts. She was wearing a very short skimpy number and of course, like all of them, she was a heroin addict.

After speaking with her it became obvious that she was in fact a he. She said that she specialised in 'head jobs' to avoid embarrassing disclosures. My partner arrested her. We put her in the back of the van and drove her to the station. On entering the station we walked her past a policewoman called Jane.

Jane was the only policewoman on the shift so she volunteered to search Sheree. She could do it in the sergeant's office (as we could view the search through a gap in the curtains). Jane was very new in the job and very inexperienced. Sheree took her top off, exposing her large breasts, then she took her pants off. Jane could see something taped up to the inside of her left leg. Jane said loudly; 'What's that?'

Thinking that it was drugs. Jane called out, 'Angus, she's got something'.

My partner and I walked into the office. Jane pointed to the object. By this stage Sheree was undoing the tape. It wasn't only her boobs that were large – 'she' was a big-boned thing indeed. At this point a large penis fell down and hung between her legs. Jane screamed and said something about men in general and stormed out of the police station. As you can imagine transvestite prostitutes tape their penises back up between their legs to look and feel more feminine to the paying public. It was just another day in the office.

MARGARET was a chronic heroin addict who constantly swapped between street prostitution and house burglaries. One day, my partner, Darren, and I decided to check out who was staying at one of the cheap motels in Acland Street, St Kilda. It was always full of crooks.

As I entered the foyer I thought I saw Margaret enter a lift. I found the manager and asked him if I could see the 'booking in' file. I described Margaret and he told me he knew her by a different name. I asked him for the master keys and he gave them to me along with her room number.

I went upstairs without a warrant, of course. I always hated too much paperwork.

Darren and I listened at the door for a while. I could hear Margaret and some male talking about their latest crimes. We both entered, screaming, with guns drawn.

I put Margaret face down on the bed. When I entered the room she was standing over a small sink attempting to find a vein to inject a syringe that she had full of liquid heroin. The male was counting out cash on the bed. It didn't look good for them.

We handcuffed them both. There was stolen property piled up against the walls. On my radio I called for the divisional van to help take all the property and the crooks back to the station.

I picked up the syringe full of heroin and walked over to the sink and started to squirt it down the plug-hole, as we had enough evidence with the stolen property and the syringe was a health hazard for police.

Margaret didn't see it that way. She went absolutely berserk, screaming, 'What are you doing? Stop! How can you do that, you're wasting about $500 worth of somebody's property, you idiot.' She was serious. It was okay for her to steal property to buy the gear, but me getting rid of it was the crime of the century.

I WAS on the van in St Kilda when we found an elderly man in an old suit and tie. He was very drunk and abusive. He was sitting in a gutter abusing the world. I got out of the van and helped him to his feet. My partner grabbed him and started to drag him to the back of the van.

I told my partner to hang on a second. I asked the old guy how he was. He told me his best mate from the war had just died and he had been to the RSL for a few beers. He said it was his last mate in the world. He had none left. I asked him where he lived.

I helped him into the back of the van and put his seat belt on. I carefully started driving towards his home. My partner asked me where I was going. I said I was taking him home. My partner looked out the window, shaking his head. He wanted to take him back and put him in the cells.

I drove him home, got his keys and helped him into his home. My partner (an old senior constable) sat in the car. I undressed the old bloke and put him into bed. I referred to him as 'Digger'. I walked back out to the van and drove off. My partner said, 'You'll have to harden up if you're gunna stay in this job, mate.'

I just kept driving. I thought I won't stay in The Job if I have to harden up so much that I stick old soldiers in the cells for having a drink. Funny thing is, now I know he was right. You do have to 'harden up'. But there's no excuse for losing your compassion, and no value in it either.

the game

'Even petty crims were prepared
to brag if someone gave them the
chance. I gave them that chance.'

THE Street was full of drug addicts who committed burglaries, stole cars and pulled armed robberies to support their habits. Then there were the street drug traffickers, their suppliers, prostitutes and, at times, their pimps.

It was the place that drew the desperate, the drugged, the lonely, the lazy and the mentally damaged. It was a different world and it had different rules.

I believed the game was ours and they were merely bit players. They would come and go, but we would remain.

When you got victims of an assault, robbery, burglary or whatever, you always did a computer crime check on them. A lot of the time the victim had more prior convictions than the crook. More than once we were called to a well-known thief's house and he'd be screaming because he had been burgled. He was actually very upset and appeared shattered, poor thing. He couldn't get insurance – it's hard to insure hot gear. No matter how hard I tried he could never see the funny side.

This environment attracted keen young cops. It was fast-track learning. In those days it was so busy that only the keenest of cops would go there. For me, there was an adventure around every corner. If there wasn't, I made one happen. My colleagues often said I could make the simplest arrest complicated. I think this was due to the fact that I always looked beyond the obvious.

I didn't just catch crooks – 'catching' sounds as if they blundered into my path. I hunted them. I hunted humans in the way a big game hunter stalked wildlife, except I had right on my side. They were not a protected species. Most of them were vermin.

Years ago I told someone that I hunted people. I remember thinking it sounded terrible, but it was true. I called my quarry the players. The players would just go about their daily routine. I would come along and make an adventure out of their misfortune (their arrest). At no stage did I ever take what I did lightly – I just tried to make it fun. I never looked at it as a job, more an extreme sport with the possibility of real bullets and real blood. The community paid me to do it. Amazing.

IN the early days after I'd been through all my training, I put in for St Kilda at the first opportunity. I arrived there in early 1985 and worked what we call general duties, which was everything from watchhouse duty, working in the car, working the divisional van, handling warrants and files and doing different jobs within the uniform section.

When I started, I'd decided I wanted to be the very best uniform member I could be. This would stand me in good stead to work plainclothes and one day become a detective. The idea was I would catch the snakes so I could go up the ladder. So away I went.

I immediately tried to catch every crook I could possibly find. I was a blue whale and they were krill – I would just scoop them up as I swam past.

I talked to burglars, prostitutes and all the 'drug-fucked scum bags' – as we referred to them – to try to cultivate them as informers.

Everybody wanted to do full-time plainclothes. It was the next best thing to being a detective, and incredible fun. I had worked in uniform, on the van and so on, for about twelve months when I was selected to work special duties, meaning full time plainclothes.

I lived and breathed to catch crooks. I was chosen to be the only full-time plainclothes member. Every two weeks another two members would come on with me and the three of us would work with one or two detectives from St Kilda CIB.

We worked the streets, or more correctly, one street – Fitzroy Street – mostly chasing drug traffickers. Then there were the burglars, armed robbers, theft from and theft of motor cars and various street offences. We would work anywhere there was a crime trend.

Very early on I teamed up with a person who is now my best friend, Darren. He was a few months senior to me and had the same aspiration – to become a detective as soon as possible.

He didn't show much enthusiasm toward working undercover, whereas I spent every minute of the day learning everything I could about the criminal sub-culture so I could just slip into it unnoticed.

The only way I could do that was to attempt to understand how crooks thought and how they worked so I could get inside their minds. I took the old saying about knowing your enemy to heart, and for me it was not easy. I had gone to a private school and had a sheltered upbringing in a nice, clean suburb. I certainly had no contact with criminals or criminal types or any contact with police. So this whole world was new to me. I was a tourist and, as a tourist, I tried to see as much as I could as quickly as I could before the novelty wore off.

I decided to make the most of every criminal I caught. When I caught a crook for anything – burglars, shop stealers, druggies, anything at all – I would do what I used to call 'suck on them like a lollipop,' to learn everything I could about their world.

In those days we had no taped interviews so you would have to sit down and type out every word – every question I asked and every answer they gave. I was, and still am, a one-finger typist, so typing took a long time. I didn't mind. It gave us time to talk.

EARLY on, I arrested a young women for shoplifting. She was a heroin addict with prior convictions for prostitution and I took her back to the St Kilda police station for questioning.

While I was interviewing her, she complained how slow I was at typing. She informed me that she had been a secretary (pre-heroin addiction) and could type eighty words a minute.

I thought that was great, so I asked her if we could swap seats. She sat with her back to the door and I sat opposite in the 'crook's' chair. I put my feet up on the desk, lit a smoke, leaned back and continued asking her questions while she typed them, followed by her own answers.

My partner laughed, thinking anything that saved time and effort had to be a good idea. The boss of the police station came into the interview room to check on the 'prisoner'. Bosses always have to do that. Anyway, the boss yelled and screamed at me for not following 'police procedure'. He wasn't a great lateral thinker. Looking back, I don't think he was a great thinker at all.

One-finger typing would cause you to interview them for hours. Back then, the law stated you could interview someone for no more than six hours and I can assure you, every single person I interviewed got the full six hours. That allowed me not to befriend, but to get close to, and build up a professional relationship with, these criminals. I was fascinated by their world and, because I was interested and not bored, many would open up and talk.

One thing I knew how to do before I started in The Job was to catch fish. I treated crooks just like I would fish. To catch a certain type of fish you would have to understand where they would be at certain times and why they would be there. That way you could use the right bait and tackle to catch them.

Being basically a pretty jovial and enthusiastic person, I was always cracking jokes with the crooks. Mostly they understood they were under arrest because they were idiots and had made some stupid mistake. They would sit there feeling sorry for themselves and I would try to boost them up and make them feel as though they were somebody.

I'd do that by getting them to let me into their world – I would talk about how they had committed their crime, where they committed it, why they used drugs, how they used drugs, how they interacted with their drug suppliers and other criminals. I found throughout my career that no matter how basic, stupid and drug-addicted these people were, they were proud of their achievements. Even the most petty crims were proud they were able to commit crime and were prepared to brag if someone gave them the chance. I always gave them that chance for my own reasons.

When I spoke to someone caught in a house doing a burglary, the last thing I wanted to do was talk to them about that burglary. There was no great need, because we had the offender red-handed. I would ask them where they'd slept the night before the burglary, what time they woke up, what they did when they woke up, where they went, which way they travelled from wherever they slept to where they were arrested doing the burg.

I wouldn't particularly want to know why they did that particular burglary. I wanted to know why they didn't burgle the hundreds of other houses they may have driven or walked past.

I wanted to suck their brains out. When I caught crooks, by the time I'd finished with them I had either driven them completely mad or built up a rapport. Sometimes both.

During the time of their arrest, I'd try to make them feel like they had something to offer, and it mostly worked a treat. I used to be fascinated at how they could steal a car and intrigued as to why some houses would be better to burgle than others.

Forget the no comment interview. I found that if you gave these criminals the chance to talk about what they did, they jumped at it. I did this purely so I could understand why they committed certain crimes, what attitudes they had towards police and other people. Most crims knew the routine in a police station and were easily bored. I tried to make the experience more fun for them by cracking gags and showing some genuine interest. That meant that many of them didn't mind me and opened up enough that I could learn from them.

One bloke I arrested showed me how he could open a locked door with a piece of string and a block of wax. I don't think I should explain how it works but, trust me, it works.

TAKE a good crook named Felix as an example. He was a top crook and once even made the Australian Top Ten Most Wanted list. Heroin brought him back to earth with a crunch – smack was a great leveller in the underworld.

I arrested him for a pissy armed robbery once. I remember trying to tell my partner that Felix had been one of the very best burglars around but he wouldn't believe me.

Working plainclothes one day, much later, I had a few beers with Felix and he told me how he used to work.

One day he dressed in a dark blue delivery man type shirt and pants. He purchased two bicycle reflectors and some double-sided tape then stood across the road from a large store in Chapel Street, Prahran, that sold video recorders, TVs and electronic gear.

He watched as the young shop assistant left the store to buy lunch. As he was leaving, you could see him take the lunch order from the shop manager. It was a lovely, warm day and the manager stood at the front door waiting for the next customer. He was only going to get one … Felix.

Our man grabbed his mobile phone and looked at the shop sign. On the sign was the shop telephone number. As he pushed the send button to dial the number, he began to walk a large industrial trolley across Chapel Street toward the door of the shop. As he got close to the store he could hear the shop phone ringing.

Felix left the trolley outside. The front door had the typical laser beam across the entrance which sounded a buzzer as a customer walked through the doorway. But Felix was no customer. He had stuck a bicycle reflector onto his pants just above and on the outside of each knee. The reflectors were at the right height to reflect the laser beam back onto itself. The reflector on his left leg allowed him to enter the store, the one on his right leg allowed him to leave silently.

As Felix entered the store, he jammed the mobile phone against his ear by lifting his shoulder. The manager's office was out of sight of the entrance to the store. Felix started to ask the manager about the price of TVs and video recorders while he picked up six boxes containing the latest state-of-the-art recorders, casually placing them on his trolley.

After putting twelve or more recorders and putting them on his trolley, he silently walked out of the store, pushing his trolley down Chapel Street. Once safe, he thanked the manager for his assistance and ended the call.

Felix was smooth, all right. Before he started using.

I ONCE arrested a bad-arse robber by the name of Shane O'Brien. He was a very fit bastard. When he was on the run, he was extremely desperate and dangerous.

What helped him become catchable was the fact that he became a junkie. When he was not a junkie he was untouchable.

I had spoken to him a lot, but I had not seen him for a while. Anyway, I saw Shane walking out of the 'Caf' – the

St Kilda Cafe. I called out to him as he was crossing the road. He looked at me, recognised me and sprinted straight across the road. I ran after him through the traffic in Fitzroy Street.

He headed for a car and dived head first through the open rear driver's side window. He did this running full bore. If it had been an Olympic event, he would have got a perfect ten from the judges. It looked as if the window was open for this exact reason.

The car was facing towards me. It took off, heading right past me and I knew I should let him go because I knew I would find him again, but I got caught up in the stupidity of the chase.

It had been raining. I grabbed the driver's side mirror and window frame.

The driver and Shane weren't in the mood to stop, even with a copper hanging on for grim death. They started accelerating up the street, dragging me along the road.

I was screaming at them to stop, I grabbed my handcuffs off a piece of elastic hanging on my shoulder holster and with them clenched in my fist I smashed the driver's window.

The glass shattered and I fell onto the roadway. Luckily I didn't go under the wheels and when I stood up I saw the local District Detective Inspector's car being driven by a constable.

I dived into their car (through the door, not the window) and we drove after them, but they lost us quickly as the DDI would not let us drive very fast, which was typical.

I soon found out that O'Brien was 'hot'. He was wanted on six apprehension warrants for burglaries, armed robberies and several car chases. I had taken the rego number of the vehicle and I was in a hurry to raid the house where the car was registered.

This was mainly because the owner of the car was a crook by the name of Andrew Dee who had just been released from prison and was on parole for an armed robbery he'd committed four years earlier.

My mentor, a very experienced detective sergeant in charge of me at the time, said it would be best to relax and let the crooks think that we didn't know the rego.

If we raid the home quickly, O'Brien would probably not be home. We had to play him like a fish.

Although O'Brien knew he was hot, he fronted at the Melbourne Motor Show. He managed to get into an office and stole the keys to a white Lotus sports car – the model used by James Bond at the time.

It was a Saturday and the big day for the show. The place was packed with people, but he calmly got into the Lotus, started it, drove it off a turntable and out of the building.

He had waited for the moment when someone opened a side door for a delivery or something. He drove the car around Melbourne, especially St Kilda, for a few days. Several car chases later he had to dump it and escape on foot.

After two weeks it was decided that it was time to raid the Doncaster address that had come up when we checked on Dee. By this time O'Brien would feel very safe. When we did a raid in those days there was no bullet proof vests, and no 'tabards' (vests with the word POLICE on them). We just raided the place flashing our badges.

About seven of us arrived at the address. It was about 5.30am and the kitchen light was on. You could see someone walking around inside as we crept up to the door. When we were all in position, the sledgehammer man looked at the sergeant and the sergeant nodded his head.

He lined up the deadlock on the door and brought the hammer back over his right shoulder. At that moment the door opened from the inside and there was Dee, dressed in overalls, carrying his lunch box and about to go to work.

Someone 'racked' a shotgun cartridge into a pump action shotgun about an inch from his nose. The metallic racking sound of this weapon is devastating when you're looking down the barrel from the wrong end. Dee instantly dropped to his knees and was placed face down, without a sound. He knew the routine. He was no fool.

Gun drawn, I entered the hallway followed by my partner Darren, while two of our team, Ross and Sandra, went toward the kitchen area.

None of us said a word until I located a female stepping out of a shower off the hallway. I screamed 'Police! Get Down.' I knew that shouting this out would alert O'Brien, but it had to be done.

A female police officer following us up the hallway immediately took over the custody of the female while I continued. I entered the next room and there was O'Brien just starting to sit up in bed, his eyes half closed with sleep.

I dragged him out of bed and put him on the floor. I handcuffed his hands behind his back. He was naked except for a pair of jocks. He was still muscular for an addict. I said something about how good we were. He just mumbled.

He was lying face down in the middle of the floor while we started searching under the bed and inside the cupboards. As the two of us were searching, I glanced over at O'Brien, who had sat up a bit. I abused him for disobeying my instructions and put him back face down on the floor. Forcefully. At this stage the other officers were searching the rest of the house. I was searching a large cupboard near the door of the bedroom and Darren was searching the drawers in the bedside table.

I heard something and glanced over my right shoulder to see O'Brien get into the sitting position. As I began to say, 'I told you ...', he jumped to his feet and into the air, passing his handcuffs from behind his back under his feet to his front. It was a pretty good trick but I wasn't all that impressed at the time. As he landed I leaped towards him.

He smashed me in the chest with both of his hands clasped together, knocking me out of the doorway into Darren. As O'Brien sprinted out of the bedroom he grabbed a black beanie from a small table and ran into the hallway. I screamed, 'Stop!' but by this time it was more of a polite request than a demand. If I thought I was holding all the cards, then he had just produced another deck.

My yell caused Sandra to walk into the hallway and look toward our room. It was a bad move. O'Brien smashed her to the side of her head with both hands, sending her flying back.

As I got to the bedroom door, Darren and I crashed into each other, attempting to chase the nearly naked, handcuffed villain. At this stage O'Brien was almost at the front door. I screamed 'Stop him, he's getting away'. As I got to the door, O'Brien was well and truly out of the frontyard and running full bore up the street.

I chased him. As I got to the front gate O'Brien was just turning the corner out of the street, out of my sight. As I turned the corner about twenty metres behind him, I saw Ross. He was knocking the front of a large baton torch against the palm of his hand looking concerned and saying, 'Shit, I think he broke my torch, I think it's the bulb.' I could not see O'Brien anywhere.

I was annoyed that Ross still wasn't chasing the offender. I asked, 'Where is he?'

Ross said, 'It might just be that little flat wire thingum-myjig is squashed and not touching the battery.'

I said, 'Where's O'Brien?'

Ross said, 'He's just over that fence. He's not going anywhere, now.' I looked over a small fence and there was O'Brien … out cold, lying face down on a rose bush.

Fortunately, our man had run to where we had parked our cars before the raid. Ross had gone to the car to get a torch to search inside the roof and was able to clock him. Both of them got their lights turned off, you could say.

Next second the police helicopter, Air 490, came screaming over the rooftops and started hovering above the light pole next to us.

The loud speaker bellowed 'Police, don't move. Lay down on the footpath and put your hands on your heads.' The whole scene must have looked pretty bad to the police helicopter crew as we all looked very scruffy and our cars were all unmarked.

I managed to show my badge to the pilot without getting shot. I picked up O'Brien's black beanie that he had grabbed on the way out of the house. There were keys to a stolen car he had parked around the corner, and a quantity of heroin.

To this day I have no doubt that if Ross wasn't 'Eveready', O'Brien would have made it to his stolen car and would have got away.

We would have been in big shit as there is nothing worse

than losing a crook. Especially a good one. Especially when he's been handcuffed, hasn't got any clothes on and there's four cops and one of him. We would have all been charged with negligence. It looks really bad on your record.

An ambulance soon fixed up O'Brien. We took him back to the station and interviewed him for numerous armed robberies, car thefts, escapes and all sorts of things. He was a good crook – but a sore one.

O'Brien got out about three or four years later and I recall seeing him in Smith Street, Fitzroy, while I was working as a detective. I was by myself, making inquiries over some other matter. We had a bit of a chat and a laugh about old times and I asked him to the pub for a beer, my shout. So we had a few beers. He explained to me how he'd gone in prison.

We spoke about one of the armed robberies he'd done and he described to me in great detail what an adrenalin rush he got from a job.

He'd done an armed robbery on a Commonwealth Bank in Kew. He and his partner were driving around with sawn-off shotguns. He described driving down the road and deciding that the time was right to do it.

It was right around the change of the police shift, about 3pm, midweek or something. He described looking at his partner and shaking hands as they do, a sort of overhand shake. They nodded to each other, meaning 'This is it – let's go.'

He described pulling on his balaclava, adrenalin pumping through him. He said he'd used most drugs in his life but none of them was as good as putting on a 'bala', jumping out of a car double-parked outside a bank, and running in.

He'd run in screaming at the bank tellers to try to frighten the living shit out of them. His mate was a big bloke and a bit too scary because when he started screaming for everyone to lie down, a couple of the women bank tellers were so scared they weren't actually listening to what he was saying. He had to push them down because they were just sort of frozen with fear.

O'Brien said he tried to scare the hell out of them so they treated him seriously, but not scare them so much that they were hypnotised. The truth was he scared the shit out of me. O'Brien didn't have to act tough and never did. He just was.

He was very proud that he had enough balls to do an armed robbery, would you believe. It was interesting to try and understand people like him because they seem to treat the risk of getting caught as we would treat paying tax. Jail was the tax they had to pay for robbing people, if they got caught. We were the tax collectors, and we all understood the rules.

That's the difference between them and us. As a detective, committing a crime such as a shop theft would be a massive risk. If I got caught I would lose my career and probably my family, the respect of all my friends and it would destroy everything I had.

But for a crim it is just part of the deal. They may not like jail time, but it is not the end of the world. So when we investigate a crime and think they wouldn't do that because they could get caught or 'surely they're not using their real name' or 'it's got to be a stolen vehicle', or 'they wouldn't have done it in their own patch', or other similar comments that detectives make, we suddenly realise we're not dealing with Lex Luther here. They are not master criminals, most of them. They're big, bad kids with guns.

Everything I heard first hand told me I had to stop thinking like a copper and think like a crook. We were dealing with criminals who live that way day to day. People often say incorrectly 'he's not a good crook – he's got five pages of prior convictions.'

I believe that's wrong, because some of the very best crooks have five pages of prior convictions – but should have three hundred pages. They get caught and they learn and it makes a detective's job harder and harder each time they get caught.

Some learn the trade so well that although they may have been caught a few times when they were kids, the convictions dry up. It is not that they have gone straight, just that they have got smart.

never bite your sergeant's pastie

WHILE at St Kilda in the early stages, Darren and I watched a movie called *Supercop*. It was basically about two cops who join the force in New York and decide they're going to be detectives – and the best cops in the city.

One of their first jobs was directing traffic in the middle of New York. What they did, while off duty, but still carrying a badge, was to try their hand at working on drug dealers.

The movie was a true story, by the way – the opening sequence of this film shows the two detectives in real life – and we loved it. The movie had footage of one of the pair wearing a Batman T-shirt standing on a podium receiving valour awards for investigating and arresting massive drug dealers.

It cut back to when these two guys joined the police force and were best friends. They were catching so many crooks that they were eventually promoted. The movie ends with them on the podium getting these commendations. The good guys win and get the girl. Everyone lives happily ever after, except the crooks. Naturally, we thought that could be us.

We watched that movie several times and it looked good to

us. We decided we were going to be St Kilda's 'supercops'. We vowed that when we left St Kilda we would have made an impression on the community and the criminal class. We wanted to be feared by the criminals and, of course, respected by our superiors.

So we worked extremely hard and long hours. We did everything possible to cultivate informers and catch criminals. As it happened, we were quite successful. I don't know if we were as good as the two blokes from New York but we weren't bloody bad. And we did it without Hollywood scriptwriters helping us out of the tight spots.

I USED to go down The Street wearing this grey cotton jacket that I still have. Every time I went down there I wore it early in the shift. I'd walk the whole length of the street.

All the local crooks knew that every day there were plainclothes cops in the street who were either going to be on afternoon shift or morning shift. I made a point of wearing this jacket and walking from the top end of Fitzroy Street and sneaking around a little bit and pretending not to be too obvious, right down the length of Fitzroy Street. The word would soon be out that a plainclothes copper was sneaking about. Wearing a grey jacket, of course.

I'd then hide my jacket in the unmarked car, change my shirt and put on a different jacket, wear a cap and just completely change my clothing. I would then go in to try to sneak into a hotel or cafe and sit there for a while and let the street cool down.

One day it was great. Darren and I were having a drink in the Prince of Wales Hotel in the afternoon after walking the street in my grey jacket and then changing appearance. We were sitting at the bar having a beer. The barmaid was a transvestite who hadn't had the cut and tuck but had great big boobs and make-up all over the shop. She asked whether we lived locally and we said, 'Oh no, we're just travelling through.'

She just said, 'Well, be careful. There's an absolute prick of a copper out and about today. You'll know him, he's wearing this large cotton grey jacket.'

I asked, 'Who is he?'

She said, 'His name's Angus. Watch out – he's an absolute prick and he'll bust you for anything.'

So, we just sort of laughed. Afterwards, Darren punched me on the shoulder and said, 'You bastard.' I was really quite proud of being known enough to make it to the ears of the barmaid. I had a reputation, I had been noticed. It might not have been headlines but it was a start. Darren was quite jealous. We left the pub shortly afterward with Darren determined to receive similar notoriety.

Not long after we were both selected to be members of the District Support Group. We had an absolute ball. And they called it work.

This was about the end of 1986 and I was there for more than a year. Then I went through my exams and had enough arrest figures to attain the revered status of 'detective'. I became a qualified detective three years and ten months after joining the force, which was pretty quick, even in those days.

When I was training to become a detective, I had to 'do a board' and sit in front of three of my superiors. Everyone tended to have a very short haircut and turn up as though they had just left the academy. I'd had really long hair up until then, after eighteen months in plainclothes doing Special

Duties and District Support Group. I had to get it all shaved off back to a short back and sides, so I suddenly looked like the typical copper again.

But I still wanted to work undercover and looking like every other plod wasn't going to help. I went down and bought a wig, a long light brown one that went half way down my back. I then thought, 'How could I disguise my face?' So I used to fill my cheeks with toilet paper – tucking long rolled-up strips of it up under my upper and lower lips. That changed the whole shape of my face. It also changed my voice because I spoke with a lisp. Try it, you'll see what I mean.

I went and got an old green japara-type fishing jacket, stupid pants that were far too big, worn-out snow boots and a big floppy jumper under my jacket. I topped it off with an old canvas bag I used for fishing, which I filled up with empty bottles and rubbish. I would often stop and drink out of a half-empty cordial bottle which was about a two-litre size.

Every now and then I'd be walking down the street or wherever I was, and I'd open up my bag and pull out this massive cordial bottle and take a swig out of it. I really tried to look like the loser from hell – an absolute drop kick half a step away from lying in the gutter. Some would say it wasn't too hard.

I rubbed fat through my wig to make it look dirty, and the smell didn't do the disguise any harm either. Show me a dead-set street derelict and I'll show you someone you can smell from ten feet away. I found an old pair of square, thick clear glasses in a drawer of an old desk when I bought my first house.

When I put on the wig and the clothes I thought I looked

like a dog – a collie. So Dean Collie was born. I got all dressed up and into character and called Darren. I actually called him back to the office. I had been doing paperwork. Darren came in and wondered who the hell it was in the office. I showed him it was me. I asked, 'What do you think?' He thought it looked disgusting – in other words, it was sensational.

We thought we'd test it out on our sergeant. I went into the interview room and sat there on the wrong side of the interview table – the crook's side.

Darren rang up Angie, a policewoman who was with our sergeant, who was called Col. They were at Prahran picking up guns or something, and Darren called them back to the office. Darren told Col he'd just arrested an absolute loser trying to break into the police cars next to the DSG office.

This was a plainclothes office, with no police signs anywhere and all unmarked cars. Anyway, Darren explained away the fact I was missing by telling Col a porkie – that I'd had to go and pick up some paperwork or do some job that left him on his own.

Darren asked Col and Angie to come back quickly. When they arrived they marched straight into the interview room. Here I was, sitting at the table, the large fishing bag around my shoulder.

They looked at me dressed as Dean Collie and I couldn't see a flicker of recognition in their eyes, so I cringed away from them. Col said, 'Christ – what's in the bag?'

Darren said straight away, 'I got no idea. I haven't looked in it.'

Angie choked a bit at that one. 'You what?' she spluttered. 'You've arrested him and you haven't looked in that bag! He could have any bloody thing.' She went absolutely apeshit. Col gave Darren a disappointed look and said, 'For Christ's sake, get the bag off him and see what's in it.'

Darren said, 'I can't.' I started to enjoy myself and thought I had missed my calling and should have been an actor. I decided to start pushing the boundaries a bit.

I started screaming at them to leave me alone, saying, 'They're not your cars so why worry about it.' I was mumbling away. Col was eating a pastie and I jumped up and tried to grab a piece of his pastie.

Now, only a fool would get between Col and his late lunch. He stepped back, pulled his fist back just about to knock me out when Darren pushed me down in the seat and out of the punching line.

I sat back down again. I was keen on Col's pastie, but not a knuckle sandwich. I felt the chair start to fall, Angie stepped around in front of Darren and again started screaming to get the bloody bag off me to have a look in it, and I kept telling her that she wasn't going to look in my bag.

I watched Col to make sure that he didn't wind up a fair dinkum punch – I was enjoying myself, but I didn't want to end up with a wired jaw over a bit of fun.

I fell on my backside on the floor in the corner as the chair flipped. I reached across and pulled Angie's shoelace undone. Well, she's just screamed at the fact that I touched her.

Angie said, 'How dare you touch me.' She kicked me so hard you wouldn't believe, it took a heap of skin off my shin and just about dislocated my knee. I wasn't expecting it and I decided now was a good time to stop before she started to River Dance on my head. Not that I'd heard of River Dance at the time, but anyway.

With my right hand I brushed off my wig and glasses. I started spitting the toilet paper onto the floor, looked up at them. Angie completely lost it by this stage. 'This guy is a fucking lunatic! He's wearing a wig.' She went berserk.

Col was screaming to get the bag off me. But no-one seemed to notice that by this stage I had no disguise whatsoever. Angie shaped up to kick me again and I yelled, 'It's me, for Christ's sake. Relax, it's me.' I was backing up into the corner in real fear of receiving a beating.

It took them fair dinkum at least ten seconds to realise that they were actually looking at me. It was a long ten seconds because I was looking like a perfect candidate for an old-fashioned interview room flogging.

I looked at them and they just shook their heads in disbelief. I said, 'Now, do you reckon I could go down the street and buy some heroin?'

Col just shook his head and said, 'Angus, you could buy anything.' It did take them a little while to calm down because they were furious at me, and somewhat embarrassed. But then they all burst out laughing.

Dean Collie was born. He had passed the test and was allowed out in the public. I started to purchase a lot of small quantities of heroin.

What was funny was that I was able to buy heroin from traffickers that I'd already charged in the past. They knew me as Angus, but in this disguise they didn't recognise me.

You must remember that we weren't dealing with brain surgeons in Fitzroy Street – they were mostly drug addicts looking to score or rip someone off. And in any case, people everywhere see what they expect to see or what they want to see. Col and Angie had proved that. I stayed in dimly-lit spots on Fitzroy Street and I only ever came out at night. I could pick and choose. I would piss off the real dead-head street dealers and only buy and bust bigger dealers.

This worked really well until one bloke who I'd charged got bail. I was wired for sound so other cops were listening to what I was saying to these crooks. I had no high-tech equipment; I just carried a police radio in the back of my pants with an external microphone under my shirt.

I would push the radio button to transmit my conversation with the crooks to my partner. They could talk to me and tell me where they were, as I had a small ear piece covered by my hair. This wasn't state of the art but, hey, this was Fitzroy Street in its heyday.

I was wanting to buy heroin from a specific drug dealer. I had been after him for some time. Anyway, as I was trying to find him this drop kick of a dealer came up and wanted to sell me heroin. I said that I wasn't interested because I was waiting for someone and I knew their 'gear' (heroin) was top quality. This guy then became very abusive towards me.

He accused me of saying that his gear was shit. He then started threatening to punch my head in. He kept on and on trying to stand over me. Just when I would think I got rid of him he would be back.

He finally stated that if I didn't buy off him he would make sure I didn't buy off anyone. He then threatened to bash and rob me. He said something like this was 'his town'. How could this be? It was my town.

That was it. I decided to make his day and buy from him. I organised to buy off him in a side street that I knew we could cover. I did the deal, then slipped away to change. He was arrested – to put it mildly. Let's just say he hit the ground quite hard. Anyway, after we arrested him he learned the hard way he was in our town and he was just a tourist whose visa had run out. It is a sad world when you realise that you can't choose who you want to buy heroin from without being assaulted. Whatever happened to the customer always being right? Anyway, as it turned out, I was right … his heroin was nowhere near as good as my original target's.

IN those days we would specifically target any dealer who had the audacity to show off any wealth. If a dealer drove a sports car, wore expensive clothing or jewellery they were shitting in our face and soon regretted their vulgar displays of affluence, even if that came naturally to the sort of vermin who push heroin.

If they were waving a flag up and down The Street that said, 'I can beat the coppers,' they never lasted long.

I'd turn myself into Dean Collie once or twice a week. One night one of Dean's heroin trafficker victims who had got bail spotted me (as Dean) and got curious about certain things. In fact, he decided to interview me as to why he happened to get arrested seconds after selling me heroin.

The trouble was, he treated it like a real interview and started behaving like a real old-style detective. He started to attack me, and wouldn't take a backward step. At first it was verbally, then physically. He took to punching me in the head and kicking me.

I had a gun under my jacket, I had a large police radio tucked down the back of my pants and I had another tape recorder as well, plus all the other things. I had to be rescued by my cover crew. Then he was interviewed until he couldn't stand up. Various police to this day still comment on how funny it was to 'sit off' heroin traffickers selling heroin to 'Dean'. I used to say I was from Shepparton and I'd just come down because I'd just started using the 'gear'. I used to get a needle and constantly jab it in the same spot. I was going out with a nurse at the time who gave me this needle and I used to jab it in my arm and make what appeared to be a track mark. At times I would have to show my track to dealers.

A track mark is called just that because it is an exact needle mark that is used over and over again. It is used so much because it's an easy way to find the vein. It's used until that vein collapses due to it being polluted once or twice a day by powders that are allegedly heroin, speed or whatever, but usually have a lot of other shit in them that don't do the system much good.

To emulate the effects of drugs I would scratch my fake track mark and rub my eyes to make them red. I would even sniff water to try to give me a runny nose. All stuff that's indicative of heroin addicts. This allowed me to buy small quantities of heroin from street dealers without problems.

But nothing lasts forever and Dean had to retire for a while. But every now and again he was good for a comeback.

Later, when I was in the drug squad I would never pose as a heroin user. I graduated to being a drug supplier.

Users were to be spat upon and avoided at all costs. Heroin addicts in particular were dangerous. They were either planning to rob you or would lag you in to the police to get bail or cut down charges. There is nothing more dangerous to a drug trafficker than an addict.

I believe even cops come second.

a cunning plan

'I love it when everything goes like clockwork'

ONCE upon a time there was a team of the best, most enthusiastic, brightest and craziest young police officers from the big four police stations of St Kilda, Prahran, South Melbourne and Port Melbourne.

The members were all uniformed police who worked better out of uniform. In the old days they were called the Crime Cars, and then they went feral.

They were re-invented as District Support Groups and ours was called the Prahran DSG. Some of the funniest rogues and scallywags to ever don the blue discount suit passed through there. Gary Silk, who was later to be murdered in Moorabbin with Rod Miller, was an old Prahran DSG boy. He was a legend. They were great days.

I was selected as one the two St Kilda police representatives. I don't know if the bosses thought this was a promotion for me or if it was simply to get me out of their hair and make me someone else's problem.

We, of course, thought we were the best and the most experienced, as we were from the hardest and busiest station. All the other stations were only busy because they worked our borders. This is what we thought, anyway. To be honest, I still think it today, although St Kilda is not what it was in the late eighties, crime wise.

This period in my career was the ultimate in job satisfaction. I was doing plainclothes work in the best training ground Australia had to offer.

There were more drug traffickers, mostly heroin, per square inch than anywhere else in the southern hemisphere. At least, it seemed like it. I guess the cops in King's Cross and the red light district of Rio might reckon their patches have their moments, too.

It was a feeding frenzy. On top of all this, I was getting paid to do it. To catch crooks, that is. Catch them in the act, before the act, during the act or after the act. Many times, you were part of the act.

At times I had to pinch myself just to make sure it wasn't all a dream. I know police are supposed to be grim-faced when talking about the crime problem, but I'll let you into a secret that only other coppers know. This protecting the community stuff can be a hell of a lot fun.

I WENT to work one morning and found that no one really had any particular jobs to do that day – including me. I thought I would cook something up. The trouble was, the idea was only half baked when it popped out of my brain.

Over coffee in the main muster room I asked everyone if they could help me out on an arrest I wanted to make. The best part was that the boss was not in that day, so there were eight free plainclothes constables and senior constables to help me, with no bosses attached. The officer in charge of the plainclothes was only ever there to kick us up the arse when we stuffed up. Anyway, they all agreed to help, although some did roll their eyes and were obviously thinking 'What the hell am I getting myself into – again.'

I said, 'My briefing starts in two minutes in the conference room.' They rolled their eyes again ... there was no conference room. This was it. The room we were in was our office, conference room, mess room and muster room. There were only two other rooms, the interview room and the toilet – and there was often shit in both of them.

With less than two minutes to spare I realised now was the time to come up with my plan. I knew from experience that whatever plan I made now would not even be remotely similar to the end result. But it is always good to have a plan.

From stuff-ups in the past I knew I could always refer back to the original plan when I hit the shit later. Hence the fact that the 'plan' always looks good – no matter what really eventuated.

The motley bunch of what appeared to be society's misfits sat before me waiting with bated breath. Make that baited breath – they smelled as if they had been eating worms. They were picking their noses, sitting with their feet on seats, smoking, playing with a basketball, and one kept shooting a small crossbow (seized exhibit) into an old dart board on the wall.

Joe was telling Ross that girls love a bloke who can touch his nose with his tongue. Paul had a small, thick circular rope with about a dozen different padlocks attached. He was practising with his 'pick lock set' – picking open one pad lock at a time. We all called him 'Harry' after Harry Houdini.

But believe it or not they were not the deadbeat losers they seemed. They were all hand picked, the best of the best. Each chosen from their station as the 'most likely to become a detective', each one hoping to be one of the few that ever make the CIB. You could look at this group and see which ones wanted to be undercover operatives, which ones wanted to be straight detectives and those heading for an institution for the criminally insane.

Undercover operatives always have this ridiculous over-the-top image of themselves – until they learn to just be themselves. They are far more effective if they drop the act and become real people, then work will follow and they will be the chosen ones. Chosen, that is, by their bosses to work undercover. But that was in the future.

I stood before them and waited for complete silence. It worked for Hitler when he stood before his half-mad troops. Eventually I said, 'I have received information that an unknown male driving an unknown vehicle is going to deliver an unknown quantity of heroin to an unknown male living in an unknown flat situated at number 147 Steven Street, St Kilda.'

Paul looks at the person next to him and says in a loud voice 'Thank Christ he knows something, this job was starting to look bad there for a while.' He was the station comic.

I pushed on, 'I also know the approximate time of the said delivery.' I didn't want to be appear unprepared.

Sandy said, 'Day time, night time?'

I said, '10am. Yesterday I was a long way off on the railway line and through binoculars I observed a male person walk to the public phone box outside the flats, ten minutes later a late model silver Ford Sedan arrived, registration unknown. A male, approximately thirty, brown hair, black leather jacket, wearing dark sunglasses, left his vehicle and walked into the flats. Three minutes later he was out of there. My information is that he does this daily.'

I sounded as if I knew what I was talking about so I continued. 'To effect the arrest obtaining the maximum amount of evidence I have devised the following cunning plan. Directly opposite this block of flats is a large park. I have arranged two large St Kilda Council trucks equipped with council uniforms, ride-on mowers, whipper snippers, branch cutters and rakes. If you have a preference for particular pieces of equipment, please see me after the briefing.'

All great leaders going into battle choose their own transport. Rommel, Montgomery, Douglas MacArthur and Guy Gibson VC couldn't all be wrong, and I wasn't going to be different. 'I will have the three-speed, four-stroke ride-on lawn mower,' I said, getting in before the rush.

Paul said, 'You're good at cutting people's grass.' Who said vaudeville was dead?

I then began to point to a sketch on the white board behind me.

'This is the park area. It is about the size of six house blocks. Our police vehicles will be left at the council offices.

'Paul, Dick, Ross and Louie – you will be in the two tonne open back garbage truck. Paul, you are in charge.

'Darren, Sandy (the only girl) and I will be in the equipment truck. Our job will be to effect the arrest of the drug supplier upon his arrival at the front of the flats. Paul, your crew is to execute a drug warrant on the flat of the buyer immediately upon the arrest of the supplier.

'Within the buyer's flat there should be evidence of large-scale drug trafficking. He is believed to be selling an ounce of pure heroin per day.'

The maths of drug dealing in the 1980s were simple and frightening. An ounce of pure heroin diluted with glucose down to five per cent pure made a pound of street quality. There are 453 grams to a pound and half grams were selling for $90 each. That equals 906 half grams at $90 each ... a total of about $80,000 a day less the payment for the ounce of pure, which was about about twelve grand. That was a profit of about $68,000 tax-free per day. Now, in 2000, heroin is sold in major cities around Australia at around sixty per cent pure, and it is flooding in.

But that day we were just worried about catching this crew in the act. I told Paul: 'Within the flat there should be ample evidence of drug trafficking. There should be a minimum of over twelve thousand cash depending where he hides his profits, cutting agents such as glucodin sugar, a coffee grinder to cut and mix the rock heroin, and foils.'

'What we are looking for is evidence of unexplained wealth – cars, properties, gold and, of course, ostriches. For some reason drug dealers love buying ostriches. Anyway, at this stage are there any questions?'

Paul then decided he wanted to be a lecturer from detective training school when he grew up. 'How do you propose to identify the flat number and how do get a drug warrant for a flat when you don't know the number?'

I answered almost as though I had prepared for the question. 'I'm glad you asked that. Sandy, you are to, er, have a plan – I mean a pram. The pram that I am to get from, um, from the Alfred Hospital and you will be looking for a flat or something and will see the buyer go to the door of his flat, then I will write in the flat number ahead of the numbers 147, because I left a little space for that on the warrant.' Obviously I was making it up as I went along, and it was getting tiring. So I cut to the chase.

'Sorry, no more time for questions. Let's do it. We are all to be on channel 52. Good luck. Er, Ross, I know how you love gardening. Remember we're council workers. I don't want anyone working too hard out there. You'll blow our cover.'

So we drove down to the council office and picked up the two trucks containing all the equipment and council uniforms. I then got a short lecture from the boss in charge of all the equipment. The boss insisted that we keep working whilst in council uniform as he didn't want any complaints. I assured him that all would be okay, and we wouldn't tarnish the reputation of his outdoor staff who, as far as I knew, weren't exactly famous for setting any records in the manual labour department. I was always an optimist, and actually almost believed myself when I solemnly told him we'd keep up the good work against weeds and litter.

I drove the front truck and parked in the middle of the park. I acted as foreman, directing who was to do what. Just before arriving in the street, I dropped Sandy off.

Sandy was dressed in a tight-fitting tee shirt and jeans. I had managed to get a practice resuscitation doll as a baby to go with the pram from the local hospital.

Nothing ever costs a thing. When you're a plainclothes cop appealing for assistance people always help out. I always promise to tell them how the whole job finishes up. This is so they have a story to tell during their next dinner party.

Anyway, we all made jokes about who the baby looked

like. We all had a great laugh. Sandy embraced the role (and thought it was very funny) although she didn't seem to me to be quite the baby type. More the babe type.

So there we were. We unloaded the gear, and got started. I was driving the ride-on mower. Paul saw a large branch on a large gum tree and decided that it better be cut down before it fell on somebody's head. In other words, he wanted to use the chainsaw because we had one.

Sandy walked around the park pushing her pram. The most difficult part of her job was to avoid nosy mothers wanting to look at her baby. We got there around 9am. I asked Sandy when she was going to breastfeed. She just gave me a look that said, 'Not in your life time.'

At 10am I had finished driving around the park and had no more lawn to mow. So I dropped the blade down a bit and started to mow the park again. I gave it a Number One cut, shorter than a first week recruit at the academy. We were all starting to get bored when I suddenly saw the buyer walk out of the flats. I indicated to the others that it was him.

Sandy started to walk over to the front of the flats. This male had a good look at us and walked to the public phone box. He made a call and returned to the flats. Our main dealer should arrive with the heroin soon, according to our cunning plan.

As he was walking back to his flat, Sandy cut him off and asked him where an old girlfriend of hers might live. This buyer was happy to talk and started to tell her who lived in what flat. The end result was that while Sandy was knocking on another door she saw him enter flat seven. Her job was over. She walked back and said, 'Seven.'

I then gave Paul the flat number and he informed his crew.

I told everyone that we were right to go. In about ten minutes our target should arrive.

I grabbed a football out of my bag in the truck and we all started to play kick to kick. All except Sandy, of course. We were having a great time up until the local busybody decided she was going to act on behalf of all the ratepayers. She walked up to our group and demanded to speak to the boss. They pointed to me, which was generous of them. I walked up to her. At this moment we were standing in between the two trucks in the front of the park.

She abused me for wasting the ratepayers' money – words to the effect of 'I been watching you and your men for over an hour and you've done nothing. You're all poncing about wasting time and now you're playing football! What's your name? I'm reporting your behaviour.'

I said, 'I am Senior Council Worker Bartholomew Aardvark.'

At that moment a large silver Ford Sedan started turning into our street, driving straight toward our position. I then said in a loud voice, 'Okay, everyone. I want you all to get back to work now.'

My crew all got the message, looking at the silver Ford drive slowly toward us. We all walked to the rear of our trucks, but Mrs Windbag followed and said, 'Not before time. You haven't gone near the play area – there's rubbish everywhere.'

The silver Ford stopped just past the flats. As the driver stepped out of his vehicle Paul pulled out a sledge hammer from under rubbish, the others removed shotguns. They loaded, then strode across the road like the *Texas Rangers,* or maybe like the *Super Mario Brothers*.

I removed my .38 revolver from its shoulder holster and held it down by my side. Mrs Windbag just looked at us with her mouth open. She walked slowly away – backwards. It was a good move. I was getting tired of her.

Sandy casually reached down and removed a .38 revolver from beneath the baby doll in her pram. Darren, Sandy and I walked ahead up behind the male as he walked onto the footpath. I tripped and pushed him face first onto the concrete foot path next to a low brick fence.

The other two covered me from any danger that might come from the target or from behind. Within a couple of seconds he was cuffed, then began whinging and complaining, but you don't worry about a crook sooking up when you are on a raid. I would have given him something to complain about but we were a little busy to get involved with gratuitous violence at that stage.

I then heard the sound of crunching and crashing as flat seven was breached. There was the faint shouting of 'Police. Don't move!' I knew the job was right.

Then there was that terrible silent pause, that massive let down as you realise the arrest doesn't live up to the excitement leading up to it.

During that pause I looked up the street. I saw a large silver Ford Sedan commence a right hand turn into the street. I looked up at Darren and said, 'Quick, drop your gun alongside your leg. Sandy, kneel down and pretend you're helping this bloke'. This job was not over and maybe there was still fun to be had.

I looked down at my prisoner. His leather jacket was not leather. It was vinyl, and the sun glasses were cheap. As an insurance policy I whispered into this bloke's ear: 'Where do you live?' He stuttered, 'Fla-, Fla-, Fla-, Flat 2/147 S-s-s-s-steven Street, h-h-here.'

I turned my head slowly and channelled myself towards this new silver Ford driver. As I walked over to the roadway I could see that this driver matched everything I was looking for. I started to limp onto the road in front of the Ford. The driver was madly looking around trying to sum up the confusion before him.

We were all still wearing council safety jackets and council pants. I screamed out, 'There's been an accident Help, Help.' As I got to the driver's door I slipped out my .38 and pointed it at his head. As I did this Darren positioned himself in the best place for someone with a shotgun – the bonnet.

Darren pressed the shotgun against the windscreen at the driver's head – it really does get their attention. All the target could see was the barrel of the gun a few inches from his face. It must have looked like a bazooka at that range. He froze and stopped the car. He was no dummy.

I dragged him out the open driver's side window onto the roadway. I started to search him. Nothing. Then I pulled off his big high cowboy boots and a white rock the size of a golf ball wrapped in clear plastic fell out of his boot.

I called out something obvious like, 'It's him' or 'got him'.

Darren mumbled something like, 'Thank Christ for that.'

I stated a great rule of policing at that moment: 'The more people you arrest the more chance you've got of getting it right.' Eventually.

Then I let myself hear the first 'arrestee'. He was bleating about the whole situation. I walked up to him and thanked him warmly for assisting us arrest a big heroin dealer. At that moment Paul walked up, stating that there was a shitload of evidence in flat seven – $50,000 cash, scales, glucodin for cutting the heroin.

I was uncuffing the innocent man when Paul said something like, 'Hey cockhead, what's your name?' He could have been in public relations if he hadn't been a copper.

I said, 'Oh no, this gentleman helped us arrest that heroin dealer. Without his help we would have nothing. On behalf of the Victorian Police Force, the Chief Commissioner himself and the people of this fair state, I would like to thank you, sir.'

He opened his mouth several times as though he was going to say something but nothing came out. He looked like a fish out of water.

I stood the bloke up and brushed him down just like 'Maxwell Smart' would do. He was pleased to be alive and he thought being free was good too.

So he left. Well he didn't just leave, he sort of ran, tripping over twice at he went. There were no complaints though – I don't know why.

I parked his car properly as he ran into the distance. After all, they call that customer service. Later on, as we were leaving I saw him peeping around the corner to make sure we were gone before he returned home.

I was on a high at finally catching our target – I love it when everything goes like clockwork.

While Darren had the crook I started to search the brand new silver Ford Ghia sedan. While I searched it, the alarm went off. Darren asked the crook, let's call him Rudi, how to turn it off. Rudi stated that he needed to push the code into the code pad. I had a better idea and said, 'What, this one?'

and ripped it out of the dashboard and then tossed it to him with a wire hanging out of it. It landed quite near Rudi's head.

I disconnected the battery but the alarm continued because it had its own hidden battery. When we stripped the car we found $15,000 in cash hidden under the centre console. The drugs and money were photographed and placed in an exhibit log, naturally.

Moments later Paul arrived with his man. We took him (our prize) back to the station. I sat with him in the back seat of our vehicle while we drove. He didn't seem to be enjoying the trip.

I said to Darren, who was driving, 'Do you know what I hate most about drug traffickers?'

He said, 'They're blood sucking leeches?'

'No.'

'They're dirty, rotten filthy maggots that live off the misery of others, and lower than mouse shit.'

I said, 'Close, but no.'

Darren said, 'They smell?' He was getting desperate.

I then looked at Rudi straight in the face and said through my teeth, 'They don't pay tax.'

I then elbowed Rudi in the chest. It hurt him, causing him to bend forward.

I then whispered into his ear, 'Tax time.'

Darren thought about it and said, 'You're right, Angus, I hate that!' It was as though he had just realised that drug traffickers don't pay tax.

We interviewed them, remanded them in custody and went to the pub to celebrate. It was a great pinch.

Drug dealers doing business or just interacting with their

families are well dressed, arrogant, confident, smooth, standing tall with their shoulders back, and always 'cashed up'.

Money is power and they are loaded. They don't have to go to work every day or struggle to pay the mortgage. They want something, they buy it. Even some people who know what they do, somehow don't mind because, in a twisted way, they appear 'successful'.

But as soon as the cops catch them, they turn into slimy little insignificant weeds that can't even look in the mirror. No-one wants to know them. They drop their shoulders and lower their heads. They don't even like themselves. We remind them at every opportunity that they are bottom dwellers.

three little pigs

'You should have
opened the door'

I WAS driving down the road with Darren one morning when
we were working at the St Kilda District Support Group
plainclothes office.

We were stopped at a set of traffic lights when I noticed the
strong smell of marijuana. I traced the smell to an old Holden
station wagon upwind from our position. We pulled it over. I
told the driver he had a big problem as it was only 8.15am
and he was already smoking dope.

The bloke was stoned off his head but still managed to
drive. I pulled him over. The only grass he had left was in his
joint. We searched and found nothing.

While we were talking and searching I got into the front
seat and made myself comfortable. I lit up a normal smoke.
Darren jumped in the back and put his feet up. It was peak-
hour traffic and we needed a break.

It was obvious to anyone that we didn't want to bust him. I
asked the bloke if he could tell us who his supplier was. He
tried to put on a serious face and explain to me that he was
not an informer. He was not a brain surgeon either.

I decided I would take another approach.

I said, 'Listen mate, as you know I'm an undercover cop. We both are. Now I'm going to have to trust you.' I looked over my shoulders to make sure no-one was listening and said, 'I'm a choof head myself. Have you got any idea how hard it is to "get on" (buy grass) when you're an undercover cop? No-one wants to know ya.'

He said, 'What a bummer, man. No-one would like ya. Bummer.'

I said, 'I just want a choof, man, that's all I want. I don't want to bust people.'

He said, 'That's right, man, wake up in the morning and you're a nark. That's heavy shit, man. That's bad shit. You need a choof, I need a choof, hey.'

I said, 'Can you help me get some choof?'

He said, 'Yeah man, but I'm empty. Be nice to people, you need to mellow out. We better take my car, Ted knows my car.'

I said, 'I'll drive.' Then I added as an afterthought, 'Not that I don't trust ya.'

I pulled over and became Dean Collie. Choofhead could not believe his eyes. The average Angus became the classic doped out 'drop kick' Dean.

Choofhead had those far away eyes of a heavy dope user. His eyes kept closing, his head kept swaying around as though it didn't know where it should be. I drove, it was much safer. He then directed us to drive back in the direction he had just come. After a short drive he told me to pull over.

He said, 'Take the keys out.'

I took the keys out of the ignition. He took them from me. He said, 'See this key ring, it has the map of Australia on it. See the letters B.B.B.A.C and a little marijuana leaf in the middle of Australia? Well this is the key to the Be, Buy, Back, Australian Club It means, "Be Australian, Buy Australian and put it back into Australia Club." Cool eh? Ted thought of that.

'Now, all you have to do is come with me into that house right there and pay $20, and you're on. Ted will then give you the medallion and you can buy gear whenever you want between 9am and 5pm Monday to Friday. He has weekends off. Come in and meet Ted.'

I had no idea who Ted was or who was in the house. I said, 'Here's $20 for the medallion and $20 to buy me a "G" (gram).'

I walked with him to the house. There was a large security door that blocked off the verandah. Choofhead rang a bell and a man appeared through the front door. They exchanged money for drugs through a small spring loaded letter vent situated in the middle of the security door.

We then returned to the car and drove off. He was very happy with himself. He asked me if he could have some of the purchase. I refused, stating that I needed it more than him – which was quite true, as far as it went. I needed it for evidence. He reluctantly agreed. Then again, he had no choice. Darren and I drove Choofhead's car back to ours and said goodbye.

As two baby Supercops we were quite happy with ourselves. We drove back to the station and made all the usual checks on the address, electricity, rates, telephones and such. We found that the house was supposed to be a centre for wayward youths and the operator was a bloke, Edward (Ted) Smead, who had two prior convictions for possessing small amounts of marijuana.

A check of Smead's bank records revealed he had large

amounts of money in several accounts and was recorded as being involved in the import-export trade.

It was all coming together beautifully. We started the day having a chat with a choofhead and we would end it with a major bust.

We planned to raid the house later that afternoon, having obtained a search warrant issued under the Drugs Act based on Dean's observations of the drug purchase. We sent another couple of cops to go down and 'sit off' the house while we set up for the raid.

Those members contacted us a short time later. They'd seen several customers buying grass from the house every few minutes, and most of them were in their teens.

I decided to raid the house at 4pm as there would most likely be the best evidence. I guessed Ted wouldn't have been able to bank the money and he would still have some drugs in the house.

At the office I gave members their duties. I informed everyone that there were no problems expected as it was a normal house in a suburban street in East St Kilda.

I hand-picked the team for special duties – the biggest one got the sledgehammer, and the second biggest got the crowbar.

We had the crowbar to force open the security door and once it was open the sledgehammer would force open the front door.

I directed one crew to intercept a drug purchaser as he left the house. Once one was arrested I would give the signal to go. I was confident it would be a text-book raid.

We drove and parked not far away. When a radio call came that one of the dope buyers had been arrested away from the premises, I gave the signal. We parked our cars just down from the address and walked up to the house in a line – a bit like the *Texas Rangers*. The crowbar man was first, followed by the sledgehammer man, followed by me and four others.

As we stopped at the security door, two members walked to the back of the house to cut off any escape. Any person watching would have known we had obviously rehearsed our roles.

I looked at crowbar man and nodded. He then started to jemmy open the security door. He pushed the bar into a crack in between the door and its steel frame. He tried and tried but could not get the jaws of the jemmy deep enough into the crack.

After scratching away for what seemed forever I indicated to him to fall back and, defeated, he moved out of the way. I then nodded to the sledge hammer man on the tried and true belief that when science failed always use dumb force. He walked forward and measured where he was to strike.

Smash … smash … smash.

You could see him vibrate as each blow struck solid steel. It was now very obvious to anyone within one hundred metres what we were doing and I started screaming 'Police, police, don't move.'

The door was about to give way any second and we were already to burst in once it splintered. You could see the hammer man was getting angry at the door for not giving way.

Smash … smash … smash. Each smash was getting harder but then each blow started to get weaker. I then grabbed the hammer off him. He bent down gasping for air, as it was very hard work. I started to smash.

The front door inside the security door opened. Ted looked at us as if we were a pack of encyclopedia salesman. He casually said, 'What's your problem? Piss off.' Ted seemed to know something we didn't.

I said, 'Open the door now.'

Smash ... smash ... smash went the hammer.

Ted called out, 'You're scratching the paintwork, now piss off.' I was beginning to develop an intense dislike of Ted.

I then bent over gasping for air. One of the other troops came back and said, 'I've been all around the house, all the windows have heavy steel bars and the back door looks even stronger.'

I then asked the next bloke to start hitting the security door. Away he went, swinging like Jack O'Toole from the backmark on the *World of Sport* woodchop, but without the same results.

I had to admit defeat. There was no way we were going to get through this solid steel security door, let alone the front door. If Hitler's bunker had been as well made he wouldn't have had to top himself. He would have starved to death before the Russians got in.

The occupants inside the house started laughing away. I heard a female voice say out loud, 'Ted, I think there is someone at the door.' They all started laughing. I felt like the big bad wolf outside the house of bricks. The cops around me then started yelling abuse – I don't know if it was at Ted or me. This was a very bad situation.

The first thing that hit me was the fact that I had never heard of police not being able to get into a house. This one was a complete fortress.

Kids kept coming to the house to purchase. They would

then see us and disappear. Then it started. Darren and the rest of the troops started stirring me. 'Got any more bright ideas, Elliot Ness? Um, what was it? No problems expected, an ordinary suburban house.'

They all started to blame me for their embarrassment. I had no come back as I had not conducted any reconnaissance to check the target's security. I had taken it for granted that it was a normal house security door.

The front door opened. It was our Ted carrying a phone. He brought the phone to the security door and said, 'Here you are, my solicitor wants to talk to the boss. Is that you?'

He passed the phone through the letter slot. I put down the sledgehammer and took the phone. I had to bend down a bit to get the phone to my ear. I said, 'Hello, yes. This is Acting Sergeant Angus of the "I" District Support Group. Yes, yes, I can appreciate that but … yes, yes, I know your client has rights. Yes, but we have a warrant to search … drugs, yes. Well, he might want to make no comment but first he must let us in. Yes, okay, bye.'

I looked at Ted. He was standing about a foot from my face, within the security of his fortress. Smiling. It was a big smile. He made sure he smiled at all of us individually. He gave the biggest smile to me. I wanted to punch that smile right off his face.

He raised his eyebrows as though he wanted me to talk to him. I refused. I said, 'Come on, everyone, let's go.' I heard one of the crew say behind me, 'But.' I said, 'Let's go.'

We all left. We arrived like *Texas Rangers* and left like Brown's cows.

Ted called out, 'Bye, see you later. Come back soon.' Did I mention that I didn't like him?

Embarrassed was not the word. Personally embarrassed, professionally embarrassed, and emotionally embarrassed. We got back to the office with our tails between our legs.

As we walked in the front door, the boss said to me, 'What is going on? I've just had two newspapers on the phone to me about you harassing a youth drop-in centre in East St Kilda.'

I told him what happened. He said, 'What do you mean you couldn't get in? What are you, a pack of Avon ladies? I've never heard of cops not being able to get in.'

I said, 'Have now.'

This was juicy gossip, and I was the subject of it. The next day everyone in the entire police force knew that I had led the charge on a house and couldn't get in.

I conducted surveillance on the house again. The day after the failed raid he was back trafficking full bore with kids buying grass flat out through the front security door.

Ted would leave the house now and then but I didn't want him without the evidence within his home. Someone always remained in the house so he never had to carry keys with him when he left to buy smokes or something. I knew that because I had him searched. Nothing.

We all went out to the pub to commiserate and Darren and I had a ten-pot conference as to what we were to do next. We spoke about how Ted had gone to the media to try to stop us having another go.

He claimed we were persecuting him and that all he wanted to do was to help and support wayward youth. I still had a search warrant that was 'unexecuted.' I needed to rectify this situation – and quickly.

We needed the heavyweights and so we called in the boys who won't take no for an answer – The Special Operations

Group. They were briefed and were keen to pop in on Ted to say hello. Our motley crew were told to wait near the address until the SOG had done their thing. We were not to get in the way.

One of them went deftly into the frontyard, climbed the side fence and jumped onto the roof of the house. He then quietly removed four tiles and stood there.

He then signalled he was ready. He was to enter through the roof once we had breached the front door. Meanwhile another Soggie dug a hole down next to the toilet down pipe.

He then got ready to hit the pipe with an axe. Once the attempted entry began it was his job to cut the toilet down pipe and catch any drugs that the crooks may try and flush.

When they were ready the SOG turned up with their four-ton front door key, a specially designed crash truck.

One jumped out, grabbed a hook attached to a heavy chain from the rear of the truck and ran up to the security grille. Another ran up to the security grille and hit it twice with a large axe. The axe made a small hole in the grille right next to the main support. He placed the hook through the hole and around the main support. One then yelled, 'Clear, go!'

The chain took up the slack, the hook wrenched at the front grille area. The wheels spun. They reversed, right back until they hit a small low brick fence. The fence fell over. The single-fronted California bungalow held firm.

They accelerated full bore, this time with feeling. The chain was as tight as it could be without breaking, then the security grille gave way. It was attached to the cement and brick veranda and the veranda was attached to the front of the house. The front of the house was attached to the roof and both walls.

The whole front of the house came off and crashed onto the front garden. One copper on the roof fell off with a scream and fell harmlessly into a large bush. They breed them tough. It was a rose bush.

And I'd thought we were only going to pull the front security grille off to let the sledgehammer man try to smash the front door down.

But now I could see right through the house. Several troops ran into the house, grabbing the three occupants. Someone yelled to get out quickly.

As they staggered out the whole house started to collapse and, as they ran clear, the unsupported walls gave way under the weight of the roof. Moments later the whole house caved in with a crash.

I looked on in disbelief at the carnage and mayhem. Ted stood about three metres in front of me, handcuffed. Through the wreckage you could hear Ted's phone ringing. He was covered in white plaster. His face was one of shock and terror.

So was mine.

But as he looked at me I recalled the face he was wearing when he had smiled at me when we couldn't get in the first time. And my face took on the same sort of smirk.

I then gave each of the arrested occupants the same smile, individually wrapped for their enjoyment. I saved the biggest smile for Ted. I raised my eyebrows at Ted, expecting him to say something. He didn't. There was nothing to say.

Actions, as the saying goes, speak louder than words. It had taken a little while, but we had acted.

I stepped forward and tucked a copy of the search warrant into the front of his shirt. As I tucked it in I said, 'You should have opened the door.' I started to walk away. I looked at the wreckage, stopped, smiled, turned around and said slowly, 'No, on second thoughts, you shouldn't have.'

WHEN we searched the remains of the house, we found three small gram packets of grass.

Locating any drugs at all, even a little bit of grass, meant that the raid was justified and the cost of all damages was the responsibility of the owner and not the responsibility of the police force.

Many a beer has been drunk re-living this raid. I maintained we used 'reasonable force'. You're not supposed to 'shoot flies with shotguns,' as they say, but we did have the failed raid behind us to back the use of more serious force.

When the magistrate found Ted guilty of possessing and trafficking marijuana, he ordered he be placed on a good behaviour bond for twelve months.

The magistrate was aware of the failed raid. He had also seen photographs of the house after the warrant was marked 'Executed'. The magistrate frowned at me. He then gave me a small smile and left the court.

After the magistrate was out of sight I started to walk out. The clerk of courts walked up to me and said, 'Mr Angus, the magistrate asked me to inform you that your job is to bring them before the court and he is the one that decides the penalty, not you.'

I shrugged. The clerk added, 'He said, "That Angus is never going to die wondering is he? Tell him to keep up the good work".'

I said, 'Thanks. Can you tell him that I really just wanted to remove the front security door, but the door was connected to the verandah and the verandah was connected to the wall, and the … anyway.'

The house itself was insured for $110,000 … but not against police acting on a lawful warrant. No insurance. Ted lost the lot.

That was the end of the 'BE, BUY, BACK AUSTRALIAN CLUB.'

a cruel barb

'The dog thought it was Christmas.
His very own person to eat'

DARREN and I were working The Street in plain clothes when a call came over the radio of 'Offenders On'. The call stated that a neighbour had seen someone break into a house across the road in a side street. We decided to run there as it was only around the corner.

We got to the house and were the first coppers to arrive. I notified D24 that two plainclothes members were at the scene. I ran up to the front door and Darren ran around the back to cover the rear.

I knocked on the front door and found it was open. A man about thirty years old walked out of a bedroom into the hallway. I had obviously startled him.

I said, 'Hello, I'm Constable Angus. We had a report that someone had broken into this house.' I showed him my police badge and asked, 'Have you seen anyone?' He looked shocked and said, 'No, I am the owner and if someone came in I would know.'

Two marked police cars then stopped at the front of the house.

I said, 'Sorry to bother you, sir.'

I then called out to Darren that everything was fine. I stopped and turned back to the owner who had just started to walk back into the hallway.

I said, 'Excuse me, sir, may I have your name for our sheet.'

He said, 'Raymond Collins ' and closed the front door.

Darren walked back into the frontyard. I waved to the uniform cops that everything was all right. They got into their cars, as one member was getting in he called out, 'Are you going to reply to D24?'

I said, 'Yeah.'

I spoke into my portable police radio, 'DSG 300 to VKC.'

D24 replied, 'VKC to DSG 300, go ahead.'

I said, 'Your last at 17 Lord Street, St Kilda, all okay, N.O.D.' ('No offence detected.')

I walked out the front gate, stopped as though it was an afterthought, opened the letter box and grabbed three letters. They were all addressed 'Mr Stephen Frederick'. This was not good.

Darren had walked out of the yard onto the street. He stopped and looked back at me. I said, 'It's him.' Those words set off a sudden sound of running steps inside the house. I said, 'He saw me check the letter box.'

We both ran around the side of the house to the back yard just in time to see him jumping the back fence. I was ahead of Darren.

We chased him through several houses, crashing full bore into fences. I was doing well until I jumped a fence straight into a large wire clothes line that was attached to the other side of the fence. It acted like a net – the more I struggled the worse I was tangled. As I was struggling, I heard Darren get bailed up by a big dog. I had already run through that yard but that must have just woken up the old dog when Darren jumped into his patch.

The dog decided that his only bit of space in the world was not going to be used as a thoroughfare. The dog thought it was Christmas. His very own person to eat.

As I was still half suspended above the ground, upside down on the clothesline I heard a very loud scream of pain. It was so loud that even the dog stopped attacking Darren for a moment. I called out, 'Stop playing with the dog and catch that bastard.'

Darren said, 'I can't shoot a Shepherd.'

I got out of the clothes line and peeped back over the fence. My partner was hanging upside down from a low branch of a gum tree. The German Shepherd was jumping up trying to bite him. Meanwhile the terrible screaming continued. It wasn't Darren. As he looked relatively safe, providing he didn't drop from the tree, I decided to continue the chase. I jumped over two more fences and found the source of the screaming. By now it was more like an agonised whimper.

Before me was our burglar. There was a two-metre high wrought iron fence that ran along the side of an old large Victorian home. The fence was made from large vertical wrought iron bars about four inches apart. At the top of each bar was a thick moulded steel arrow head.

The arrow heads were meant to be blunt, but the fact that the owner of the house had run an angle grinder over each one and made them sharp. The top of each bar was now sharp – and rusty.

Our burglar had run up to the fence and placed the middle of his right palm on top of the arrow head. In his haste he had put all his weight on it, the arrow head had pushed through the fine bone and flesh exiting the back of his hand. He and the fence had become one.

He was standing on his tip toes in an attempt to take the weight off his right hand, his eyes were closed, his head back.

As I ran up to him I swiftly whipped my hand cuffs from a strap on my shoulder holster, grabbed his free left hand and hand-cuffed it to the iron fence. Then I proudly pronounced, 'Gotcha. You're not obliged to say or do anything and all that shit. You understand?' He said through the pain, 'You're sick.'

I turned and screamed out, 'Darren, I got him.' The crook managed to whisper, 'You didn't get me, you arsehole.' I really didn't care if he wanted to argue semantics. I was happy with the result. He wasn't.

Several uniform members then arrived. They all laughed, of course. We were all laughing. Some of the coppers were wincing at the thought of all that pain, but then again he was just a burglar. I explained to all the new arrivals that I had caught him. Among other things, the crook kept saying was 'You didn't catch me.' He didn't get the joke.

I grabbed a portable radio and called for an ambulance. The radio operator said, 'Is it a member or the offender, and what is the injury?'

I said, 'It's not serious, the offender has hurt himself.'

The offender seemed to disagree. 'Not serious! Hurt himself! HELP ME!'

It was funny because the crook started to call out for other people, members of the public, to come and help him. For some reason he didn't have confidence in the police members present. It was an insult. One of the uniform police stepped forward and offered him a bullet to bite on. Again everyone laughed – except the skewered suspect.

Someone said loud enough for the crook to hear, 'All that rust on the top of the arrow can't be good for you – you don't want that in your blood stream.' Cops laughed in the background.

A few minutes later an ambulance arrived. The two ambulance men looked at the victim, I mean the offender. By now he had lost interest in the debate. He was quietly sobbing. The boss ambulance man said, 'I can try and reduce his pain.'

The offender whimpered, 'Reduce the pain, reduce the pain.'

The ambo guy said, 'But I can't get him off the fence. You will have to call the fire brigade.'

The offender screamed, 'Call the fire brigade, reduce the pain!'

I requested the fire brigade to attend. Darren was talking to a girl or someone on his mobile phone, relaying the story. He just caught the words fire brigade. He said, 'Hey Angus, is he going to catch fire now?' I ignored him. How cruel to make fun of a man in pain.

While we were waiting, I began to explain to everyone how I caught this crook. This annoyed 'the crook' no end. It was quite obvious to all that the only person who caught the crook was himself. But he didn't get the joke. No sense of humour.

The fire brigade arrived and used an angle grinder to cut off the steel fence spike just below his impaled hand. By this time the owner arrived on the scene. He asked me why I put the bloke on the fence. It was a fair question, when you think about it. I told him that the crook did it himself, that he was a burglar I was chasing. The owner said, 'I thought by sharpening the spikes it might put a burglar off, you know, but I didn't think it would actually catch one.'

The owner of the house went inside and came out with a camera. He took a heap of photographs. The crook was not impressed, again.

The owner offered to give me some photos after he had them developed. He was having a great time.

After the fireman cut the fence spike, the owner said, right in front of the crook, 'When you get that out of his hand I want it back 'coz I might catch another one.' We all laughed like drains.

The ambulance man said, 'We will clean it up and get it back to you.' The owner said, 'The rustier the better.'

Throughout the whole incident, no matter now hard the crook tried to make the situation serious, he couldn't. I bumped into him years later in Collingwood. Only then could he laugh about that day. But not as much as I did.

no way out

'We're not the problem, mate,
and you're not the solution'

IN THE St Kilda days I recall I was looking for a prostitute named Cindy Chapman. Darren and I were in plainclothes and we looked like real shitheads. We were attached to the 'I' District Support Group. I had known Cindy for a couple of years. She was about twenty years old, bottle blonde, with a bubbly personality. She always acted happy in life and was typical of many young street prostitutes before it all caught up with them.

Being a heroin addict, she needed to prostitute herself to make money and, being young and attractive, she made lots of it. The more money she made the more heroin she could buy and use. Having 'track' marks on her arms made her ineligible to work in massage parlours, so the street it was. All she had now was her body.

She was the girlfriend of my old crook mate, Bones. Cindy lived in a shitty old room in a shitty old boarding house. Bones, her boyfriend, and her customers all used the same bed.

Anyway Darren and I decided to go and find Cindy as she might have been with our man Bones. We were after him for an armed robbery or something, or he could have just been a suspect for something. He was always doing something wrong so he was always worth finding. Anyway, we walked to the door of her room. Our guns were concealed in our shoulder holsters. I lifted up my right hand intending to knock politely. For some reason I decided to step back and just kick the door in. After I did, I stepped through the doorway and saw a naked man in the middle of getting his money's worth from Cindy.

This man got a hell of a fright, jumped off Cindy and jumped through a closed glass window. We were on the first floor of the four storey building. Directly below the window was the footpath of The Street.

Cindy and I casually looked at each other. While this man had been getting his money's worth, she had been lying on her back naked on the bed eating an apple.

This sex stuff obviously meant more to him than it did to her. The door being caved in and the customer diving out the window hardly got Cindy's attention.

She gave me a look that indicated that she was disappointed in my behaviour. It made me feel awkward. I rectified the situation by reaching out with my right hand and knocking on the already open broken door three times.

Cindy let her head fall back onto her pillow and smiled. She said, 'Come in.' I said, 'Thanks. Hello Cindy.' I felt it was important to uphold the polite social conventions no matter what the situation, a bit like the missionaries dealing with the natives in darkest Africa.

I walked across the room and looked out the broken window.

I said, 'Seen Bones?'

She said, 'He's out scoring. Should be back soon.'

I jerked my head towards the window where the jerk had launched himself into space. 'Do you have that effect on all your clients?' I asked.

She said, 'I wish I had that effect on you. He's just a mug. Must have thought you were going to rob him. He was probably right.' I smiled.

Being naked didn't worry Cindy. She calmly picked up all the mug's clothes, removed $90 for her service fee and $40 for the broken window. She then threw the clothes through the broken glass. The clothes landed on the bloodied naked man who was rolling around on the roadway trying to hold what appeared to be broken ankles.

Next to the bed was a small box with a little tabby kitten in it. Cindy picked up the kitten and said, 'Angus, you want a kitten?'

I said, 'I've just bought a house, I'd love one.'

She said, 'His name is "Indi" – Indiana Jones.'

I said, 'It would need to be.'

That was 1988, twelve years later I still had Indi. At the time of writing he has been run over four times, he has a large scar on his head which causes his right eye to be permanently open, his left front leg was amputated after our next door neighbour found him almost dead in their frontyard after he was hit by a car. He has half a tail after getting it caught in our side fence.

Maybe Indi should have been called Lucky, because he has used up about eight of his lives.

Cindy only had one. She was to die of a heroin overdose in May, 1989.

DARREN called in sick one day. I should have stayed indoors to do the paperwork, but I wasn't in the mood. In my unmarked car I drove down The Street and slowly went past the St Kilda Cafe and all the shops.

Then I saw Cindy, and accelerated up to her before skidding to a stop. I jumped out of the car, slamming the door, and strode up to her. The Street was packed. Cindy turned in time to see I was coming for her.

She tried to run but I cut her off, pushed her face first onto a rubbish bin and cuffed her.

I said, 'You're under arrest for conspiracy. You're not obliged to say anything, so shut up.' She went ape shit. She used words I'd never heard before. At least not that week.

I put her in the back seat. Meanwhile, several crooks gathered around started to protest about my behavior. They abused me all the way to the car. I sped off.

Cindy abused me, too. I turned and smiled at her and said, 'I thought I might rescue you from those dickheads. You feel like a drink?'

Cindy said, 'You going to pay for my rent, you arsehole? That mug I was with wanted me for an hour.' I threw her the cuff keys. She fiddled around in the back seat trying to undo the cuffs, and eventually managed it. She lit a smoke and climbed into the front seat. No problem in a short skirt.

She looked at me and smiled. 'How's Indi?' she asked.

I said, 'Off the planet, costing me a fortune.' She just smiled again.

We drove to a nice quiet hotel and had a few drinks. We spoke about different cops and different crooks. Most of our conversation was light and happy. At one stage it got a bit heavy.

I spoke to her about her childhood, which she said hadn't been happy.

I spent some time with Cindy. It was a nice break for both of us, for different reasons. A couple of hours later I took Cindy back and dropped her off near The Street. She went back to her world and I went back to mine.

Cindy respected me. Not because I was a copper. It was because I liked her company. She lived off her body. It was all she had left. She used to sort of flirt with me at times. I often thought it was because she was testing me, to see if I would indulge. When I didn't, it gave her a boost to think that someone liked her just because they liked her.

The look we gave each other said it all. No sex required.

ABOUT a month before Cindy died I found her sitting at a table in the St Kilda Cafe. I had gone in there looking for some idiot. Cindy saw me enter and stood up. She walked up and stood in front of me. Her cheeks, upper cheeks, chin, nose, eye lids, lips, neck and arms were covered in disgusting so-called 'love bites'. They were really purple welts. She looked as if she had been violated to the max. The sight of her made me feel sick.

I said, 'Who did that?'

She said, 'A couple of mugs.'

I reached out my right hand and touched her on the upper arm. A sort of feeble comforting gesture. I looked into her eyes and saw nothing but desperation and pain.

She was asking me for help without asking. How could I help her? I was not her pimp. I couldn't protect her. I couldn't get her off the heroin that caused her to prostitute herself in the first place.

I lowered my eyes, looked away. I felt ashamed, but I was not sure why. I thought it was because I couldn't help her. Then I thought it was because I was a male.

I stopped and wondered how cops can protect illegal prostitutes trying to make money to buy heroin. Unfortunately, whenever I think of Cindy I think of her covered in those bites, deliberately violated. When I look at Indi the cat, I often think of her.

A NEW solicitor came to St Kilda. We met in the foyer of our station. I said, 'Constable Angus of St Kilda Police' and he introduced himself as 'Simon Henderson of Henderson, Barker & Associates.'

I had arrested a street prostitute named Linda. Someone had seen me pick her up and called Simon to represent her. Linda and I knew she was guilty of the heinous crime of 'possess heroin.' I had been a cop for about three years and that made me an old hand. The new solicitor thought every one of his clients, including Linda, was innocent. The only innocent one was him.

In fact, the only thing Simon thought Linda was guilty of was being a victim of the police. The young lawyer came to The Street thinking the whole game was his. He was so wrong. I'd like to think it was ours, but what I did know for sure was that there were no rules. Simon instantly thought because he was a solicitor and I was a cop, he was superior. To me that was like a stone fish thinking it had it all over a shark.

The day after I met him, I heard a call come over the radio. The call was to attend at his new office. My partner and I attended and Simple Simon met us at the door. Totally embarrassed and obviously out of his depth, he showed me through to the rear of his office. He carefully opened a small toilet door.

There, sitting on the toilet, pants down, legs apart, was Linda. Eyes open, head back, tongue hanging out, saliva down her chin, needle hanging out of her inner right arm. Overdosed on heroin. Obviously guilty and very dead.

I turned to the new smartarse solicitor and said, 'We're not the problem, mate, and you're not the solution.'

Several months later I was interviewing a crook. This crook was desperately trying to give me information so as I would be inclined to allow him bail.

While he was trying to sell his mother, he told me he had committed a large burglary on a liquor store in Prahran. We were talking about how pissed he got when he let drop that he had given his solicitor six bottles of Grange Hermitage in lieu of payment for his legal representation. The crook stated that his solicitor had put them on a shelf in his office.

The perfect part of this story was that his solicitor was Simon Henderson. And they reckon only coppers are always looking for a drink. This was great. I decided to keep this information for a rainy day, as you would.

wrestling with
the drug problem

'This is better than sex, the hunt'

THE great thing about working plainclothes in St Kilda is that the bosses gave as a bit of a free hand. We weren't burdened down with too many instructions. We were told to get out amongst it. We weren't given specific targets – we just had to go out and get figures.

We targeted whoever we wanted. We targeted the drug dealers. Most coppers went out and got the users and the odd street offender, but it took hard work and time to catch the dealers.

Now, I want to stress that this time was about the best time of my fifteen years in the Police Force. This was the ultimate – we could go out and do what we wanted – when and how we wanted to do it.

I think that heroin traffickers are one of the worst and lowest form of criminal filth. They actively go out and destroy lives and kill people – kill people quickly by deliberately overdosing them and kill people slowly by addicting them. And they just do it for profit, pure greed. I loved to hunt them. It was fun and we were doing good at the same time. Anyway, back to the scene of the crime …

On this particular day we chose to hunt in The Street. We were equipped with our portable radios, guns, cuffs and plainclothes – of course.

I had obtained keys to a large building directly across the road from the St Kilda Cafe. As I have said, the 'Caf' was then the meeting place and the centre of all heroin trafficking in the St Kilda area. It was to drug dealers what the RSL was to old soldiers.

We climbed up the stairs up the back of the building and, using the key I had got from the owners, opened up a door leading to the roof. We crawled flat on our stomachs along the roof to the very edge.

If this job had been in summer we would have been stuffed because there was a line of trees blocking our view, but, being the middle of winter, all the leaves had gone and we could see through the bare branches.

Looking over that edge onto The Street I felt like a kid in a lolly shop. There were so many targets slinking around attempting to hide amongst the 'Joe Citizens'. The crooks tried to blend in with the squareheads, but they always stood out.

I loved to read The Street and see what was happening. It was like looking into a mountain stream and seeing trout hiding in their natural habitat.

I would look at and separate the 'Joe Citizens', the drug users (buyers), the drug traffickers that trafficked purely for the purpose of using themselves (i.e. if they sell four foils of heroin, their dealer gives them one free) and the real target, the greedy blood-sucking parasite known as the non-drug using profiteer.

It was from here we could identify our gallery of targets.

I prided myself on being able to pick them out but there was one that any fool could see. We called him Fat Tony.

He was a very porky pig-faced heroin trafficker and he looked totally out of place. He was in fact an ex-manager and chef of a major restaurant in Prahran who found there was more money in smack than fine dining. He spoke very well and considered himself smarter that everyone.

He came across as being very well-educated and he had a big gold tooth that was always visible due to his incessant sickly smile. Chefs' hours were obviously too long, traffickers' hours were much more reasonable. The profits were much greater and tax free, too.

He had as much class as a fat rat with a gold tooth.

I asked Darren to refresh my memory. 'Didn't we ban him from St Kilda?' I asked.

We had. But there he was, as large as life, walking down Fitzroy Street as if he owned it when, in fact, we did. He turned straight into the fun parlour next door to the St Kilda Cafe. This was an amusement parlour where certain traffickers were known to operate from.

Try as we could in the past we had been unable to charge Fat Tony with trafficking and that pissed us off. Tubs of lard that sell smack should not be able to beat Victoria's Finest.

We'd tried to get prostitutes to purchase smack from him and set him up. We'd tried surveillance of the amusement parlour and using an undercover operative.

I tried every single thing I could think of, including a hidden camera across the road. But there was no way we could get evidence of Tony trafficking.

What he did was traffic from within the amusement parlour so that he could get behind the counter or out the back. He had the heroin hidden in his mouth at times or hidden in the parlour. If we had raided it we would have found a quantity of heroin in the public area under or in one of the many pin-ball machines. We could never prove that it was Fat Tony's.

While we sat on the roof I could feel the beginning of a cunning plan start to form in my cunning head. I loved it when that happened.

The answer was dressed in a big brown leather jacket and jeans (let's call him 'Jacket Man'). He walked nervously up to the entrance of Tony's lair. He saw Tony inside, walked in and about a minute later Jacket Man and Fat Tony appeared at the entrance.

Jacket Man lifted his left arm and pointed to his watch with his right hand. Tony put his arm on Jacket Man's back as though to say, 'trust me, everything will be okay'. They both nodded.

I didn't need a listening device to known what was going on. I interpreted their actions as Tony telling Jacket Man to come back in a few minutes to buy the gear.

Face down, lying on the roof, I smirked at Darren, a look he had seen many times before. 'Don't do it to me,' he said. 'Every one of your brilliant plans turns out to be life threatening, illegal, or both.'

I know that Darren was only joking (I think) and that he actually loved it when the game was afoot. I quickly turned and started to crawl off the roof to the stairwell. Darren followed – a tad reluctantly, I thought.

As we started running down four flights of stairs I heard him yelling at me: 'I hope you've thought this plan all the way through.' He was such a worry-wart. I knew I had to beef up his confidence so I yelled back, 'I've got the first part down pat – we'll just have to ad-lib it from there.'

My long-suffering partner responded: 'Plan's good, ad-lib's bad.'

I was beginning to think he was a pessimist.

We burst out the back of the building so the crooks would never know where we were concealed, hit the back street and kept running. As we did that we passed our unmarked police car.

I puffed to Darren; 'Mate, take the car – he's headed towards Dalgety Street, I'll meet you there – we need him.' I kept running. As far as I could work out, all was going beautifully.

As I arrived in The Street, I spotted Jacket Man turning up a laneway. I stopped running and tried to look casual, walking through the traffic as fast as I could without making too much of a fuss.

I didn't want Jacket Man to see me coming. As I got close to him in the laneway he turned around, realised I was probably a Jack (slang for copper, which is slang for police officer) and started to run. I chased him down onto the roadway as Darren pulled our car up next to us. Jacket Man started screaming, 'I've done nothing!' Why do they always do that?

I informed him that I was going to search him under the Drugs Act for drugs. He said, 'I haven't got any fucking drugs.' He went right off the planet as I began to search his pockets. In his front right hand pocket were five $20 notes. As it happened, $100 was the going price for half a gram of heroin on the streets of St Kilda at the time. Now it is much cheaper, but that is another sad story. He told me his name and other details on request. I looked at Darren and said, 'Can you watch him?' Darren took custody of him while I walked back to our unit to check his current criminal status and see if he was wanted on any outstanding warrants.

I had the $100 with me when I went back to the car. I sat in the car checking out his record, then walked back to Jacket Man and said, 'There are some warrants, you're under arrest.'

I then told Darren to hang on.

I ran back to the cop car and listened to the radio – the crook was too far away to earwig so he couldn't hear. I came back to the crook with a sour face and said, 'This is your lucky day – just go. Darren – armed robbery in progress Carlisle Street, East St Kilda.' I threw the $100 at Leather Man who picked it up and scurried off.

We ran back to the car and Darren did a huge 'burn out' into another side street. We screeched into Acland Street, then Barkly Street, just missing several cars. More method acting at its finest – or so I thought.

I said, 'Okay, that's far enough. Stop.'

Darren looked sideways at me and said, 'But, we're nearly there.'

I quickly confessed, 'Stop, I made it up, drive back to the building we have to see what happens next, quick.'

Darren said, 'What about the armed rob?'

I don't think he was listening. 'Look, I made it up. Just get back, we have to see their next move.'

Darren said, 'Angus, what are you doing?'

I said, 'What we always do, follow the buyer, let the buyer take us to Fat Tony.'

Darren drove to The Street, and parked behind the building

where we first conducting the surveillance. Darren was still shaking his head. I had seen that look before.

He made the point (in a most colourful way) that we were back where we started – at a surveillance post without any evidence.

I was trying to play chess while Darren was still playing draughts.

He said: 'We are just going to sit up this building like every other day and prove nothing'.

I said, 'Wrong.'

We went up the stairs, back on top of the building where we were, crawled along the building, peeped over the side and looked.

I lit a cigarette and blew a confident smoke ring. 'This is better than sex, the hunt,' I confessed. I don't know if Darren agreed with me.

About five minutes later – you guessed it – Jacket Man peeped his head around a laneway into Fitzroy Street to see if it was safe to come out. He was like a moray eel in a leather jacket.

Looking at Jacket Man I willed him out into The Street. 'Come on, Jacket Man, the coast is clear.'

As he carefully walked towards the parlour he took his jacket off as though it was an afterthought. He rolled it up, but had nowhere to hide it. He was no brain surgeon but then, few of them are.

Jacket Man, minus the jacket, was nervously walking up The Street. There was something we could always count on in our hunt for druggies: their desire for heroin was always greater than their sense of self preservation.

As if he was following a piece of string, he made a line

directly to the parlour. As he went out of sight through the doorway, we were on about a forty-five degree angle across the road up on a building. I gave a running commentary to Darren.

Even though I couldn't see, I had a fair idea what was happening. 'Right, he's in. He's taken six steps up to the fat boy.

'Tony walks up and says, "Got the right money? Come over here".

I then spoke in a higher voice for Jacket Man: "Yes Tony, I've robbed the living shit out of everyone. I'm a good little piece of shit that you can suck the guts out of, and I'll do it again tomorrow and the next day".

'Tony says, "That's my boy." They exchange money for gear. Tony pats him on the head and Jacket Man should appear any second.'

You guessed it, just at that moment Jacket Man peeped out the doorway into The Street with Fat Tony right behind him.

The deal was done and Jacket Man took a deep breath as he prepared to run the gauntlet.

I looked at Darren and said: 'That's our cue, let's go!' He rolled his eyes as we moved, keeping low so we couldn't be spotted. 'What's next, Elliott Ness?' I felt a touch of sarcasm creeping into Darren's voice, but perhaps I was being overly sensitive.

As we ran down the stairs he yelled for the thousandth time: 'What are we doing?' I told him our new mission, 'We've got to get the gear, understand, the gear'.

We ran through a few side streets and back out into Fitzroy Street so no-one knew where we came from. As we got close to The Street we stopped running and started to walk. Sure enough, there was our Jacket Man minus the jacket. He was well clear of Fat Tony and he was walking with a pathetic little spring in his step because he had his gear.

I started to stroll across the street. There were two lanes on each side of the tram track that runs up the middle.

I said to Darren: 'Watch this.' I called out to Jacket Man, who was about thirty metres in front of us across the road, 'Hey you.' Jacket Man peeped over his shoulder. 'Yeah you, without the jacket, stop right there! Police.'

I held up my badge to him. Jacket Man exploded into a desperate sprint and I began the chase. Darren followed, but he was clearly starting to lose faith in The Plan. I knew this because he was yelling, 'Are you mad?' I think it was a rhetorical question.

It was obvious we could have walked up behind him and grabbed him by the arm. But Dazza didn't understand that I wanted him to run.

As we ran full bore, he crossed a small road and nearly got run over. More importantly, I nearly got hit as well which was definitely not part of The Plan.

I yelled all the usual lines: 'Stop, Police' and all the rest, and he kept running. I knew he would.

When he realised I was catching him – a copper who smokes should be able to run faster than nine out of ten weedy junkies – he reached into his pocket and tossed a little folded-up piece of paper onto the footpath. I stopped chasing him and picked up the foil of heroin, but as I was bending down I saw Darren whiz past.

I called out: 'Stop, let him go, I've got it.'

Darren had enough of the chase, me, Jacket Man, Fat Tony and The Plan.

Darren was filthy. As I started to walk back toward the parlour my long suffering partner mumbled away behind me, 'Up the stairs, down the stairs, there's an armed robbery, there's no armed robbery, chase this guy, let him go, chase him again, let him go again.'

I think he had low blood sugar. That was what was making him cranky. I couldn't see what else could be the problem.

The way Fat Tony packaged his heroin was quite distinctive. It was a square cut out of a magazine, which contained the gear.

Instead of a foil, (Tony never sold heroin in foils) he sold it in what the drug world calls a 'bindle'. It was cut from a Vogue magazine or similar. Cocaine is normally sold in a bindle, heroin isn't. The heroin bindle was Tony's trademark, basically. He truly was a fat goose.

I said, 'Let's go back and get Tony.'

Darren shook his head (again). 'So we've got enough to arrest Tony now have we? We've seen jack shit, we've got nothing. No buyer, just the 'gear'. We can't prove that Tony sold anyone anything including, that.' He was pointing at the bindle.

I was beginning to think that Darren should get out more often.

I said, 'Watch.'

We walked up and into the parlour. Immediately the place went dead silent. Everyone in there knew who we were.

I reached into my back pocket. Holding up my police badge high in the air I said, 'Relax, it's the police. We are here to protect you from the evils of drugs.'

I walked past several people up to Tony. The tub of lard

was wearing a big golden grin even when I informed him, 'Tony, you are under arrest for trafficking in heroin, you're not obliged to say anything at all, if you do you'll only confuse the situation.'

I turned Tony around and removed my cuffs from the back of my belt. I managed to handcuff one of his wrists but I couldn't get the other cuff on because his other wrist was too fat. This was all much to the amusement of many crooks who were watching. I needed one of the giant leg irons they used to tie up elephants in Thailand to hold him.

By this stage he was wearing an even larger smile. I grabbed his free hand and said, 'All right, just keep your hands together.'

Darren was still just shaking his head in disbelief. Did I tell you he often did that?

Tony said, 'What the fuck are you on about? You've got nothing on me, you know that.'

I walked Tony a few paces toward the door. I stopped him and told Darren to just keep him here for a second. I walked out of the parlour and into a second hand dealer's nearby.

I said, 'G'day, give me that blue light you've got behind the counter there.'

The woman behind the jump said, 'What blue light?' (Why do they always say that?)

I jumped up and over the counter, and she wisely moved back. I reached under the counter and grabbed the ultra-violet blue light.

I said, 'This one.' (Why did I always say that?)

Ultra-violet crayons are commonly used to mark video recorders and such, which helps police identify stolen property. Being a second hand dealer in St Kilda in those days, she used the blue light to see the crayon writing – and then clean it off. She was a scallywag.

I walked back into the parlour, unplugged a large pinball machine and plugged the blue light in. Tony kept on saying in a calm, smartarse voice, 'You've got nothing. My solicitor is going to sue your arse off, you twerp.'

A few of his mates in the parlour seemed to agree, but I wasn't too worried because they didn't look as if they had law degrees. They were saying things like, 'What a load of shit, Tony's done nuffin.'

I faced Tony toward the machine and said in a loud voice, 'Let's test the evidence'

I removed a large fat wallet from large Fat Tony's back pocket. Inside was a large fat amount of cash.

One by one I flipped over each side on the notes, most of the notes were $50s, $20s and $100s. As I started I said, 'Let's look for Exhibit Number One.'

Tony's face changed to a bewildered nervous glare.

As I pulled out each note and held it under the ultra violet blue light I said, 'Gimme number one, come on number one.'

Then 'Bingo, Tony congratulations you're a winner, give the man Exhibit Number One.'

I slapped down a $20 note with the word Exhibit No. 1 written on it. Tony's eye's nearly popped out of his head. I slapped down five $20 notes each with the words Exhibit No.1 written on them. Tony stood there and mumbled 'But, But.' He had lost his big, fat, rat grin.

Darren could not believe it either. The reason we had caught Jacket Man the first time was to mark his money with the invisible ultra violet crayon I had pinched from work. In normal light it is invisible, but under a blue fluorescent light it stood out like a beacon. Tony was in shock and just stood there trying to work it all out.

I said, 'But no, there's more – along with those you get Exhibit number two free.'

I slapped the bindle of heroin down on the pin ball machine. Tony closed his eyes in disbelief. He looked like a cane toad having a power nap.

Tony, Darren and I walked out of the parlour and down the road to our car. I said, 'Tony, I told you not to come back to St Kilda, what goes round comes around – you play in the fast lane long enough, you get run over, mate.'

He shook his head and realised he was gone. He knew that someone set him up and that he'd purchased off an undercover cop. I knew Tony was trying to remember who Jacket Man was. Tony had so many customers he couldn't quite do it.

As we walked down the street Tony started to talk in a low voice sort of from the corner of his mouth. He said things like, 'Listen, just help me and I'll give you anything. Just give me bail, let me go, I'll give you anything.'

I said, 'Anything?'

He said, 'Yeah, what.'

I said, 'I can never make my roast potatoes crispy. I roll them in oil, scratch them with a fork, everything, but I can't get them really crispy.'

He said, 'Please Mr Angus, I'll give you a big dealer.'

All Tony wanted to do was save his arse. Later, he told me that I only had to add a little bit of water to the bottom of the pan just before they finish cooking. He wasn't all bad.

Tony said of Jacket Man, 'So he was a cop, but I thought I knew his sister, or did he just set me up?'

I said, 'Does it matter? You're stuffed either way.' At this time I was on cloud nine – I was absolutely wrapped because I could see in Tony's eyes and I could see in his demeanour that he was a different man, he wasn't the smartarse arrogant fat prick anymore. He was now a big fat nothing.

Tony then started trying to make a deal in the middle of the street. He starts wanting to set up his dealer. He would have sold his mother.

Darren looked at me from behind Tony's back. He was just smiling, still shaking his head, as if he was thinking, 'How the hell did he do that?'

On the way back to the station Tony kept saying, 'Give me bail and I'll set up my main man, he's a big dealer. I just need bail.'

I told him that bail was out of the question. He's just getting locked up and that was that.

In desperation Tony said, 'Listen, my man is coming to my motel room at eight tonight to drop off. I'll set him up, I'll buy off him, just give me bail.'

I refused any such deal, but I found out how to roast spuds properly.

LATER we drove to Tony's motel. We took him up to his room but, by this time Tony was a shattered man. He gave us permission to search it without a warrant which saved a lot of time.

Just to make sure he didn't change his mind I produced a tape recorder from my bag and tape recorded Tony giving us permission. I used a small recorder that takes a normal size audio tape. Tony was trying to be as helpful as possible so we would go easy on him. This sort of tape can be very useful at times. During the search we found the magazine – it was a Cleo or something. You could see where he had cut out lots of square pieces to package the heroin – including the piece that we had.

Tony kept asking, 'Was the guy an undercover cop – was he from interstate, was he from here?'

I just never confirmed nor denied what Tony said. By not confirming or denying the fact that this Jacket Man was an undercover policeman, it convinced Tony that he was absolutely gone, that the weight of evidence against him was massive.

Tony went on to make full admissions to trafficking for the previous three months. By the end of the interview Tony had resigned himself to the fact that he was getting locked up and became his old jovial self.

Darren, Tony and I had a smoke and laughed about all the dickheads we knew around St Kilda. At one stage I asked a young policewoman to sit in the interview room and mind Tony for a minute while we did some of the paperwork.

Tony broke into song. Being an Italian, he appreciated beautiful women. Tony sang an Italian love song in a loud operatic voice with a strong Italian accent. His voice bellowed through the whole station. He was actually very good. The policewoman sat back, enjoying it. I have heard of crims singing in the interview room but not like this.

When the interview was finished it was about 5pm. The court was closed so Tony was remanded in custody by a Bail Justice overnight to front court the next day. Darren and I finished our paperwork and left the station.

As we left I called out, 'See you at Tony's joint later.' Darren said, 'No worries.' I looked at my partner and there was something different about him. Then I realised. He wasn't shaking his head.

Later that night I was making myself at home with my feet up drinking one of Tony's Crown Lagers in front of the TV. There was a knock at the door. It was Darren,

I said, 'Help yourself. There's beer in the fridge, he's even got some spirits and, can you believe it, he's even got an ice maker. I would love a fridge with an ice maker.'

I said, 'Can you believe he had *Scar Face* in his VCR.'

Darren said, 'He cops his right whack in the end.'

The dealer was supposed to turn up at 8pm, but drug dealers are nearly always late. At about 10.15, just when *Scar Face* was about to get really good, and we were a bit pissed, there was a faint knock at the door. Darren jumped up and went into the bathroom. I turned the TV down a bit, I then heard Darren start to run the shower.

I took a deep breath and called out, 'Who is it?'

A deep voice said, 'Alex.' I should have guessed, as every trafficker's name seemed to be Alex.

I carefully opened the door and peeped up and down the hallway. I said, 'Quick, come in.'

Alex was Romanian or something. He had the gold chains happening, black leather jacket and the usual gear on. I still don't know why drug dealers always seem to dress like drug dealers. Maybe there was a shop where they all bought their clothes. It could be called: 'Big Bucks No Taste.'

Alex quietly came in. I held out my hand and said, 'I'm Wayne, Tony's brother-in-law. Well, ex-brother-in-law. Well, she's not Tony's real sister, she's a ...'

Alex cut me off. He wasn't interested in my ramblings.

'Where's Tony,' he asked suspiciously.

I said, 'In the shower.'

We could see steam coming from beneath the bathroom door.

I said, 'I'll get Tony, but he's really pissed off that you're late.'

Alex said, 'Well, fuck him.'

I said, 'Hang on a sec.'

I was just about to open the bathroom door when Tony's voice burst into the air. I opened the door and through the steam I could just see Darren. We had Tony's stereo system on his toilet and we had taped Tony singing to the police-woman at the station.

I made out I was talking to Tony in the shower.

I said, 'But I don't want to get involved – but, but, okay, Christ.'

I left the bathroom and closed the door. The tape started again and Tony's voice sang out again, 'Mi, O, Mi, AHHHH, COME HOME TO MEEEEEEEE.' That sort of thing. It loses something in the translation.

'Tony told me where the money is and he wants me to do the business.

Alex hesitated, and said, 'I get it.' I don't think he did.

Alex left and returned seconds later. We sat on the couch and Alex put three ounces of rock heroin on the table. I reached over and picked up a large vase in the middle of the table and turned it upside down. Nothing came out so I shook it again. My police badge fell onto the table. I picked it up and showed him. And said: 'You're under arrest.'

Alex reached over and took the badge from me and looked at it closely. He was the studious type. I pointed out and said, 'See that writing, it says TENEZ LE DROIT. That means

UPHOLD THE RIGHT.' I touched my chest with both hands and said, 'That's what I do.'

Alex was convinced. He jumped up, pushing me away. I had a huge struggle with him. Not a stand-up punching match, just an all out full-on, old-fashioned Greco-Rumanian wrestle.

At this point Darren should have burst out of the bathroom to assist because what is the point of having a partner if he is not there to help gang up on the crims?

But there was no Darren. He was still sitting on the edge of the bath in the steam-filled bathroom with Tony's voice blaring away full blast.

It was like an opera in a Turkish bath. Darren couldn't hear me calling for help. After several minutes I managed to handcuff Alex's left ankle to his right wrist. I was stuffed and he wasn't much better.

Darren then peeped out of the bathroom. I saw his face and said, 'Yeah mate, it's safe to come out now.'

He said, 'You've got the bad guy.' On the table was a large amount of heroin. We were proud of ourselves and we had every reason to be.

As usual, we didn't have handcuff keys so we had great difficulty in getting Alex down the stairs of the motel and into the cop car, and going into the station was fun as well. He looked like a giant Rumanian Pretzel.

We worked through the night interviewing and charging Alex.

When we fronted court that morning we both looked like death. The crooks looked better than we did. It had been a big twenty-four hours.

Tony's case was up first and I applied to have him

remanded in custody. It was very funny because at court when I was in the witness box giving evidence, Tony's Legal Aid barrister asked me the identity of the mysterious Jacket Man.

I told the Court that his name was Mark Bowers. I went on to say that I had in fact checked him after I'd seen him approach Tony, and that I thought he was going to return a few minutes later and buy heroin from the fat man.

I told the court how I marked the buyer's money without him knowing, and then gave the money back to him. Tony's face started to change as he woke to what had really happened – he started to realise that the whole thing was a scam.

I then went on to say that from the roof, I observed Bowers re-attend at the parlour and walk in towards Tony. I told the court that when he came his demeanour had changed and he had a spring in his step.

I told the court the whole story of how we caught Fat Tony and how he made admissions of trafficking for the past three months.

Tony just shook his head (he must have caught the habit from Darren) as he realised the whole thing was a smoke and mirrors job and that he'd put himself in.

The penny dropped that he'd convinced himself he was stuffed when in fact he wasn't, and if he hadn't made any admissions he would have walked away and not been charged. With all the evidence we had gathered, when you put the whole thing with his admissions, he was absolutely gone. The magistrate found it amusing. So did I.

Tony's barrister, the poor dear, tried his best by accusing me of tricking Tony and lying to him. I looked at the magistrate with a George Washington look and said: 'I certainly did not lie. When he asked me several times who Jacket Man was, I just refused to confirm or deny the fact that he was, or was not, an undercover operative.'

I informed the court that I had some concerns about Mark Bowers (Jacket Man) looking like an informer and setting up Tony. I told the court I wanted to make it quite clear that, at that time Mark Bowers had no idea that I had marked the money and he had no idea I would return that paper bindle full of heroin back to Tony. Of course, on top of it all, the cream was finding the magazine that matched this square piece of paper.

You could also see other squares had been cut out of the magazine. They often said that solving crime was like putting together a jigsaw. This time they were right.

The magistrate remanded Tony in custody. As Tony was leaving the dock he stopped as Alex was led out of a door in front of him into the dock. Tony looked terrified as he turned and looked at me. I gave him a wry smile and lifted my eye brows as if to say, 'Life's a shit sandwich.'

I think he agreed with me.

ONE day Darren and I were working plainclothes when I received information from an old crow about an old guy whose name was Eddie Tout, who was known around The Street as 'the Trout'.

He was about seventy-three years old and still sold heroin from the St Kilda Cafe. What he did was keep his heroin in those stainless steel straw dispensers that sat in the middle of the counter within the cafe. It was a pokey little cafe with six tables and chairs and the the main counter.

Anyway, he would sit on a stool in the middle of the

counter. He'd sit there with heroin concealed inside this stainless steel straw container. He paid the owner $20 an hour to sit on the stool in the cafe, waiting for junkie customers.

So we looked for him that day, but every time we went there he was missing, so we decided at the end of the shift to stay back and do surveillance.

We finished work, went and bought a six-pack of Fosters and sat directly over the road from the cafe on a window sill in the frontyard of a big old house.

We sat on the window sill with our feet dangling about a foot off the ground drinking cans and having a smoke, determined to catch this old bloke as the pinch seemed pretty simple. In front of us was about five metres of lawn then a small front fence. So there we sat.

Anyway, it started to get a bit dark and then, of course, we ran out of cans and any off-duty surveillance was out of the question without lubrication, so we had to go to the Prince of Wales hotel for another six-pack. We had to get our priorities right.

When we returned two females kept standing in front of us while we were trying to look at the cafe. We kept looking around them, trying to look across the road, but we both wished they'd piss off out of our way.

Then, all of a sudden, a great big, young bloke of around eighteen who we'd never seen before, walked up and started talking to them. Then they were all right in our way. So we kept leaning around trying to see. If he hadn't been so big we would have told him to piss off.

So there we were – contorting ourselves, bending over, looking around them wishing they'd piss off, when the big one said, 'Right, what do you want?'

I nudged Darren. He looked at me and said quietly, 'You're kidding?'

One of them said, 'We just want one – just a half.'

He said, 'Sweet – no problem.' Anyway, they either didn't see us sitting on the window sill or they didn't give a shit about us.

He started to reach down inside his jocks when one of the females said, 'Hey listen, can you spot us $10, we've only got $80' (because a half of heroin was $90).

The big, fat, young bloke turned around and said, 'Get fucked – pay the price or fuck off' or words to that effect. She started, 'Please, please, we're $10 short, we'll give you an extra $10 next time.'

He's saying, 'Yeah, yeah, sure. You're full of shit.' They start arguing and bargaining and as two girls tried to get a discount – it was just ridiculous. It was all there right in front of us.

So we're looking at each other. We think, 'Oh well, what the hell'. We skolled what was left of our cans. By this time the bloke had finally agreed. He was not happy about it. The girls started to count out the money into his hand. He started to get the heroin from the inside of his jocks.

I whispered words similar to, 'The girls are on my side – I'll take them.'

Darren said, a bit sarcastically, 'Oh, leave me the fat bloke?'

I whispered, 'I'm a lover not a fighter,' or words to that effect and Darren called me a bastard, or words to that effect. At least he didn't shake his head this time.

Darren had to take the big bloke. I've just jumped out, held my badge at the two girls 'Get on the ground, don't move!

Police.' Darren, of course, drew his gun on the big fat bloke and told him to get on the ground. But the fat bloke was young and stupid and decided to argue the toss.

I got the girls down on the ground without much problem.

I stepped around behind the big bloke to stop him getting away. Darren realised that the gun wasn't having the desired effect and reluctantly started to put it back in its holster, realising it was going to be a fight. It was time for Plan B.

I knelt down on all fours behind the fat bloke, Darren shirt fronted him with his shoulder and tried to push him backwards so I would trip him over, but the fat bloke didn't budge and Darren bounced off him onto the ground. The fat bloke just stood there and pushed me out the way with his foot and started to walk off. So much for Plan B.

We both jumped up onto the fat bloke and I screamed at the two girls, 'Stay on the ground, you're under arrest.' At first the girls obeyed and lay there face down. The fat bloke just kept pushing and pulling us off him and dropping us over the small brick fence.

I recall being very careful not to punch this bloke. The first reason was that it would have no effect on him, anyway. The second reason was that I didn't want him to punch me back. So a wrestle it was.

After a minute or so the two girls ignored our screams not to move, stood up, brushed themselves off and quickly walked to freedom. Darren and I were by no means winning the wrestle. In fact, the fat bloke started to walk off down the street dragging us with him. It was like two flyweights attacking a Sumo.

People came over and watched. We should have sold tickets.

In the middle of the wrestle Darren screamed, 'Cuff him, cuff the bastard.'

I screamed back, 'I don't think he's at the cuffing stage just yet, you idiot.'

Darren and I were exhausted.

Then I started trying to pull his pants down. The fat bloke thought he was being attacked by a crazed homosexual copper. I finally got them over his belly down to his ankles, which stopped him walking and tripped him over. Once he was on the ground it was a bit easier to wrestle him.

I said, 'Get your cuffs out.'

Darren said, 'I haven't got cuffs, you're supposed to have the cuffs, I had the radio.'

I said, 'Use the radio.'

Darren said, 'I forgot it.'

I yelled, 'You don't bring the cuffs because you've got the radio, but you haven't got the radio!'

Darren and I kept arguing while we fought this bloke.

After about five minutes I got sick of it. The big fat guy was face down. I pulled out my gun and pushed it hard into his right ear. I was puffing so much I could hardly breathe. I said, 'NOW, I'm ready to shoot you. Give me two big blinks if you believe me.' Fat guts gave me two big blinks. I was very happy.

The next moment about five police cars with their lights and sirens going pulled up. All the coppers who turned up laughed at the sight before them.

Meanwhile a large crowd of people had built up around us.

I said to Darren, 'Have you got the gear – the foil?'

Darren said, 'No, I thought you were picking it up.' We argued again about who was going to pick up he foil.

We crawled around in the tan bark and found one of the foils. We took fat guts back and charged him with trafficking heroin.

We'd gone hunting a wily old trout and landed the great white whale.

THE following day we again worked, but still couldn't find the Trout. After the shift we were still determined to crack the case (and a few cans). We headed back to the window sill. We were on our first can when this old grey-haired bloke wearing a suit walked into the cafe.

We gave him a couple of minutes to get set up, followed him in and there he is sitting there at the counter with a straw dispenser right in front of him. We sat either side of him, and went into the routine.

'G'day mate – how's it going? We're plainclothes cops,' I said, and we showed him our badges.

I looked at the straw dispenser. 'What are we going to find in this, mate?' I asked. He looked at me and said, 'What do you reckon?'

I tipped it upside down. About a dozen foils of heroin were stuck to the bottom of the straw dispenser with blue tack. He said, 'Never seen them before in my life.' For some reason we didn't believe him.

Because the straw dispenser was stainless steel you could see fresh fingerprints on it. I said, 'Well, whose fingerprints are they, do you reckon?' He just looked at me in silence.

I said, 'You're under arrest for trafficking in heroin.'

As we walked him out and down the street. He said, 'So I'm fucked, aren't I?' and I said, 'Yeah Digger, you are'.

We had hooked the Trout.

He gave me the impression he would have been a real good crook in his day. Anyway, we got back to the station and he was being quite friendly and talkative. He explained how he'd been a crook most of his life. He spoke of being in the war and about his past.

I got him a hot cup of coffee. He took two sugars.

'Do you know this cuppa is the first thing I have ever taken from a copper in me life? Besides a beating, that is,' he said.

He then let out a long sigh and said, 'I'm too old this crap.'

A short time later I interviewed him about trafficking heroin. He made full and frank admissions to trafficking for the past week out of the St Kilda Cafe. But he did it without lagging anyone else.

At the end of the interview I sat in front of him and had a chat. I said, 'What's your caper? Records state that you only ever say 'No Comment' when interviewed. Should we feel privileged or what?'

He said, 'I'm too old for this shit. I've been interviewed by some of the best in my day. I remember that bastard Detective Sergeant (name deleted) from Coburg CIB interviewed me about a safe break. I told him nothin', so he threw me out the interview room window head first and charged me with escape! I still told him nothin'.' The Trout started to cry.

Reading his history was interesting. His antecedents said that every cop who ever met him said he was unco-operative, would never say anything or admit to anything.

He had been an armed robber in his younger years, then a safe breaker. He had been in the war and his wife had died. He had two priors for trafficking heroin which resulted in jail terms.

He was now seventy-three. He was proud of his age and told everybody. I found it strange that he was making full admissions at the time.

Maybe I was the friendliest copper he had ever run into over all those years. Or maybe he was just getting old and sentimental and I got lucky.

When we finished the paperwork we bailed him, because of his age and the fact we had proved where he lived and his identity. He left the station. Darren and I left for home a bit later. The next morning we came to work and a policewoman said to me, 'Oh, did you hear what happened?'

No, we hadn't. The policewoman said, 'That drug trafficker you charged last night, Eddie Tout. Did you hear?'

I said, 'No, what?'

She said, 'You let him go a 19.30 and he hanged himself at 19.45.'

Fifteen minutes after we let him go he walked back to his car, drove home and hanged himself in a tree at the front of his house. One of the neighbours found him.

Even to this day I think he was trying to make some sort of a little statement by doing it so openly. I realised why he was so co-operative and why he made full admissions for the first time in his life. He had reached the end.

I was disappointed that I hadn't picked it up in the interview. I'd known something was wrong and I found it strange he was making admissions, but I didn't put it all together.

To be honest, you try not to care if they just go and shoot themselves, deliberately overdose, hang themselves or whatever, and often you don't. But this old guy – I often remember him.

Some time later I read his autopsy report. It turned out he had forty-seven puncture marks in his thighs. There was only one explanation for that, and I would never have picked it. He regularly injected heroin. He was a junkie.

The more experience I had as a copper, the more I realised I didn't know.

I WAS driving down Grey Street with my mate Darren when we saw a well known prostitute called 'Katrina.' She saw us approaching and started to walk away, but I called her over.

Katrina was a quite attractive. Tall, slim, twenty three years old, with long legs in high heels. She walked straight up to the passenger side window, which was open.

She lifted her tight little top and thrust her large breasts into Darren's face and said, 'Please don't book me, please.'

As a few members of the public could see what she was doing it was quite embarrassing, being a cop with naked tits hanging in your window.

I smiled and said, 'Katrina, put them away, you could poke someone's eyes out with them. Any new dealers around that you want to talk about?'

She pulled her top down and said, 'There's an old "Straight Head", got heaps of gear. He turned up last week. Called Stan. About seventy, grey hair, well dressed. You'll find him first table on the left at Joe's Pizza.' I thanked her and we left.

We sat off Stan and watched him deal for about half an hour. One of the people he sold heroin to was a shit head named Blackie.

I walked up to Stan and said I was a mate of Blackie's. Stan sold heroin to me. When Darren and I arrested him he said, 'Oh, I guess I'm in a spot of bother, I'm terribly sorry.' We took him back to our office. Stan was strange. He was very well-spoken and obviously didn't belong in Fitzroy Street. He had never been in trouble in his life. He was a mathematician or scientist who had been a university lecturer. He presented as most professional. Get this, the reason he was selling heroin was that he reckoned he had found the answer to winning at roulette.

He had found the secret formula of how to place his bets to win every time. It's just that he had been losing a lot, but he would fix that if he could just bet again. His pockets were full of notes and formulas. He sold heroin to make money to prove this formula.

He was an addict, but not a smack-head – he was a gambling addict.

He had 'discovered' he could sell heroin and make a lot of money. Darren and I were the first cops to meet him. I asked him where he got his heroin from and he told us he got it from a high level Rumanian drug dealer by the name of Alex. Another Alex – a smart Alex.

This Alex was about thirty two, with the mandatory moustache, leather jacket and dark sunglasses. He drove a late model flashy car, delivered only on the outskirts of St Kilda, would never go near The Street and he delivered nothing short of an ounce of pure, which was about twelve grand at the time.

We decided to get Alex.

A new policewoman named Jane had just arrived at St Kilda. She'd been at our station for about two days. She was a young, slightly plump, attractive girl who was nineteen and looked fifteen.

She was short with a very pretty young face. I saw the

Sergeant, told him that we had this guy who was buying ounces at a time who was willing to set up a dealer. I needed an undercover girlfriend and Jane was perfect.

I convinced him that we could teach her and that she could do it. The Sergeant agreed we could have her for a couple of days. He also asked us to be careful with her. Us careful? Of course. We then went and saw young Jane, sat her down and told her we would like her to assist us and be my girlfriend undercover.

She thought it sounded great. She also said she knew nothing about drugs. I said, 'Well, we'll go out for a drink and I'll teach you all you need to know'.

We gave her a crash course on drug dealing, how it's bought, the slang terms, how it's cut up, etc. I explained the following levels of drug users and dealers:

1) The heroin user buys 'caps', also known as 'foils'. These contain anything from .15 of a gram to .5 of a gram of heroin depending on the purity.

2) The next level is the heroin trafficker who gets about five foils from a dealer. If he sells four he can keep one for nothing. He then gives the money he got for the four foils and gets given another five. This keeps repeating. This is the common 'street dealer' or 'user dealer'.

3) Then there is the dealer who may supply several other street dealers. He too is often a drug user himself, but can also be making a tidy profit, which is mostly spent on using larger amounts of heroin, gambling and cars.

4) The high level drug trafficker that deals for pure greed makes large amounts of money. He can afford to purchase large amounts of heroin very cheaply, and often dilutes it to maximise his profits.

5) Last of all, you have the importer. The importer can purchase a pound of pure rock heroin in Thailand for next to nothing. Once in Australia it can be sold for about $105,000 wholesale.

Profits are huge, but you risk the death penalty bringing it out of Thailand. Your profits can be even larger if you can sell the heroin yourself down the trafficking pecking order because the closer you can sell to street level the bigger the profit, because you cut out the other levels.

I explained all this over drinks. We then formulated a plan. The plan was for Jane and me to act as heroin purchasers from Perth. We came from Perth because the heroin is a lot cheaper in Melbourne. This time we would want just one ounce of pure rock, but next time we came over we would want a lot more.

The bait, as always, was greed.

We set up in a motel room. We would stay only for one day and then, our story went, we would be flying back to Perth. That way they couldn't stuff us around for long. Professor Stan was to organise the meeting and the first introduction would be in the motel room.

The following day, Darren, myself and Jane were given permission to work on this one job full time. We then went down to the local motel and spoke to the manager who we knew and trusted. We got a room for nothing.

We then set up the room. We bought heaps of shit in there to make it look as if we had just arrived. Jane got some stuff in from her home and it looked as if a couple had just unpacked.

Stan came over and we told told him all he needed to know. He then rang Alex from our motel room and arranged for him to come over in an hour just to organise the deal. Alex was a pretty switched-on drug dealer. He liked the idea of meeting with Jane, but refused to meet the boyfriend. At the end of the call I asked Stan why he didn't want to meet me. Stan finally admitted that he had told Alex that I was a jail escapee from Perth and was 'hot to trot'. Alex (they didn't call him Smart Alex for nothing) thought he might get robbed.

The last thing we needed was an elderly mathematician turned roulette nut turned scag seller trying to make things up as he went along. I laid the down the law to Stan, telling him not to say a word unless he was told.

Stan's story made things quite difficult as Jane had to do it alone and we needed to cover her closely.

As a drug dealer the most dangerous thing that can happen is getting robbed and undercover operatives are not exempt. All precautions must be taken to cover this possibility. Rip-offs are part of the scene.

Alex said he'd come about an hour after Stan gave him the name of the motel and room number. We then started briefing Jane, getting ready for the meeting. Here was a kid just out of the academy who was now going undercover with a partner.

Within about ten minutes there's a knock at the door – Alex was the only dealer in the history of the world to be early. I then looked at Jane and mouthed the words, 'Who is it?' and Jane called out 'Who is it?' on cue.

There was this deep Rumanian voice that said, 'It's Alex – open the door'. I jumped into the shower recess and Darren jumped into the toilet. Old Stan was still there, of course.

So the door was opened and in he came for the meeting.

He appeared to like Jane very much as she certainly didn't

even look old enough to be a policewoman. He trusted Stan because he was a good dealer and had dealt with Alex for quite some time. Alex told Jane how they met at the casino playing roulette.

Now the deal was that Jane and I were from Perth, that heroin was more expensive in the West, that Stan had spent a lot of time in Perth previously and Jane's boyfriend was like a grandson to him.

It sounded like crap, but Alex seemed to cop it. Everything was going fine, then Alex asked to see Jane's air tickets. Fortunately I had gone to Tullamarine and got the woman at the counter to make me up a couple of bodgie tickets that showed us flying in a couple of days earlier.

This fitted our story perfectly so Alex was assured when he saw the tickets. Jane arranged to buy one ounce of heroin for $12,000 at St Kilda Pier, at the cafe at the end of the pier, the following night. The deal was set for 7pm.

While I was hiding in the shower I was wearing a grey jacket that I always wore and it had a sort of belt thing at the bottom of it and two steel rings that hang down at the back. I know a lot about drug dealers, but not a lot about fashion.

Anyway, while I was in the shower recess I moved and tapped the two rings against the tiles of the shower and for a moment I thought the experienced member was going to blow the operation while the rookie was starring. Luckily, Alex didn't seem to hear anything.

We were happy for Jane to be up front because she was perfect. She had a bubbly, lively personality and sold the whole thing beautifully.

Alex left, we came out and told Jane she'd done a great job. Jane just about collapsed, fell back on the bed in this motel room and said, 'That was sensational'. She loved the experience. She'd never dreamed she was suddenly going to arrive from the academy and buy $12,000 worth of heroin undercover.

Anyway, the next day we organised buy/bust teams. We got plainclothes, the CIB, the dog squad, everybody we could think of to bust Alex.

We had search and rescue on stand-by. We had cops everywhere to try to follow him and pick him up. Our plan was to find out where Alex was getting his heroin and to arrest his supplier. We didn't just want Alex, we wanted his supplier so we could go up the ladder.

I briefed everyone that Alex might be early so we were set up and were ready by 5.30pm. Time passed, and by 7.30pm I could not hold on to my little police army any longer. The bosses would not authorise any more overtime.

It was a 'no show' on Alex's behalf. Nothing. We didn't have his phone number, only a pager number. I paged him several times, but still nothing.

Eventually, to my embarrassment, I had to tell everybody the deal was not going ahead, and they could all leave. We left the pier. It was a disaster. Everybody was laughing at us. Somehow, I was getting used to it.

Stan couldn't get on to Alex either. I was about to take Jane home when she told me she left her keys back at the motel and I had to go back there anyway to pick up our gear.

I told Jane that we had to be quick to make sure we didn't bump into Alex. You only want to deal with a dealer on your terms. The problem was that Alex might want to go ahead with the deal and all our covering cops had gone home for fish fingers in front of the TV – *Blue Heelers* was on, I think.

We threw our gear into bags and left the motel room, but as we approached reception, you guessed it, Alex arrived. Jane said, 'You're too late, Alex.'

I tried to get on the front foot, 'So this is the bloke that stuffed us around.'

Alex said, 'I spoke with Stan, he said you were upset. I'm sorry, we can still do it. Somebody stole my car in Dandenong, I was stuck.'

I said, 'You left me on the end of a pier with twelve grand. I'm not interested in you, you're fucking unreliable, you're full of shit. You only understand day time and night time. I need to know when it's happening because I've got business to do. You're late – no business. Simple. I've got a reputation, we have to get it somewhere else.'

Alex said, 'But I've got it now. I will pay for your airfare – please.'

I said, 'Just get out of my face, I've organised it with someone else, my word is my word; you're a fuck up.'

He pleaded so much it was obvious that he had committed himself and had to sell the gear. He may have got it on credit or something, because he was desperate.

I called out to the receptionist: 'Can we have the same room for another night?'

She didn't look up. 'Yes, certainly.'

I said to Alex, '10 am tomorrow, here, one 'Aussie' (slang for an ounce) Take $900 off for airfare and this motel, I'll give you $11,100. Your boss delivers it – if I see you anywhere near here the deal's off, do you understand? If all goes well this time that means I can trust you again, you do it next time. Tell your boss if I'm happy with this one, I want six ounces of rock every Friday.'

He said, 'Yes, that's okay, but I can do it?'

I said, 'You heard me – yes or no?'

Now Alex was on the back foot, 'That will be fine. Ten tomorrow. Trust me.'

We returned back to our room and Alex left. Jane said, 'Well, you might have done that before. I don't think this was your first time.'

I said, 'Once or twice. These cockheads have to show a bit more professionalism. Some of these idiots give drug dealers a bad name. The bottom line is "Money talks, bullshit walks".'

We dropped all our gear on the bed, sat down and cracked a couple of cans of bourbon and coke. I telephoned Darren and told him the good news. He muttered something about trying to convince everyone it would happen again tomorrow. I couldn't see him, but I bet he was shaking his head.

The next morning we set up surveillance all around the motel. We had an arrest crew set up in the motel room next door. We waited until 10am came and then waited some more. You don't have to be told – no show.

Eventually an unknown man walked past our door. Everyone thought he was not our man, but he turned and knocked on our door. I opened it and he came right in. He was a long-haired smartarse, wearing sunglasses indoors, a leather jacket, all the usual dealer shit. He said, 'Call me Peter.'

I said, 'You can call me Paul.'

He smiled and said, 'I'll call you Lenny'. I let him think he knew more than I did.

I pulled out the cash and dropped it on the table. Peter said, 'I'll come back.'

Peter left to get the 'gear'. Surveillance had reported a late model Ford circling the motel. Peter met the driver out the front and the driver handed him a small package. Peter returned to the room.

And as soon as he shut the door he, Jane and I were arrested by a bunch of screaming, lunatic coppers. Sometimes I think we would be safer being raided by crooks. Another unit arrested the bloke in the car.

Cops always over-do it. There is always too many of them and they always get too excited. For some reason they love hurting undercover cops in the arrest.

Maybe they didn't like me or maybe they were just bored. They probably think there's method in their madness, in that they try to sell the idea they're arresting real crooks all round, and biff the undercovers to make it look good. But, having been on the receiving end of such fraternal enthusiasm more than most, I reckon it's more a case of too much madness in their method acting.

Anyway, what's a few bruises between friends when it all works a treat? It was a great pinch. The heroin turned out to be about ninety-one percent pure, the highest seen at the Victorian Science Laboratory at that time.

Back at the station Peter became most upset when I walked into the interview room being led by Darren. I had my head down, hands behind my back in the handcuff position. Peter said, 'Anything is his. I know nothing, if you have drugs or something it is his. I am innocent, I have a family, I do nothing, I swear on my mother's grave he do it, not me.' Peter was crying. I nearly believed him. Nearly.

I lifted my head, moved my hand in front of me and lit a smoke. Darren and I sat down in front of him. I smiled and blew smoke into his face. I said, 'I thought I could trust you. If we can't trust each other how can we ever do business?'

Peter's face dissolved as his life flashed before him. He closed his eyes as he realised he was about to spend several years in jail. Darren, Jane and I had a laugh. It was a very good pinch. We halted the interview to go and search Peter's house. It was a huge joint. He had money to burn and, of course, that's what he did. You should have seen the shit he wasted it on. Such as the huge, purple, velvet-covered stereo bedhead. To ethnic drug dealers these bed-heads were mandatory. He should have got five years for bad taste.

We found a small quantity of heroin and some packaging, but nothing of any great importance.

After the interview we conveyed Peter over to the local court. Word had spread, via his upset wife no doubt, and the court was packed with Peter's cousins, uncles and brothers. They all looked like younger and older versions of Peter.

We were all smiling at Peter's misfortune. Until Peter called out to one of his relatives in Rumanian or similar. I could not understand a word – except the name Alex.

I had decided not to charge Alex with conspiracy or attempting to traffic heroin because I wanted to protect Stan. If I charged Alex it meant Stan was the informer. If I let Alex go then no-one would be positive.

During the remand hearing at court I saw several relatives leave the court. I had to stay.

About half an hour later Peter was remanded into custody. We left the court. I drove over to Stan's home and spoke with him. He told me he had spoken to Alex about thirty minutes before and that Alex had no idea Peter had been arrested.

Darren, Jane and I drove to Alex's house and found him at

home. He was lying dead in his doorway. He had been badly beaten and a syringe was sticking out of him. I checked him, returned back to the car and called it in to VKC. I requested homicide attend.

All three of us imagined Alex trying to tell Peter's criminal associates that he didn't set Peter up. Nothing we could have said to Peter after his arrest would have helped Alex. I signed Alex's death warrant the second I kicked him out of the drug deal.

I'm not sure if I did it without realising the consequences or I just didn't care. I did know the sight of Alex's body wiped the smile off my face. It brought home the fact that all this is not a game. The death of a drug dealer is a death, is a death, is a death. We all felt we'd been touched by it.

I knew I wasn't responsible, but I wasn't innocent either. Welcome to The Street, Jane.

A TOP mate of mine was Chooka. I worked with him at St Kilda. He was newly married to a police woman named Karen, who also worked at St Kilda. She was one of the boys – and one of these girls that could melt you with a smile. We used to go fishing – well, it was actually a big card playing weekend at Chooka's parents' holiday house at Inverloch.

No girls, just us blokes. We would get pissed for three days and come home. Anyway, we got back from one of our annual trips to find trouble.

When Chooka got home, his newly-wedded wife Karen asked him to leave for good. He was devastated. Chooka left home and stayed with his sister in her flat. Karen said she was totally sick of all his bullshit. Chooka worshipped the ground she walked on. Everyone knew she was a great catch, especially for Chooka, but he was a real lad, one of 'the boys'.

Anyway, Karen was working at our plainclothes office. She was slim and attractive, very serious and frighteningly intelligent.

She didn't just think she was never wrong, she was never wrong, and could turn you into stone with a look. Really tough, smart women always scare the living shit out of blokes, including me.

About three days later Chooka came to work pissed. It was 8am. I fronted him to find what was wrong.

I told the sergeant I was taking him home to look after him. So we went straight to the nearest pub instead, to sort it out (as you would).

I then discovered the real problem. Chooka told me that he had gone home the night before to pick up a few things. He found that Karen was living with another policewoman from St Kilda. He found that the spare bedroom was not set up. He had said to Karen: 'Is she staying in our bed, our wedding bed just like you and me?'

Karen had told him, 'Yep, she's what I want, she gives me what I need.'

Well, that nearly killed him. He still loved her. To have her leave him for a woman was devastating, not to mention highly embarrassing.

He decided to fix the problem by getting pissed every day forever. It was a Monday when I discovered this gem. It was always going to be a big day, as it was Filthy's last day in The Job.

Filthy (his real name was Phil) had been a copper for thirty-

Me as a fresh-faced copper at my graduation, mid-1984.

CYNTHIA
CHAPMAN EDNA.
DKT Nº AAC 449
17-12-64

NAME CHAPMAM CINDY
DOB. 17 12 64 DKT 729 80
SK. 11 82

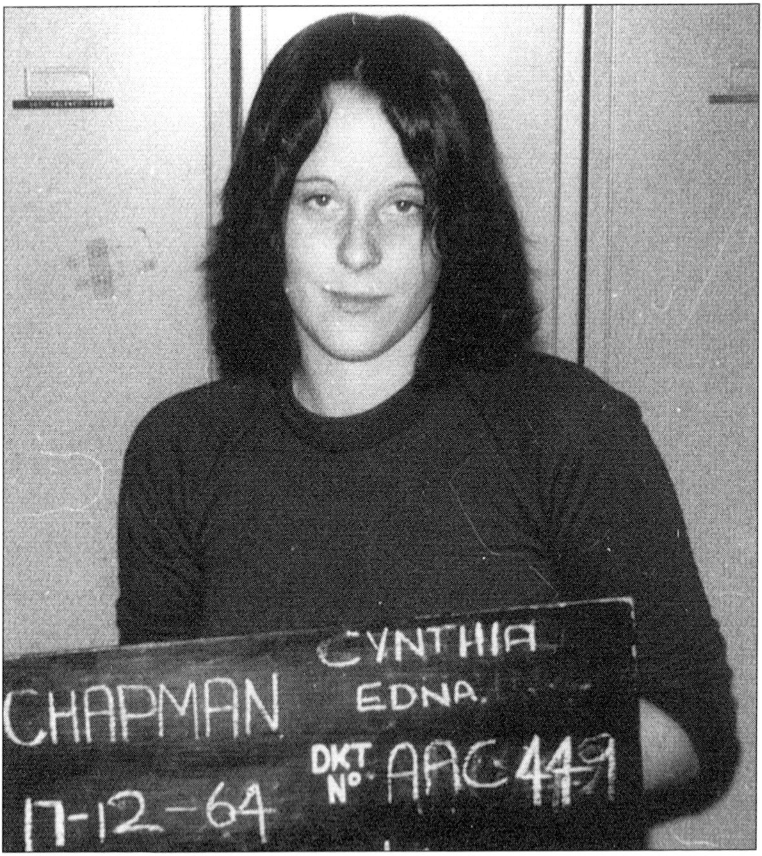

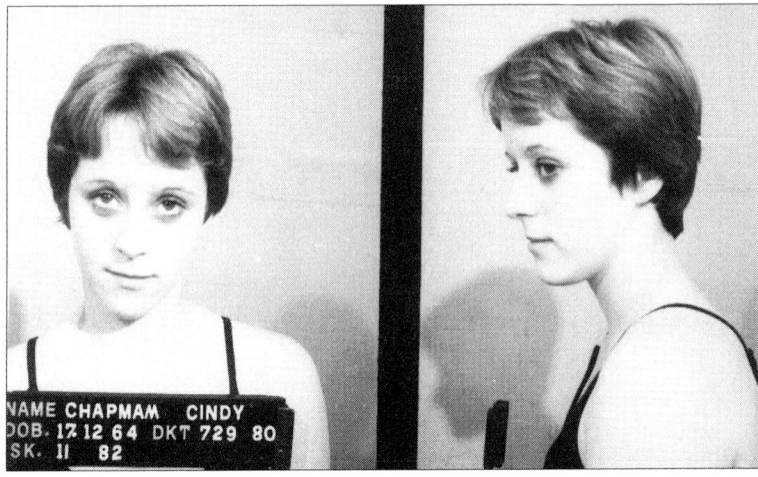

The
needle
and the
damage
done …
four
faces
of Cindy
on a
one-way
trip.

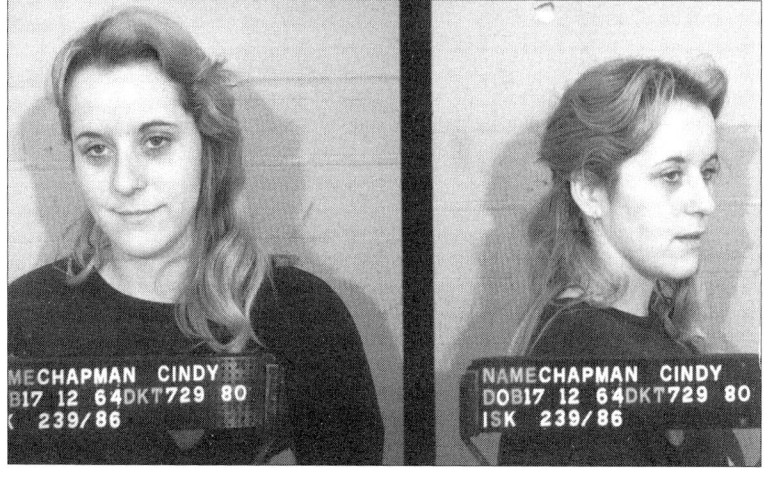

NAME CHAPMAN SINDY
DOB 17 12 64 DKT DUCASSE
ISK 7 / 83   729 80

ME CHAPMAN CINDY
B 17 12 64 DKT 729 80
K 239/86

NAME CHAPMAN CINDY
DOB 17 12 64 DKT 729 80
ISK 239/86

Me masquerading as an innocent, uniformed cop.

Me masquerading as an ignorant slob – Dean Collie

Indy the cat ... had nine lives, which was eight more than Cindy, the girl who gave her to me.

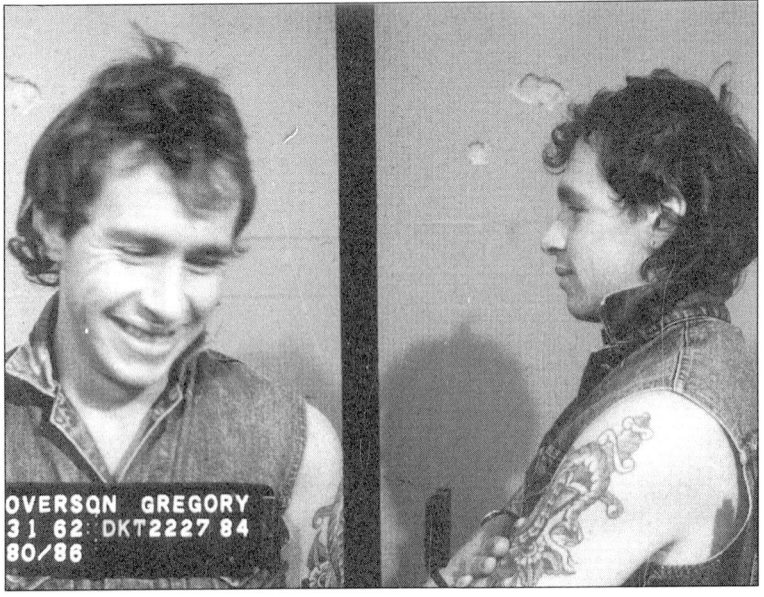

OVERSON GREGORY
31 62 DKT2227 84
80/86

Greg ... we went to school together, he went to jail alone.

Drug raids can be messy. We said we would clean up the town, not drug dealers' hallways after we sledgehammer their doors.

A bandana and a coloured contact lens ... just another day at the office, working undercover.

Sometimes, crooks brought us to our knees.

Toys for bad boys ... a Luger with a silencer, a machine pistol, a machine gun and a couple of glorified water pistols.

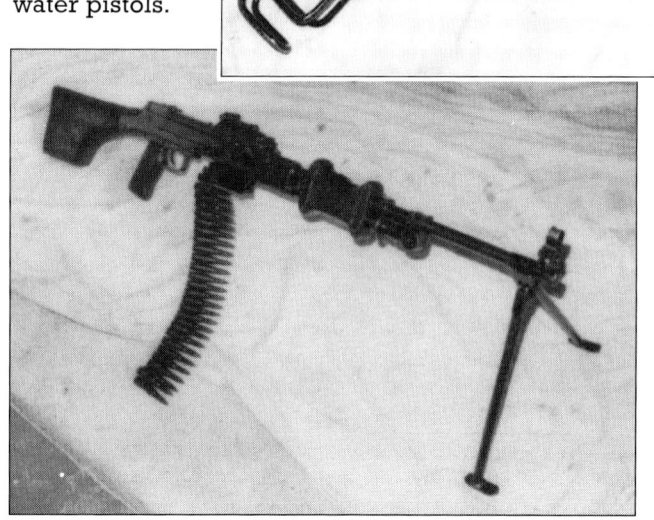

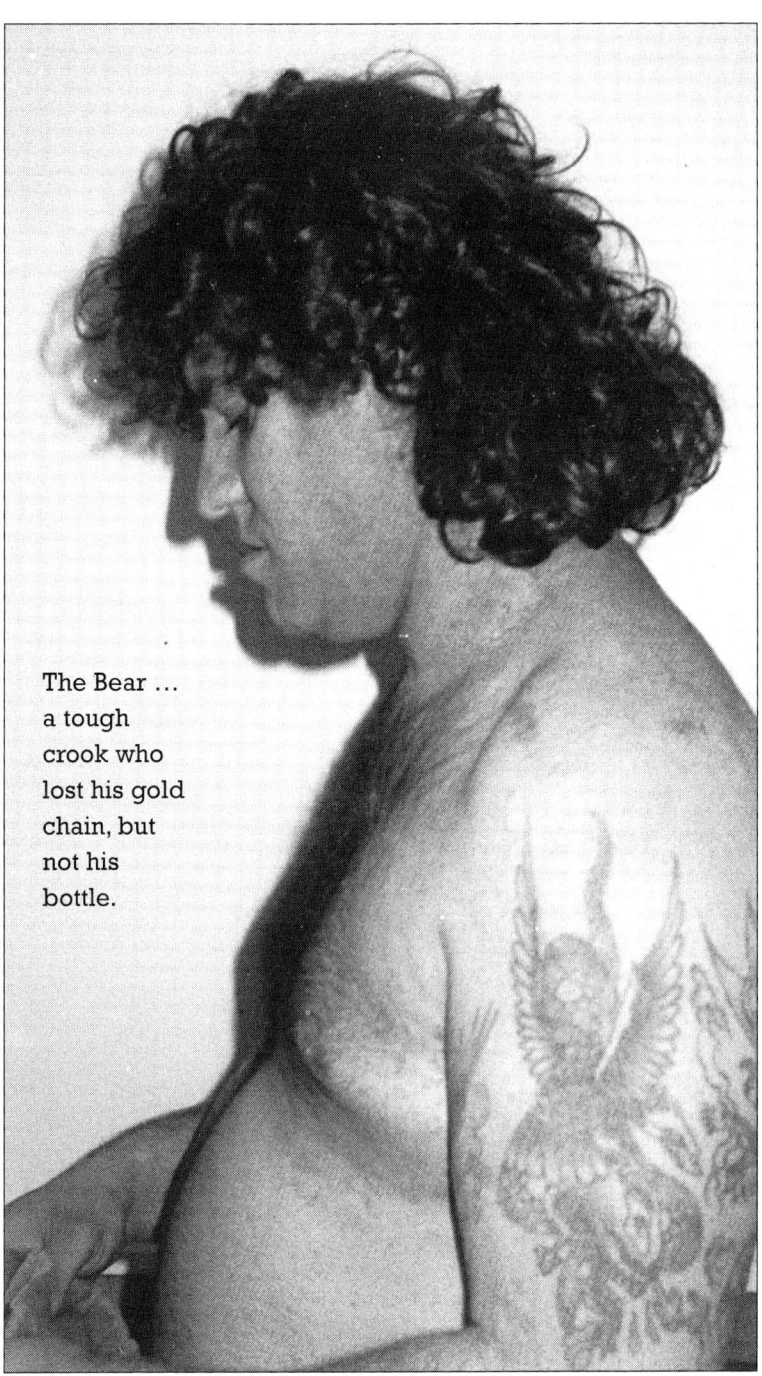

The Bear … a tough crook who lost his gold chain, but not his bottle.

Have you busted a Ford lately? Me with a drug dealer's pride and joy.

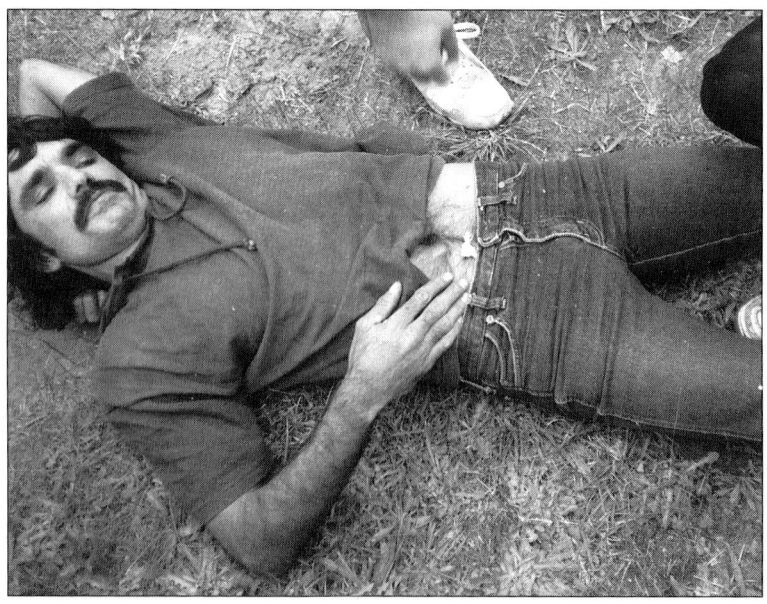

Taking it lying down ... an unhappy dealer shows where he keeps his gear.

Me, serious for once, the day I rescued a child from a deranged man.

Setting a white pointer to catch a fish finger ... our undercover agent, Marielle Porter, in the celebrated flasher case.

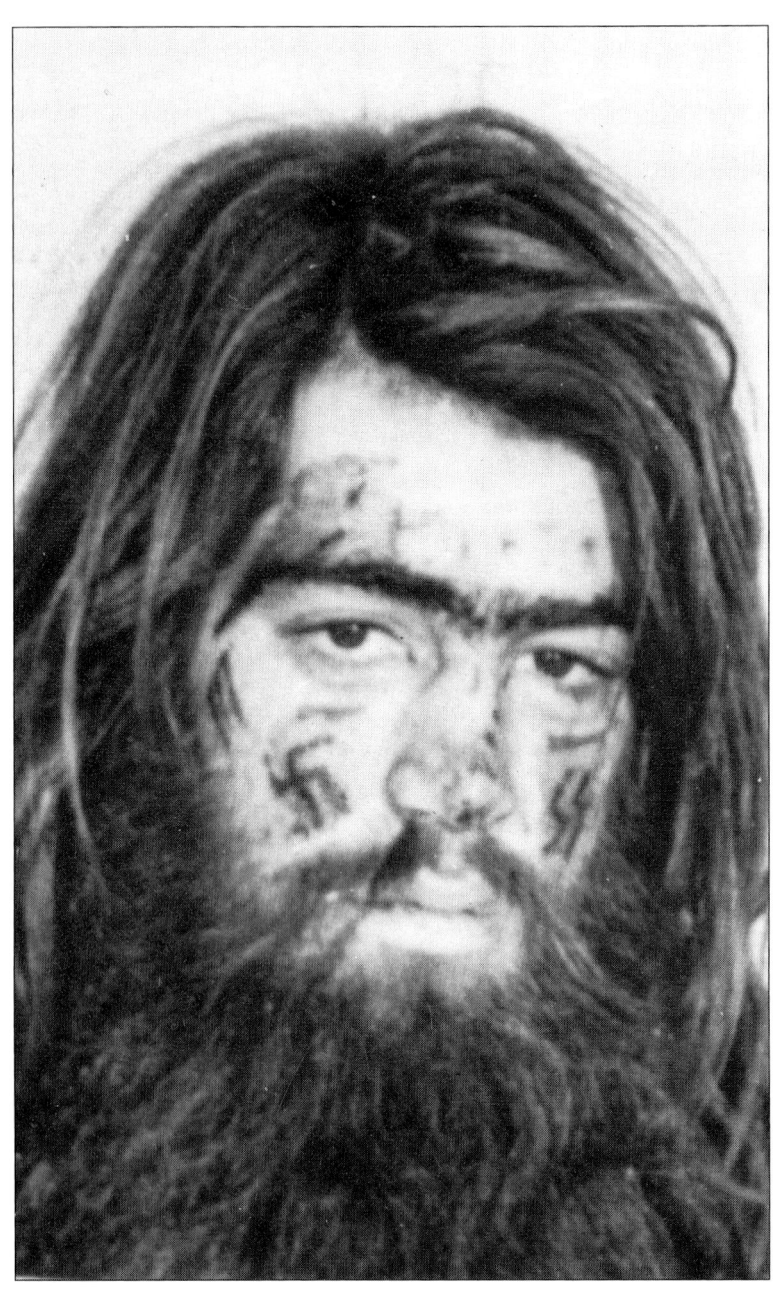

Werewolf? Charles Manson? Undercover cop?
No, just another loser.

one years. He was one of the first cops to seriously work undercover. Phil had made sergeant fifteen years before and was happy to stay at that rank.

He was an Aussie, but he looked more like an old Italian fisherman than a cop. He was a lovely bloke, but could never just have a couple of drinks and go home. Once he started that was it, he drank till he dropped.

It didn't take long for Filthy to hear that Chooka and I were down the pub already. Filthy's last day drinkathon was not due to start until 5pm but here we were, getting into it at about 9am. (I got the publican to open the bar early for us.)

I was drinking Coke, and every now and then I would have a light beer. I had decided to be sensible – at least until 5 or 6pm.

Anyway, about 6pm six of us decided to change pubs and head to the Prince of Wales in Fitzroy Street. So six very scruffy undercover cops poured themselves into an old 'Rent-a-Bomb' Ford Cortina.

Filthy and Chooka were 'maggotted'. We were all squashed, sitting on each other's laps. As the driver, I was constantly telling everyone to just calm down and not be silly.

As we were driving along everyone in the back seat decided that Filthy looked as if he was about to vomit. To be on the safe side they took the risk of moving Chooka – who could also vomit at any moment – out of the way so they could shove Filthy over to the rear seat driver's side window. I was stuck in traffic, unable to pull over.

I decided that Filthy didn't have another pub in him. I had to take what was left of him home. I drove down Carlisle Street, and stopped at the intersection with St Kilda Road in heavy traffic. Filthy was attempting to vomit out the rear passenger window. All of a sudden he went quiet. I turned around, thinking he might have just died.

Even though he was so pissed he could hardly scratch himself he was looking toward a car parked next to us. Filthy said, 'Have a look at this bloke. I don't like the look of him. What's his story? I don't look the like of him.'

The vehicle next to us was a late model Holden sedan. The driver was dressed in a suit, had short hair and looked like a middle-aged, typical businessman. But he looked at Filthy with a disgusted glare. Filthy glared back, but was too pissed to do it with meaning. I said, 'Don't worry about it Filthy, you're a citizen now, let it go.'

I thought this poor old Joe Citizen would die if he knew we were coppers.

As I started to drive off Filthy made his move. He couldn't stop and harass this driver so he did the next best thing. He spat a great big 'greenie' onto the middle of Joe Citizen's passenger side window.

I heard it land, and cringed as I turned and saw the disgusting blob slowly slide down the window. The target responded instantly.

This driver lifted his bum off the seat, pulled out his wallet and began to open it. All of us in the car knew what was coming – we had all done it many, many times. We knew he was not about to offer us money.

Just as we expected, he opened his wallet and flashed us a police badge. I saw my police career flash before me. Everyone thought he was an inspector or something, and urged me to just do a runner.

All of us in the car attempted to hide our faces, dropping

low in the seat. Filthy let out a big, 'Oh Shit!' But the totally drunk Filthy was the only one to actually have a look at the badge. Filthy cried, 'Stop, stop! Look at the badge – it's bullshit.' I looked and noticed that the badge wasn't quite right. It was a fake.

Everyone stopped hiding their faces and actually looked at the badge. We all let out a cheer and started doing the badge shuffle, removing our badges from our rear jean pockets and simultaneously thrusting them at this wanker.

The wanker was so shocked he could barely drive across the intersection. He parked. We all managed to climb out of our little car. Tim, the youngest most-junior cop of us all, was ordered to be in charge of him.

Tim patted him down for weapons then removed his wallet, revealing the offensive fake badge. We were all laughing. I opened the rear passenger side door and lifted a towel lying on the back seat.

There, in front of me were a couple of hundred 'Buddha Sticks' – top quality cannabis all wrapped in aluminum foil, all tied up in bundles. Each bundle had a label attached with words like, 'DAVE $900' or 'STEVE $1,100.'

I called out for everyone to have a look at all this shit. It was all very amusing. We all started patting old Filthy on the back, saying things like, 'Why retire now, you're at your prime. Sensational.'

Filthy said, 'They don't teach that shit at the academy nowadays.' He looked at young Tim and said, 'Instincts, son – you need to trust your instincts.'

Tim handcuffed our catch. We started loading all the grass into our car. Darren then elected to drive Joe Citizen's car back to the station. Joe started saying, 'Excuse me' all the time. Everyone ignored him. I told him several times, 'You don't have to say anything, so shut up.'

As I started to put Joe in the back of our car he stopped, again saying, 'Excuse me, sir.' I finally said, 'For Christ's sake, What?'

Joe said, 'I think you better have this.' He then turned and lifted the back of his suit jacket up and revealed a black leather holster containing a .38 six-shot revolver.

I ripped the gun out of the holster and pushed him face first against the car.

I opened the breech and emptied six live hollow-point rounds into my hand. Suddenly what seemed so hilarious wasn't. I looked at Tim. Looks can't kill, but guns can.

He said, 'But ...' then thought better of it. I said in a very quiet serious voice, 'There's no but.' We got a cold shiver down our spines, realising we were all unarmed. I recall being more angry at Tim for missing the gun than I was at the crook for having it.

We took him back to our plainclothes office, then executed a search warrant on his home. It was a normal, well-kept place in suburbia but it was full of stolen goods and the roof was packed with hydroponically-grown marijuana. All up it was a great arrest – and from outside it looked like a text book operation. But we knew different.

At the very end of a very long day the four of us who were still awake opened cans of Fosters. We were in the first floor muster room. Filthy and Chooka were curled up asleep on the floor. Tim looked asleep at his desk, about four metres from us, his head down on his forearm, facing out the window.

He had been very upset with himself. I looked at the reflection in the window and saw that his eyes were open, and that he was far from sleeping. I walked over and tried to make him feel better.

I said, 'It could be worse, we could all be lying shot in the gutter.' Tim said, 'Yeah, thanks. I feel much better.' He didn't look it.

I said, 'Have a beer, we've all made mistakes – well, not as bad as yours. Like I've never nearly had my boss and all my work mates killed.'

Tim looked at me and smiled. He said, 'You're never serious, but you would never make a mistake like that.'

I touched him on the shoulder and said, 'Just learn from your mistakes. Always remember, when you do something, anything, do it one hundred percent or just don't do it at all. Policing is a very serious business, I just never take myself seriously when I do it.'

I felt sorry for the next poor bastard Tim searched.

DURING my undercover days I used to get right into it. I used to have to feel like a low life scum bag so I could act and look like one.

At this time I was convinced I had to act, but I wasn't acting, I was being a scum bag. You just can't act, it doesn't hold water.

Anyway, I had a set of clothes I would put on that would transform me mentally into what I was to become. I knew that if I believed I was a low-life heroin-using parasite, I could convince others I was one. So I developed a person that was between the normal Angus and disgusting Dean Collie. I would become Lex.

Lex was hip but not trendy, with-it but not cool. Imagine a

'Fonzie' from the series *Happy Days* with a bad hair cut and no cool. That was Lex.

I was Lex when I wanted to work undercover down The Street. I could blow my cover as Lex without a problem. I did not have to protect him like I did Dean Collie. I needed Dean to keep in touch with The Street.

There were Lexes everywhere; they were a dime a dozen. He was the typical scum bag. I recall Lex wanted to wear the old blue and white check Miller Shirt with the silver thread in it, but I could never find my old shirts. Mum must have thrown them out. She always had good taste.

And, yes, Lex was known to wear an old pair of tight fitting black acid washed stretch jeans with the worn-out patch on the right side where he always scratched his balls. It's a bloke thing, you do it just to show people you've got them or something.

I would rub oil through my hair, wearing the same old jeans. And I would never, I mean never, wash the jeans. You can wear jeans for years and not wash them. The best part about it is they don't fade.

I found the downside was that when I got home from work my girlfriend wouldn't let me in the house. This meant I would arrive home after a hard day's work, ring the door bell and start to take all my clothes off on the front porch. My girlfriend would throw a towel at me, I would wrap the towel around me so the neighbours would not see all my 'rudie bits' and walk back inside.

I would then jump in a hot shower and wash The Street off – or try to. I think it was in the blood. But the warm water and soap could wash The Street out of my mind. It allowed me to be me. The problem was that I started to lose who me was.

This never affected my police work as much as it did my social life. Now, years later, I realise that Lex, Dean and me were in fact all parts of the same person – no acting required.

I BELIEVE the difference between an also-ran detective and a good detective is massive. I believe if you're going to do a job, it's all or nothing. I tend to put my whole self into it. Sometimes it pays dividends and sometimes it gets me in the shit.

When you are an investigator,d 'avenues of inquiry' are the roads in which the investigation travels. For example, a crime happens, we then do door knocks, use the media to find suspects and maybe set up a police caravan at the crime scene. These are avenues of inquiry.

Being a cop is fantastic, being an investigating detective is even better. I got to live in my very own TV murder mystery, often without the murder but a mystery all the same. It is up to you to solve the case.

As an investigator often you are given a crime, and the easy part is finding out who did it. The hard part is finding a nexus between the crime and the offender.

Then you have to collect it in such a way as it can be used in evidence. Keep an open mind. Always look for 'avenues of inquiry.'

As the saying goes, 'The mind is like a parachute, it only works when it's open.'

in the dock

'I'd always wanted to be a
hard bitten detective. Now I was'

I WAS working plainclothes duty with Darren one day when we got back to our office and found trouble. Our boss called a meeting and we were told we all had to be there. It could only be bad news.

The boss started by saying, 'A United States warship, believed to be nuclear powered, will dock at Station Pier in two days time. Due to intelligence received, we expect large demonstrations.

'The District Commander has directed that all leave and rest days have been cancelled forthwith. I don't care how you do it, but you will all be wearing full, yes full, uniform on Friday. You, of course, may choose to go off sick – saying your dog got run over, you have gonorrhoea, diarrhoea, your dick fell off or whatever – but in that case, as soon as you are fit to work, you will be in charge of the property office, brief book and buying lunches.

'Any questions?'

All quiet except for a few muffled mumblings.

The boss said, 'Dismissed,' and we were.

Friday rolled up and so did we. Some moustaches had to go

or were heavily trimmed, hair got cut, some just got heavily gelled and shoved under caps.

Uniforms were too small, too dirty, and often with belts and tie pins missing. Some of the black uniform issue shoes had been replaced with black privately purchased casual shoes. We looked a shambles – like rejects from *Police Academy*.

We were picked up at our office in a large bus and conveyed to the Port Melbourne Docks. We had all worked in plainclothes for so long we had gone a little feral and felt weird back in uniform.

I whispered to Darren, 'Don't look now but I think you're a Jack.'

THE pier was packed with screaming protesters. Our bus pushed its way through the mob and stopped after going through a large gate that closed behind us. After a while the Commander appeared to give the coach's address.

'We are here to protect our naval visitors from America. The issue is that the sailors have the right to come and go from their ship as they like.

'For the past two hours these protesters have not allowed free passage to and from this pier. We are here to remedy this situation. Listen to your sergeants. You are not to arrest anyone unless specifically directed by your sergeants. Listen to our commands and take care.'

The Commander strode off.

I took this to mean that this was serious shit and that shit was going to happen.

The upside was that we were looking forward to meeting some of the women protesters that gave the old Diggers such a hard time at an Anzac Day Parade a few weeks earlier.

Our lot was mixed in with about a hundred other real uniform police. I told Paul and Darren they better behave because there were cops everywhere. We tried to mingle but from the looks we got from the real cops it appeared they thought we might be enemy infiltrators.

Darren, Paul, Sandy and I did dag it up a bit, anyway. I had to produce my police badge three times to police who thought we didn't belong.

Paul looked the funniest. He was a very thick set boofheaded bloke with black hair and a large black droopy moustache. We called him the Turk as he looked exactly like a Turkish terrorist. Now he looked like a Turkish terrorist in a bodgie police uniform. No cops asked to see his ID because he looked too scary to approach.

We all found ourselves in the front line in this serious demonstration. The protesters were full on. Many of them very tough 'Women Against War' types. They really hated men full stop. Men in uniform tended to set them right off – the wrong way.

We stood there in a straight line stopping the protesters getting near the ship. In front of us, about one metre away were the protesters, all screaming things like, 'Fascist Pigs' etc. Right in front of me was a particularly annoying bongo drummer. I thought the piano accordion was bad.

This bloke had hair down to his bum and kept on hitting the drum making this senseless moronic tune, singing, 'Coppers are pigs, fascist pigs' on and on and on.

Every now and then he would pause to spit on me or another copper nearby. God it was hard to stand there being spat on.

I looked over to the Turk. I noticed even the protesters were keeping well away from him. Every time a protester got anywhere near him he peeled back his lips and snarled, then they would melt back into the crowd.

As a police officer you realise that they are not attacking you personally, so you don't take it personally. You just turn the other cheek and smile. You don't take sides, you just do your job. Insults are water off a duck's back.

I whispered to Darren, 'Pass the word, the bongo drummer is mine – don't touch the bongo drummer.'

I then started to try to work out how I was going to shove the bongo drum up his arse. I was getting really pissed off at several other cops that also thought they could have the bongo drummer. I said, 'Don't even think about it. He's mine.'

As the spittle dripped down my shirt he just kept smiling, spitting, drumming and teasing, totally unaware of the imminent extreme violence planned against him.

I was prepared to overlook and ignore several other extremely annoying bastards just to get the drummer. I knew I would have to fight several other cops to do it, but that was a small price to pay for revenge. Not that I was taking it personally or anything.

This drummer was smarter than I gave him credit for. As our superiors started to give us orders to attack, sorry, I mean walk forward and calmly and safely clear the pier of protesters, the bongo drummer did a runner. He stayed out of my reach as the 'clear the pier' order was given.

I had almost got to him when he wisely leapt off the pier into deep cold water, definitely safer than having a close encounter with an enraged copper. The cunning, wet bastard.

A short time later a very careful observer would have seen

a particularly nasty protester get led along by an angry policeman, the policeman bending her arm up her back in an effort to control her. The arm bent too far and went in a direction arms weren't meant to. The policeman immediately let go and pretended it didn't happen. He then picked another target.

After several battles won and lost the cops were given the order to go home. A senior officer walked up to our bus as we were getting onto it. He said, 'I want four volunteers to stay till eleven so the night shift can take over.' I was right in his face. I tried to turn away but there was nowhere to hide.

No volunteers put their hands up so the officer said, 'You, you, you and you, report to the gatehouse now. Thanks for your assistance.' A sergeant unknown to us, Darren, Sandy and me were it.

When we got to the gatehouse, it was raining and the pier was totally deserted. The odd US sailor came and went, but there were no protesters. We sat there watching ourselves on the late news, cheering as the police did the big 'charge'. I even got a glimpse of the bongo drummer as he dived off the pier to safety.

All the navy sailors had passed and walked through the gate by themselves. A short time later I heard an, 'excuse me officer.' I looked out the window and saw a women with her daughter. Her daughter was about eighteen years old and attractive.

The mother explained to me that her daughter had met a lovely sailor and wanted to visit him before he left. I started to telephone the ship, but I paused for a moment when I thought I heard a distant bongo drum. I did, I did hear a bongo drum.

It was like being in the jungle waiting for the savages to attack except when we heard the unforgettable words, 'Coppers are pigs, fascist pigs,' again and again. We put up with it for a minute or so until he started to get into the face of the young girl and her mother. He then started singing new disgusting little songs aimed at them.

I looked at my sergeant, the look said, 'please?' The sergeant, who I didn't know, was clearly a wise and decent man. He said, 'He's yours, go.'

I immediately looked away, uninterested, in an attempt to catch him off guard. Then I turned and leapt head first out the large open counter window.

The bongo man might have been a tuneless idiot, but he could recognise danger when he saw it, particularly when it dived through a window at him. He was off, straight up the pier with me running full bore after him.

He maintained about a three metre lead on me for the length of the pier then he turned right and headed for an old deserted house.

As he got close he yelled out for help, but I didn't care as I knew it was deserted. Just as he got to the front of the house I leapt, grabbing a handful of hair. I came to the ground knocking over several large tins of paint. One paint tin was pink oil paint, it opened, we rolled in the paint as he struggled to get away.

Bongo yelled, 'Help!' Knowing there was no-one to save him I yelled, 'Help!', mocking him.

I yelled, 'Help, Help!' even louder than he was yelling. Of course, no-one came. After all the abuse, all the spitting, he was finally mine. It was one of those moments when it was great to be a peacekeeper.

Then the front door of the dark deserted house opened, and about twenty 'Women Against War' ran at me screaming. This was not good. Bongo Man must have belonged to them.

I wrapped one hand around his long hair and hung on. The women kicked, poked, scratched and spat on me. With my one free hand I tried to keep them back, then I realised I was in trouble. I was losing badly and getting hurt.

My free hand then started to punch these women as hard as it could, I recall even poking one of the she devils in the eye to get her to let go. These were desperate times.

Until now I had never hit a woman in my life, but this was no time for chivalry. They were using their feet, fists, nails and teeth against me. It was like being attacked by a pack of wild dogs, although the dogs would have smelled better.

I'd always wanted to be a hard bitten detective. Now I was.

Through the women I saw two large American sailors who could see what was happening. They could not intervene as this could cause a diplomatic incident. I couldn't have cared less – I was in serious trouble. I wish they would have nuked the bitches. One of the sailors ran back toward the gatehouse to get me help, the other stayed.

At one stage I got to my police radio, curled up and screamed, 'End of Princes Pier, urgent! I'm in trouble!' A woman grabbed the radio from me, pushed the button and screamed, 'No he's not, we'll look after him.' That was against the rules.

Bongo Man was in agony, he was screaming at the women to stop and to let me go. I had so much of his hair in my hand that it wouldn't pull out. If it did his whole scalp would come off. He just wanted the whole thing to stop.

Eventually several other cops came and jumped in, then

cop cars screamed up. They got to me and Bongo. By this stage Bongo and I were stuffed. Someone cuffed Bongo Man. It wasn't me – I didn't have the strength.

I staggered to my feet, sore all over, badly scratched and bruised with the makings of a black eye swelling already. Several other police were assaulted by the women as they arrived. I staggered forward and grabbed one of the women that had been 'up close and personal' throughout the attack, she was still screaming abuse. She was one of many that assaulted me, but was the only one that I could identify.

The rest of the women retired back into the dark, undeserted house. As we drove away I heard over the radio that several cops were missing equipment such as police caps. The women must have taken them into the house.

They joked about who was going back in there to get them. No-one was game.

I was taken to hospital to have my injuries checked. As I was taken into casualty the nurses thought I had been ripped apart by a lion. I was happy to stick to that story.

But Darren, my trusted and loyal mate, opened his big mouth and told them it was a bunch of women. The nurses thought that was hilarious, so did the doctors, cops, cleaners, patients and any other bastard that happened to be passing by.

Darren told me they had arrested and charged four of the women that had attacked me. They gave Bongo Man a heap of charges too. He also said they had got statements from the mother and daughter at the gatehouse. I would have smiled if it didn't hurt so much. I slept and was actually off work for three days.

I carried the classic female scratch marks for two weeks, four deep scratches about a centimetre apart down the right side of my face. They were the worst injuries I got in sixteen years in the job.

ONE afternoon I was with Darren working plainclothes and we were doing what we loved – hunting crooks in The Street. It was getting dark when we saw the divvie van pull up near The Cafe. Then Helen and Simon, two uniform cops, got out and sat in the caf to have a smoke and a coffee.

Now how are we meant to catch crooks with them around? I wanted them to piss off, they made The Street nervous. I then saw something that could brighten our day.

We walked over the road to the post office where Morrie had just staggered out of the phone box. He was in his fifties, totally pissed and very angry at the world. Sober or drunk he would be shadow boxing the whole time, ducking and weaving non-existent punches.

Morrie had just got out of prison two weeks earlier after doing a twenty-two year stretch for armed robbery and murder. His body wasn't used to alcohol so just a few drinks made him blind drunk. He was short and stocky with a flat face and nose. Twenty-two years in prison made his language disgusting.

He scared the shit out of the general public and it was our duty to protect them.

We walked up to Morrie, told him we were police and that he was under arrest. He thought that was great, he had someone to fight. He was swinging punches at me but we were able to lead him over to the back of the police van. I opened the door and we only just managed to get him inside. He went off his head when we closed the back door and locked it.

We quickly disappeared and took up our our surveillance position again. We laughed as we could see the van rocking wildly. After a couple of minutes the van became still. Morrie had fought his three rounder and was asleep again.

Simon and Helen casually walked up to their van. Now, Simon was a very serious cop, with short red hair, freckles and a short temper. He was the sort of cop that talked tough because he wasn't. Helen was tall and thin, immaculately presented and looked more like a beauty consultant.

Darren and I left our surveillance post and walked to The Street. As they got into the van and closed the doors I said, 'Shhhh'. They were directly opposite us as they began to drive off. We were both laughing. They closed their doors. Simon gave way to one car and pulled out into heavy traffic. Just as he did that Morrie woke, screamed at the top of his voice and smashed the inside of the van.

Simon slammed on the brakes, then Batman and Robin dived out of the van and took cover behind their bonnet. Simon drew his gun and screamed, 'Who are you?' He must have thought he was in the *X Files*.

It was funny to see two cops approach the back of their own van, guns drawn, as if they expected a lion to jump out of it. Morrie was going crazy, the van was rocking, and he was not listening to any of their demands. Traffic built up around them, and a crowd gathered. The crowd wondered why the cops didn't know who was in the back of their van.

Simon was very upset and angry. He screamed, 'What are you doing in our van? Why are you in there?' Finally Simon got up enough guts to put his face to the window and peep inside. Simon recognised Morrie and started to abuse him.

We had moved position. Simon decided that he didn't care

how he got in the van, he was taking him to jail. As they drove up The Street I waved to Helen. I think my cheeky grin gave me away. She screamed to Simon, 'Look at Angus, it was him. That bastard!' It looked as if she was trying to get Simon to stop the car to abuse me – or shoot me, maybe.

We went back to protecting the public.

I ARRIVED at the Prahran Magistrates' Court. Two of the women arrested on the night of the bongo drummer incident had pleaded not guilty to assault and other charges. One of the women I knew nothing about, as someone else had arrested her. The other one was the one that was up close and personal, attacking me to force me to let go of Bongo Man. I walked into court and saw the two women. You couldn't miss them – they didn't look like social workers or barristers or even hookers. They had a look all of their own.

It was a beautiful day and I was in a hurry to knock off early to go fishing. The prosecutor told me the women were up first, then stood up and called the defendant's name. The defendant walked forward and sat behind her barrister. The prosecutor then bellowed, 'I call the informant.'

That was my cue. I stood up and marched into the witness box. The magistrate nodded to me as I gave my full name and the oath.

I gave my evidence in the usual way. Well, then it started. The barrister was most upset with me. He accused me of lying to the court, misleading the court, fabricating evidence, exaggerating. He disagreed with everything I said, as usual. The defendant seated behind him was saying under her breath, 'Lying male bastard, prick, Nazi.' Twice her own barrister had to tell her to shut up.

I told the court how she had spat on me, kicked me, scratched me, poked me in the eyes, and taken my police radio. Eventually it was over. The magistrate obviously believed me and understood what a difficult job the police had to contend with. The magistrate had read the statements of the mother and daughter, as it was the same beak who had heard the guilty plea from the Bongo Man the day before.

I sat back down in the court waiting for his decision. He convicted and fined her about $500, a good result all around. I was about to leave when the prosecutor stood up and called the next case, he called the defendant's name, then he said, 'I call the informant.'

I looked over to another copper named Scotty who had his head in his hands peeping at me through his fingers. Something was terribly wrong. He just shook his head at me.

I could not work out what he was on about. I stood up about to leave when the prosecutor said, 'I call Constable Angus.'

My heart stopped, I looked at the prosecutor. I thought this could not be happening. It was true. I had got up out of my seat and into the witness box so fast Scotty had missed out. I looked at Scotty, who just shook his head again.

I had just given evidence against the wrong defendant. No wonder the barrister and the defendant were abusing me so much. I reluctantly got back into the witness box and swore myself in. My mind was running at a hundred miles an hour. What could I do?

I couldn't just say, 'Okay, time out, excuse me everyone, I just gave evidence for the last hour against the wrong person.' Especially when the magistrate had just convicted her.

I did the only thing possible in the circumstances. I gave very similar evidence to the previous case. Surely a little bit more bullshit wouldn't matter. I peeped at Scotty who was, by this stage, almost under his seat. From the corner of my eye I saw Scotty almost crawl out of the court, not wanting to have anything to do with me or what was happening. The police prosecutor had a strange perplexed look on his face, as did the magistrate. I danced around in the witness box again for a while. My evidence was nowhere near as good as the first time.

But it was good enough. She was convicted. I ran from the court. I found Scotty lurking in some bushes out the front.

He said, 'What happened?'

I said, 'Guilty, $600 fine. They shouldn't look so much alike.'

He said, 'Their names don't look alike, you idiot.' He had a point.

Anyway, I'd protected the public enough for one day. I went fishing to recover.

picking up chicks

'Maybe he was just
giving it a cuddle'

IT was a public holiday and The Street was deserted, except for a few die-hard addicts looking to die the hard way, as most eventually do. There was a call for a police unit to do a job, but all the other St Kilda units were busy.

Darren picked up the radio and said, 'St Kilda 450, we'll do that job for you.' The D24 operator said, 'Thanks 450. Your job is a "story to tell." Mrs Adams Flat 19/36 Milton Street, Elwood.' Darren responded: 'Roger that, 24102.' (We always had to give our registered number when we took a job.)

We pulled up out the front of a four-storey block of flats and walked to the top floor. We knocked politely and the door was opened by a lovely old lady who said, 'Come in.'

I said in my best official voice, 'What seems to be the problem?'

She said, 'Well it's terrible really. The problem is chicken noises. Now, chickens can make a lot on noise, especially when they get clucky – you know, when they sit on the eggs. I used to have chickens as I child when I lived in the country.'

Well, off she went with her life story, well away from the problem at hand. She was putting the chicken before the egg so to speak.

I interrupted her and said, 'Just contact the body corporate. I'm sure your neighbours are not allowed to have chickens in the building.' I wasn't sure as I was not up on chicken legislation, but it sounded right.

She said, 'No, not in this building, over there.'

She led us over to her kitchen window. 'I was doing the dishes here with the window open. I heard the noise so I looked out down to that house there, see that house with the chicken coop, and there he was, he had his pants down doing a terrible thing to that chicken.'

She then pointed to a chicken that was lying motionless on the ground within the cage. It looked well and truly stuffed. She went on to say she rang the police because she thought, 'That poor chicken.'

I looked at Darren, who was silently mouthing the word, 'Chicken'.

I said, 'You saw a man actually doing something to that chicken right there.' I pointed to the only motionless chicken in the pen. She said, 'Oh it was terrible, when he finished he put it back in the pen and it hasn't moved since.' I wasn't surprised.

I said, 'How many men live in that house?'

The respectable old lady said, 'Only one, his name is Eric. I thought he was a lovely man, he helped me when I had a fall back in January. It was Eric with the chicken. My hearing's not too good, but my eye sight is perfect.'

I informed her that I would need a statement, but we wouldn't do it at that moment. Darren and I left quietly – we were on the case. On the way down the stairs Darren said, 'Maybe he was just giving it a cuddle.' He was always an optimist.

I said, 'I'm not a pheasant plucker, I'm a pheasant plucker's son and I'm only plucken pheasants while the pheasant pluckers gone.'

Darren walked along saying, 'Chicken?' over and over again. That was the great thing about being a copper, every day was different.

We knocked on the suspect's door. The door opened. An attractive woman said, 'Hello' in a cheerful voice.

This made me take a step backwards. For some reason I didn't think a chicken fucker would have a girlfriend or a wife, but you always should have an open mind. Parachutes and all that.

We identified ourselves. Her name was Sue. We walked inside. It was a lovely house. I asked to see Eric. She said, 'Certainly, I think he's out the back. I'll just get him.' I motioned for Darren to look at the wedding photo on the wall. There were no chickens in the wedding party. In fact, no poultry was visible at all.

Moments later Sue introduced us to Eric. They both seemed quite happy and intrigued to know why we were there. I told Sue we just might go out into the backyard to talk with Eric.

Sue wanted to know what was wrong, but she eventually left us. As she was leaving I asked her if she had been home all morning. Sue said that she had, but she went out shopping for a little while. I asked Eric what he did for a job. He was an executive in a large accounting firm.

I asked, 'Fond of chickens, are you Eric?'

He said, 'What's this about?' He started to get shitty, and looked like he was about to panic.

I said, 'Come over here.' We walked to the chicken coop. I pointed to the dead chicken lying on the ground.' I said, 'What happened to that chicken?'

He said, 'It's dead. Chickens die all the time.'

I said, 'It looks fucked.' With that Eric went right off tap. He demanded we leave his home immediately, threatening to get his solicitors onto us.

I grabbed him and forced him face first against the wire. I put the handcuffs on.

I said, 'Well, we could have done this nicely, but it's your choice. You're under arrest for having sex with and killing this chicken. The charge is bestiality.'

He turned and whispered, 'It's my chicken.'

I corrected him, 'Was your chicken.'

We walked Eric through the house. Sue demanded to know what was going on and almost started fighting us. She screamed that her husband had done nothing. She saw the dead chicken I was holding. She then screamed, 'Why are you taking my husband and that chicken?'

I said, 'I'm terribly sorry, but it's evidence.'

She said, 'Evidence? Evidence? What evidence?'

We took Eric out to the car, but Sue was still demanding to know what was going on. We put him in the back seat. I looked at Eric and said, 'Well, this is going to test the relationship.'

He closed his eyes and dropped his head. I put the chicken in the boot and walked back to Sue. I felt like I was about to deliver a death message.

I said, 'Sue, your husband is under arrest for having sex

with a chicken'. Her face just dropped and she said, 'You're not serious. Sex?'

I said, 'While you were out shopping a person up in those flats saw him pay a visit to the chicken coop, and do the business with the chicken. The chicken went berserk and died.'

She said, 'You're kidding. How can he have sex with a chicken. It's impossible?'

I said, 'I think that's why it's dead.'

Sue started to put it all together in her mind. She said, 'I found one of our other chickens dead last Saturday and I couldn't work out why. Eric loved those chickens. Well, you know what I mean.' I could see Sue thinking.

I said, 'We'll take Eric to the St Kilda Police Station.'

She said, 'You can take Eric wherever you like, I don't want him. How am I going to tell my friends about this. A chicken? He prefers a chicken? Christ, what do I tell mum?'

I was lost for words. Sue finished up by saying, 'You blokes, a crack in the concrete isn't safe.' She put me in the same basket as the chicken fucker. I was a touch offended. She pretended to talk to her mum, 'Hello mum. Oh everything's fine, Eric's just been arrested for rooting one of our chickens -- the cops took my chicken for evidence.' She then walked off. All in all, I thought she took it pretty well.

In the car and back at the station Eric was being a real prick. It was a bad mistake. The whole station had to come and see what a chicken fucker looked like. A lot of chicken jokes flew around. Sandy said, 'Angus, you'd have killed a few chickens in your time, I reckon.'

Whilst we were interviewing Eric, the wife was at home getting over the shock of it all. Not.

I heard over the radio the fire brigade had been called to a fire in Milton Street. Sue had lit a bonfire on her front lawn. I walked back into the interview room and told Eric, and he sat there shaking his head. I said to Eric sympathetically, 'You fuck just one chicken.'

Eric pleaded guilty. The court heard how this stupid act had cost him his job and his marriage. Sue had telephoned his work, his friends, even the press. The press loved it.

A woman once said, 'Women need a reason, men just need a place.'

Anyway.

jumper leads

'The boss preferred not to know.
He was smart like that'

IT was a cold winter's day. I was working as a detective one morning when a Mr Philips, aged about sixty, came into the station. He was talking of a person named Timothy.

He said Timothy was a con man, about thirty five years old and he had a set of stolen number plates in his office. All he knew was that the number plates were stolen. He knew nothing else. This bloke seemed to really hate this Timothy, so I had to be careful as it might well have been a domestic situation. He said Timothy was smooth.

As a cop you never believe one side of the story. I didn't know either person so I decided to pay Timothy a visit. His limousine company was nearby, so I walked down there by myself. I walked into a plush foyer and spoke to the receptionist. I told her who I was. She telephoned Timothy and then said I could go upstairs. At the top of the stairs was a large, beautifully-furnished office.

Timothy stood up and shook my hand. I was impressed. He was about six foot one, immaculately dressed in a $1000 Italian suit. He didn't have a hair out of place, spoke with an educated voice and oozed class.

I felt I had to stand a little taller and pronounce my words carefully. I attempted to match his class. I could now see why it was Timothy and not Tim.

I sat at the huge desk. I said, 'I've received information suggesting you have a set of stolen number plates in your office.'

He said, 'I would say that a Mr Philips has come to you recently. I sacked him two days ago. I'm sure you understand he is upset, but business is business.

'He was a driver of mine. I had to let him go. He has a drinking problem.'

I said, 'I see. He suggested to me that your business is in dire trouble.'

Timothy: 'We have bad times but you battle on.' He then told me that he was very busy and that he had to attend to business. I thought obviously Mr Philips was trying to use me to get back at Timothy. I started to leave, we shook hands again. I apologised for any inconvenience.

As I walked out of his office Timothy said, 'Detective.' I paused and turned back to face him. He said, 'I know it's cold outside but take my advice, if you're going to wear a suit, wear a suit'.

He waved his right hand in an up and down motion. He continued, 'That jumper just doesn't suit.'

I smiled and said, 'Yes, I suppose you're right.'

He said, 'I am. It's the first thing I noticed as you walked in the room. That is a fisherman's knit jumper – keep it for fishing or some such thing.'

I said, 'Thanks for the advice and I am terribly sorry to have caused you or your staff any inconvenience. I won't bother you again.' I left.

I walked down the stairs and left the building. Tim had been doing well until he mentioned my jumper. It was my favourite; my mum had knitted it.

By the time I got back to my office, I was furious. I mumbled away as I typed out a search warrant based on the information from the extremely reliable, totally truthful, never ever wrong employee of the year, Mr Philips.

I asked our receptionist, Deb, what she thought of my jumper. She agreed it was lovely. So there. I gathered a posse together and we all walked to see Mr Fashion Plate. I told everyone his name was Tim.

Six of us walked in. I placed the search warrant on the receptionist's table. I said, 'Hello, I'm back, please stay seated.'

I walked straight up stairs. No Tim. Or Timothy.

I immediately started searching his office. Next to his seat at his desk was a loaded double barrel 'Purdy' shotgun. This is a hand made, top of the range, work-of-art gun.

I had checked if he had gun licence. He didn't. I admired it as I made it safe. I said to Darren, 'Tim must have other enemies besides me. He may have insulted somebody else's dress sense.'

While we were searching I found the receptionist talking to Tim on the blower, then hanging up. After a while it became obvious Tim was not coming back because Timmy knew what we would find.

We found that he had written about two hundred valueless cheques and re-financed two Mercs worth about $120,000 each.

He had taken out a loan for $120,000 to buy a car, then changed the number plates and took out another loan to buy the same car. Totally illegal. So I had him for theft of $240,000 plus the value of all the valueless cheques he had written and an unlicensed shotgun. I was happy – and nice and warm in my jumper.

We left the building with boxes of paperwork. Some I didn't need, but I took them just to upset him.

We checked every address known to man. No Tim. From receipts, I found that he had a Qantas Gold Card and regularly flew all over Australia to play in the casinos. The bastard disappeared. I had four days to go, then I was on leave. I was going fishing interstate with my jumper so I needed to catch him soon.

His ex-wife contacted me. She was stunning. She cried in my office as she told me the story of how her parents had gone guarantor in a big business deal Tim did. Result: they lost their big house in Brighton.

She told me Tim would be very hard to find. He was smart and would not put himself in a position to go to jail. What I needed was a cunning plan.

I turned my mind to locating him. I thought 'avenues of inquiry' – where would he absolutely have to go? I located a post office box where he got some of his mail sent. I went to that post office and looked in the box. There were several large cheques made out for cash. I knew Tim would be busting to get them. A man who dressed so well couldn't live without a large cash flow for long.

I got the surveillance 'dogs' (crime surveillance unit) to work for me for one day. It was now my last day before leave. I was desperate. I got the dogs to sit off the post office box, his parent's place and the casino.

I had nowhere else to look. At lunch time I got a telephone

call. He said, 'Hello, I'm barrister Simon Fortesque of
Fortesque and Briggs, I'm acting on behalf of my client
Timothy. What is your current situation regarding him?'

I said vaguely, 'Timothy? I know that name. Oh, Timothy,
of course. Well, as you know I executed a search warrant at
his business premises and he wasn't there.

'Can you inform him that I am extremely sorry for the
embarrassment both professionally and personally that I have
caused him. My superiors would like to apologise on my
behalf for my incorrect assessment of offences that I thought
he had committed.'

He said, 'Well, I should think so, Timothy is highly
regarded and I am astounded at your behaviour.'

I then went on to tell the barrister that I needed to return all
the documents to him as soon as possible as I wasn't
interested in civil matters.

I said, 'I am a detective. We only deal with criminal
matters, so please apologise to him. He was right. I should
never have listened to Mr Philips. Although I do have a
shotgun belonging to him, and he is unlicensed, please wait
whilst I check my diary.'

I pretended to look up dates. I said, 'Well, I'm busy this
week but how about 2.30pm next Wednesday at my office'.
He said, 'So you do not wish to speak to my client now.'

I said, 'Yes, I do, next Wednesday at 2.30pm. Can you call
me back to confirm that appointment?'

He said, 'So, that's it then. You don't wish to speak to my
client now?'

I said, 'No, I would appreciate a call back to confirm next
Wednesday.'

He said, 'Certainly.'

I put the phone down. Just as I started to think about what I had just done the phone rang. It was Tim.

I said, 'Hello, Timothy, I'm terribly sorry about everything.' Timothy was on the attack. He said, 'Well, I have spoken to my barrister and we are very upset about how you have handled this inquiry. It was only ever civil. You have completely embarrassed me both professionally and privately.'

I said, 'I would appreciate it if you could come and sort the unlicensed firearm out next week.' He agreed and hung up the phone.

I immediately telephoned the leader of the surveillance team.

I said, 'Smurf, it's Angus, just bullshitted my tits off to Tim and his barrister. He's on his mobile and should be there any minute to pick up his money.'

I put the phone down and walked into the boss's office. The boss looked at me and said, 'What? I can tell you've done something wrong.' He was a trained detective.

I said, 'No, boss. We're about to catch Tim. It's just that I did something – "wrong" is a bit harsh – I think naughty is the word.'

The boss really wanted Tim arrested as we were going to charge him with about three hundred cheque offences. The only thing the boss was interested in was the crime figures. It's the 'Clean Up Rate' that counts.

Darren walked into the boss's office and said, 'Excuse me, Angus, the dogs just grabbed him. He double parked his Porsche outside the post office, he was arrested at his mail box. They'll be here in two minutes.'

I said, 'Fantastic, what about his Porsche.'

Darren said, 'That might take a bit longer. Smurf's driving it back here.' Probably via Sydney, I thought to myself.

I said, 'Boss, please remember, whatever happens I'm just protecting the community.'

The boss looked perplexed. I left. The boss preferred not to know. He was smart like that.

Moments later, Tim appeared. He was led into an interview room. I had a huge smile. I was happy, he looked sad.

I uncuffed him and sat him down. I could see and hear Tim's teeth grind with anger. I waited for him to speak. Nothing.

I said, 'G'day Tim, got anything to say about my jumper now?'

He said, 'You lied.'

I said, 'Correct.' At least we knew where we stood. I read out the full formal caution to him.

One of the other officers had put his wallet and his mobile phone on the interview room table. Tim picked it up and started to ring someone. I went to take it from him. He snatched it away and said, 'How dare you touch my phone, I am not a criminal.'

I stood there, smiled and said, 'Watch this.'

I walked to the interview room door and said, 'I can go in.' I stepped into the room. Then I said 'I can go out' and I stepped out. I repeated this several times. I walked over to Tim and removed the phone from his hand. I said, 'You can only go in.' I walked out.

Darren then told me that a barrister by the name of Fortesque was in with the boss. He was more upset than Tim. Darren and I organised the paperwork and the charges.

I had already got our secretary to type up all the charges,

three hundred and two in all. The total sum of the deceptions was over two million dollars, once you added the cheque offences together.

He had stolen so much from so many people it was amazing. He would write out a cheque and receive top of the range hotel accommodation, furniture, car hire and repair, clothing – you name it. He had the gift of the gab and a fantastic ability to impress people. After all, he was always well-dressed.

We charged and remanded him into custody. Mr Fortesque appeared at the remand hearing and treated me with total contempt.

He said, 'You lied to me, causing me to tell your lie to Timothy. This is the most unprofessional act I have come across.'

I said, 'It's no offence to lie, and I'll do it again if it protects the public from blood sucking leeches like your client, plus I have to go away fishing tomorrow.' I left. Timothy remained in custody for two weeks while he arranged a large surety for bail. At the County Court Tim got a huge fine and a long community based order. At least he tasted jail.

What I did was naughty, not wrong. And I don't regret it.

EARLY in our plainclothes days we decided to go up to the snow for a weekend – well, a Saturday night actually, then come home Sunday. Darren, Sandy, Paul and I drove up to Mt Hotham. We planned to do a bit of skiing but it was mainly a drinking-bonding session. At the end of skiing we ended up at a nightclub. We were all having a great time.

Darren was a dolphin trainer, I was a deep sea diver maintaining the telecommunication cable between Tasmania and the mainland – scraping the abalone of the cable, stuff like that. Sandy was a solicitor, Paul went one better, as a senior barrister. We spun bullshit to women most of the night.

The dolphin trainer brought his young lady home. She was about twenty or so, still at uni doing an arts degree. Home was a large 'A' frame house on the edge of a huge gully. We had great views.

Unfortunately, Darren was sleeping in my room. I stayed up for a while and eventually had to go to bed. As I tried to get to sleep I could hear them giggling. I put a pillow over my head and fell asleep.

I woke to a heap of yelling and screaming. I climbed out of bed to see what it was. I looked across the lounge and through the large glass windows. The young woman Darren had brought home was stark naked, standing on the thin rail of the balcony threatening to jump. It was snowing hard and freezing cold. Darren was pleading with her to get down. I screamed at him, 'What's her problem.'

He looked at me and said, 'I told her I was a cop.'

She screamed, 'I slept with a cop! I hate cops, cops killed my father.'

By this time Sandy and Paul were up too, asking questions. She had nothing more to live for, so it was goodbye cruel world. She covered her eyes and leapt off the balcony. We ran forward to see where she was going to land. Fortunately she landed in a deep snow drift. Darren was in shock. He thought he had caused her death. I told him he should never blow his cover.

She was perfectly all right. Sandy gave her a hot shower and she went home.

We all stayed up and drank. It was a lot safer.

ONE morning Darren came to work late. He missed the weekly meeting, the whole meeting stopped as he entered the room. When it finished I asked what happened. He said, 'I got booked for speeding – ninety in a sixty zone.'

I said, 'Didn't you flash Freddie?' Freddie being the police badge. Darren said, 'I think I was trumped. Have a look who gave it to me.'

It was the signature of the Chief Commissioner, S. I. Miller. Sensational. We jumped in the car and took it to straight to a picture framer, and waited until it was framed. It looked great. He then paid the fine.

Darren decided it wouldn't be a good career move putting the chief in the witness box to contest it.

THE problem with being a heroin addict is that you're a crook and you have to rely on other crooks to give you the heroin. The industry is full of criminals. Everyone that touches it are crooks, right up until it is either used by crooks or seized by police. Dirty, smelly, stupid, treacherous crooks.

They finally get enough money together to buy their daily dose of heroin. Even though the opium resin was collected by filthy rotten criminals who wouldn't wash their hands, sold to more filthy criminals working in an unclean clandestine laboratory mixing it with toxic chemicals while turning it into heroin.

It's then been up two arseholes, a stomach and a couple of fannies, then sold to you by a bloke that kept it in his mouth. It's good shit so they can't wait to whack it up their arm no matter where it's been.

I WAS working plainclothes down The Street one day and,

when I was buying lunch, I heard some screaming and crying. It was coming from a female toilet in McDonalds. I found a young women crying over a body.

The corpse had a familiar face. It was Josie, a young street kid turned prostitute. I checked her pulse, nothing. A syringe stuck out of one arm.

As the ambulance took her away one of the officers told me it was the third death that day in the St Kilda area. I took the survivor back to our police station. She was off her face on heroin and didn't make much sense.

She told me through her heroin stupor that they bought the gear from a black bloke named Norman. We left her to straighten up. Darren and I went hunting.

I saw Cindy hanging around the Caf. I double parked. She saw me coming and tried to slink off, but I grabbed her and searched her handbag. Hidden in the lining was a foil of heroin. She swore and carried on. I cuffed her and put her in the back seat. Darren and I drove off.

As we were driving I smiled and threw a cuff key over my shoulder onto Cindy's lap. Cindy had to spread her legs to allow the key to fall on the seat then squirmed around to grab the key and uncuff herself.

While she did this she was abusing me, muttering, 'You arrest me for an offence, that will be the day.'

I threw the foil I had said I found back to her. She opened it up. It was empty. She said, 'Christ!'

I dropped my voice to a serious tone. 'Cindy, do you know a new bloke, a black guy named Norman?'

She said, 'Am I a dog (informer). Do I look like a dog?' I didn't answer.

But she realised that I had never asked her for information

before. She suddenly became serious and said, 'What's wrong?' I said, 'It's Josie, she's left The Street and won't be coming back.'

Cindy knew there was only one way you leave The Street. She didn't say a word and just looked out the window. Tears welled in her eyes. One rolled down her face onto her lips. She said, 'When I was a little girl I used to think tears were salty to stop me crying.'

I stopped at a red light. In a different voice, Cindy said 'Leave your phone on.' She stepped out of our car and walked off. About fifteen minutes later she rang me and said, 'Where do you want him?'

I had thought of a cunning plan. To avoid Cindy having to give evidence I arranged for her to get Norman to do the deal in the driveway to her units. There was a large gate half-way up the driveway. She does the deal on the outside of the gate, we wait on the inside, see and hear the deal through a hole in the gate and arrest him.

Half an hour later Darren and I waited for the deal to take place and a little while later Cindy was waiting in her driveway. All of a sudden a motorbike pulled up in the driveway. Cindy looked back at us, as she knew there was nothing she could do.

It was Norman. Wearing the matching, colour co-ordinated full leathers and helmet. Norman was trendy, on a brand new racing CBR 500 motorbike. She reluctantly did the deal, and he drove off. We were on foot. It wasn't even worth us trying to arrest him. Norman was supposed to be on foot. At least we saw him.

Cindy was upset that he got away. I reassured her that she did a great job, that we got a look at him. I took the heroin she bought and thanked her. We drove off with our foil of heroin for testing at the Forensic Science Laboratory.

I met with Sue the scientist and told her the story that we expected it to be very high quality because we believed this Norman guy was responsible for heroin deaths.

She tested it, and it was pure, top quality, one hundred percent sugar. I knew we must have the wrong bloke. But selling Cindy sugar purporting it to be heroin is trafficking heroin. That's case law. I then wondered if there could be two Normans, both black, one trafficking heroin and the other sugar in St Kilda. Surely not?

We went back down The Street. We were very disappointed and still had no idea who he was. The motorbike registration came up as 'unknown' on the computer data base.

We thought even if we see him how the hell do you stop or catch a motorbike? We parked our car in Lock Street, just off Fitzroy Street, and walked up the road.

We had driven around looking for him for ages, then decided to have a break. Sure enough we heard the unmistakable sound of Norman's motorbike coming up the road toward us. Darren said, 'Shit, you're kidding.' We both turned and, sure enough, it was Norman.

I walked onto the edge of the roadway and looked toward Norman. He was accelerating up the road toward me. As he drew close I reached down and grabbed my imaginary heavy fishing line and lifted it to head height and pulled it tight. I braced myself ready to take off Norm's head.

He saw my actions and panicked. He ducked, slammed his brakes on skidding along the road to a stop. I started to laugh and mimic Norman's actions.

I pretended to be riding a motorbike trying to avoid the

imaginary line. Darren just stood there. Norman realised I was only joking, he then accelerated straight at me, skidded on the grass nature strip, kicked the stand down on his bike, stepped off and strode straight at me. Norman was pissed off.

I smiled and stepped backwards holding both hands in the air obviously surrendering. Norman was wearing a black full face helmet with the visor down. I couldn't see his face, but I suspect he would have looked cross. I backed up to a fence and stopped. Norman brought back his fist about to punch me right in the face. As he got to an arm's length I ripped out my little Saturday night special .38 calibre revolver and smashed it straight into his helmet just below his visor. The visor lifted just enough for my whole hand and the snub-nosed gun to disappear into his helmet.

My hand was so far into the helmet that my gun must have been in his mouth – or his eye socket.

I said in a very loud voice, 'Can you hear me?' The helmet nodded. I said, 'You are under arrest for trafficking heroin, so shut up.' He lay down, I turned to Darren and said, 'You got cuffs?' He stepped forward and cuffed him. I only ever had cuffs or keys, never both.

I said, 'Do they still teach that arrest procedure at the academy?' Darren said, 'I must have been sick that day'. He then said, 'I can't wait to read your statement.'

Norman was mumbling away in his helmet. His mother obviously didn't teach him that it was rude to speak with your mouth full. We searched him and in his boot was a black film canister full of foils of white powder. Darren and I celebrated a good punch – I mean pinch.

We took him back to our office. I told the boss that I had

him as the main suspect for causing up to three deaths that day. The boss told me that seven users had died in the previous three days.

We interviewed Norman. He was not a heroin user himself. Just making money.

He was making full admissions and all was well. At this stage I didn't want to mention the overdose deaths. I just concentrated on the trafficking.

I asked him how he packaged, cut and mixed the heroin. He was a professional and went into great detail how he purchased and how he mixed the heroin. He called it 'mixed'. He explained how he would buy the rock heroin, put it in a coffee grinder and turn the hard rock substance into a fine powder. He would then place the Glucodin into the grinder. He then told me how he would put each of the powders into foils and mix them all together.

I said, 'Hang on a second, could you tell me that again.' The interview was being taped and I needed to clarify something.

He said, 'I would buy the rock heroin and make it into a powder. Then I get the Glucodin sugar and put that in the blender too … it would then become fine like talcum powder. Then I put the heroin into foils and the sugar into foils and mix them all up.'

I said, 'You mix the 'foils' up, is that right?'

He said, 'Yes, that's how I was taught to do it properly.'

I could not believe what I was hearing.

I said, 'So you mix the foils of pure heroin with the foils of pure sugar?'

He said, 'Yep.'

I said, 'Do you ever use heroin?'

He said, 'Never. I'm not stupid.'

I walked out of the interview room. Darren shook his head and said, 'This guy killed seven drug users because he fucks up the recipe.' It was Russian Roulette, pure heroin or pure sugar.

We got a coffee and told the boss. We could not believe that his stupidity cost so many lives. I then went back into the interview room and interviewed him for several counts of manslaughter. He ended up with five years jail.

Anyway.

a bear with a sore head

'One golden rule of policing is that you never hit anyone else's crooks'

COPS and robbers live in a tough world. Being tough comes with the territory, but acting tough gets you into trouble. Men only ever act tough when they aren't. Some cops think that the superman suit makes them tough. They're wrong.

A good crook once told me, 'You don't get respect, you earn it.' He was right.

When I first joined the police force I had to direct traffic in the city. Whilst there I came across a bloke named Sam, although everyone knew him as Bear.

Bear looked like a shortish fat Mexican from an old western movie. He had long fuzzy hair and a long moustache. He was a key member of the Lebanese Tigers. They were a street gang that owned the footpath outside McDonalds in Swanston Street in the middle of Melbourne's central business district.

Sam was the 'gun' fighter of the Tigers. He was a bit smaller than me but he was tough. In those days Bear had to fight all the West Side Sharps, the South Side Sharps, the Tribe (Aboriginal gang) and the Carrum Boys, just to mention a few. Sam was my age but from a different world.

He had the old time crook mentality built in. He didn't have to learn it, he was born with it.

Sam lived by a code. You don't touch the very old or the very young and you treat anyone with respect who shows you respect. When I dealt with him he always knew he was a crook and that I had a job to do.

The thing I liked most about Sam was that he never had to say or do anything to 'show off' in front of his brothers like so many other street thugs. To me he deserved some respect.

Several years later I found him living around The Street. He was past his gang days. He sold a bit of gear, mostly cannabis, and handled heaps of stolen goods.

I could never catch him.

One Saturday night I was working plainclothes with Darren. Over the radio came 'Brawl outside the Wales Hotel, any units clear?'

Several police units came up on the air to attend. Darren and I just followed the speeding cop cars because they had blue lights and sirens and we didn't.

At the scene I found Bear. He was wearing his huge solid gold chain around his neck. This was no ordinary chain, each link was about the size of a ten cent piece. The whole thing weighed five ounces (140 grams). It was the biggest gold chain ever. You could have tied up the Queen Mary with it.

Bear told me that some people buy a house, but he bought a gold chain. His theory was that it was always there if he needed a large amount of money quickly. He always carried winning TAB betting slips to the value of about fifty thousand dollars that accounted for the purchase of the gold chain.

He would often say to crooks, and the odd copper, 'If you

can take it off me you can have it.' He kept it. I was standing there having a chat when Constable Tyson walked up to Bear with his note book. Tyson had taken it upon himself to take the names and addresses of everyone in the area. Tyson was a very good-looking, six foot two inch, ultra fit, immaculate, egotistical smartarse. He thought that the name Tyson meant he was tough and invincible. I don't even think he could bowl fast.

His walk alone told you everything about his personality. Tyson walked up into Bear's face and said, 'What's your name, dickhead?'

Bear looked at him and said, 'No.' He then looked at me and raised his eyebrows as if to say, 'It's not my fault, I have to do it.'

Bear then slowly lifted his right fist to get Tyson's attention then with a straight left punch hit the smartarse in the middle of his face. Tyson was out like a light before he hit the ground.

I grabbed Bear and handcuffed him. He said, 'I never showed him disrespect and he did to me.'

I said, 'I understand, Bear, but you can't just smash cops. I know he is a dickhead but you just can't.' Bear was calm and chatty. We walked off talking about the old days. Other cops walked up and saw Tyson on the ground, they all thought another cop probably did it – he was a well-known dickhead. We had to back him up, but the truth was Bear was a far better bloke than Tyson. But when you put on the uniform you have to back up everyone in blue – smartarses included.

DARREN and I were driving down Grey Street when we saw Chantel, one of our local street prostitutes. Chantel had long legs, long blonde hair with a nice bust. The whole hooker package.

Just after I drove past I looked in the rear vision mirror. A brand new BMW stopped next to her. The driver and hooker had a chat, then Chantel got into the passenger seat. I decided to have a bit of a chat to this loser.

I slowed my unmarked car down and the BMW accelerated past us, went down a couple of side streets and stopped in a deserted business car park. We pulled over. I told Darren we had time for a smoke. The plan was to let them get right into it before we bust them. I told Darren that a BMW driver was likely to pay for 'a hamburger with the lot' with extra relish.

I also allowed them extra time because it was a BMW and this meant possibly it was a European driver, likely to fiddle around a lot more. An Aussie would just get right into it, was my theory.

We got out of the car and walked up to the bouncing vehicle. They were right into it. I crept up to the driver's side door and smashed on the window. The driver nearly jumped through the roof and it wasn't a soft top. I opened the door and said, 'Relax, it's the police.'

The driver was a slimy, smooth well-dressed Greek, about twenty-five years old. He went straight onto the attack.

He said, 'What do you think you are doing?' I think it was a rhetorical question.

I said, 'I'm here because it is illegal to use a prostitute in this state.' He said, 'I hope you know this is my girlfriend. I'll have your job for this.'

I said, 'That is impossible. Not the bit about having my job, the girlfriend bit.' I looked over at Chantel and said, 'You're a bloke aren't you, Dave?'

Chantel said in a deep voice, 'Thanks, Angus.'

Up until now Chantel had spoken in high voice and sounded like one of the Bee Gees. Now she sounded like a lumberjack.

The driver nearly died. He had been having sex with Dave from behind. Dave had taken female hormones so he had breasts. He was a good looking bastard, the old Dave.

Anyway, after the initial shock, the driver fought to survive. It was as though accusing him of having sex with a prostitute was equal to murder. It was all Greek to him.

Him having just boofed a male prostitute made it hilarious for us, but not to BMW man. He wasn't sure whether to commit suicide or to kill all the witnesses.

He started to rub his head and eyes like he was trying to wash all the sexual thoughts he'd just had out of his brain.

I felt sorry for him so I said, 'Pine-o-Clean is the go, give it a good wash in Pine-o-Clean.' It was a joke, Pine-o-Clean would burn the hell out of his dick. Don't ask me how I know that.

We let Dave go and took the driver back to the station. I only ever got any fun out of the mugs in flashy cars. I used to do it because no mugs using street prostitutes meant no street prostitutes and that must be a good thing. It was our job to clean up the streets, and no-one said we couldn't have fun doing it.

VANESSA was a thirty-year-old prostitute and heroin addict. Everyone knew she was a prostitute, but you would never see her working the streets. She was a serious sort of bird with a dry sense of humour, a great body and a weatherbeaten face. It was obvious she was very intelligent by the way she spoke and the fact she could be seen reading newspapers, a very rare sight in The Street, I can tell you.

In a conversation she could snap back one liners that cut you to the quick. I often got the feeling she was streets ahead of everyone else around, including me.

She kept looking at me as though she was up to no good. I realised she wanted me to follow her. I caught up to her in a carpark around the back of the caf. She said, 'I'm getting out of this shit hole. I met this really nice truckie who lives in Alice Springs. I'm moving in with him so I leave on Friday.'

I said, 'Well, I'll see you in a month or so.'

She said, 'I don't ever want to come back. I've been thinking if I burn all my bridges here I won't be able to come back.'

I said, 'Like what?'

She said, 'Set someone up.' She was prepared to give us a good crook so she couldn't come back again.

Vanessa said, 'Pick someone good, I'll do it.'

I told her, 'I don't pay for information. I'll give you nothin'.'

She said, 'I'm doing it so I can't ever come back. What do you think?' I said, 'Well what about Cliffy?' I always wanted Cliffy.

She said, 'I don't get on with him. What about Bear?'

I said, 'You want to set Bear up?'

She said, 'Yeah, he's worth catching.' I jumped at the chance.

'You're on, ring me on my mobile at midday tomorrow. I'll come up with a plan.' She agreed and bounced off.

I stood there thinking there must be a catch, that something was wrong. I would have to watch her closely. Anyway, the following day she rang up. I worked out a cunning plan and ran with it.

Darren went with the arrest crew to the bust site. I got Vanessa to telephone Bear and tell him we wanted six pounds of cannabis at $4500 a pound. The story was that Vanessa was going to Sydney for about three months and her new boyfriend was paying for the gear.

When she sold that she would be back for more. The arrest was to happen at a service station on the outskirts of St Kilda. I drove out to pick her up. She was in Frankston.

I was running late as I had to pick up a hire car as well. I picked her up. She was her relaxed self. I was nervous, making sure everything was right. She sat there talking about how good it would be in a whole new world.

I was driving flat out, trying to get back to St Kilda to make the deal on time. As we were driving through Parkdale, Vanessa said she wanted to buy some cigarettes. I reluctantly agreed and pulled over as a small milk bar.

As she was getting out of the car she asked me for some money to buy the cigarettes. Typical. I handed her seven bucks, the required amount. She bounced away. I waited, and waited. I thought, how the hell can buying cigarettes take so long. As I burst out of the car to go and get her she burst out of the milk bar carrying two white plastic bags of goods.

I said, 'I told you no fucking stealing. Take that back.' She jumped into the passenger seat and opened the bags.

She smiled and said, 'Look I've got chips, Twisties, three packets of smokes.'

I asked, 'You robbed the milk bar man?'

She said, 'No, I boofed him.'

I said, 'We're late for a drug deal and your boofing the milk

187

bar man.' It was ahead of its time as a way to beat the GST. The barter system was alive and well.

All the way to the drug deal she would pull some new goodie out of the bag and say, 'I've got two Bertie Beetles and look, Redskins. I love Redskins. Look, they still put the little spoon in the Whiz Fizz.' She was like a kid looking through a show bag. We got to St Kilda and I dropped her off. The plan was for her to meet up with Bear, make him sweet so he would do the deal.

I got a plainclothes cop from another station to do the deal with Bear.

We parked in the pre-arranged location and waited. Vanessa and Bear appeared out of a laneway and walked toward the car. Bear was carrying a large sports bag. He jumped into the passenger seat, Vanessa into the back.

The undercover pulled out the money, they did the deal. We drove up in cars and did the arrest. Bear turned to Vanessa, knowing it was a set up. He didn't fight, he just abused himself for falling for the whole thing.

I checked the money and the drugs. They were all there, thank Christ. Darren took Bear away and I spoke with Vanessa.

I said, 'Thanks, you did well. With his prior convictions he should get four or five years.'

She said, 'I'll send you a post card' and left.

I was wrong about Vanessa. She really did just want to get away from the street. With Bear the way he was, there was no way she could ever come back. I went back to the station. It was a good pinch.

Bear was very, very unhappy about the whole thing.

He said no comment to everything in the interview. At one

stage Darren went and made a coffee. We came back a few minutes later.

Bear was bleeding from the nose and obviously had been bashed. I asked him what happened, and he said, 'Nothin.'

One golden rule of policing is that you never ever hit anyone else's crook. You're allowed to hit your own but never someone else's. I had seen Tyson in the hallway. He still had a black eye with a cut above it. I knew Bear wouldn't complain. He wasn't the type.

We forgot about it and moved on. Later, he was remanded in custody. I had to take him to his cell and Bear was not his jovial self. He was seething mad over what Vanessa had done to him.

As I was closing the door to his cell he spoke, 'You should be charged with being an accessory and conspiracy.'

I said, 'How do you work that out?'

Bear said, 'Don't you know?'

I said, 'Know what?'

He said, 'Just before we walked up to the car and got busted Vanessa asked me if she could wear my gold chain for a second, and I let her.' I said, 'You're kidding?'

We both laughed. I pulled out a smoke and gave him one.

Bear smiled and said, 'She got me twice, that smartarse bitch.'

I said, 'What a pisser, so that's what it was all about.' We laughed. Bear knew I knew nothing about her plan.

Vanessa had about $30,000 worth of pure gold. The truckie in Alice Springs had scored a treasure trove. Presuming, of course, that's where she went.

The moral of the story is never trust a street crow who reads newspapers.

DARREN and I were on the move in an unmarked police car, when we noticed a vehicle driving without its lights on. I did a U-turn, Darren put the blue light on the roof, the car pulled over and we drew up alongside.

The driver was a young, beautiful Japanese girl. Darren wound his window down and said, 'It's dark, isn't it.'

She said, 'Yes it is.'

I drove off. She sat there for a moment. In my rear vision mirror I saw her headlights go on.

She then chased us and pulled us over. She said that she had been having trouble with a peeping tom. We followed her to her flat, which was on the first floor. She brought us inside, and showed us her bathroom. She pointed out her window, which overlooked a small laneway.

She said that when she had a shower in the morning a man would stop and watch her from the lane. She told us that she had her shower at 7.30am each day. We said we'd be there.

The following morning we arrived in the lane early. We stood there and watched her take her tiny little nightie off and get into the shower. She was stunning. Drop dead gorgeous. We stood there mesmerised. We could see her beautiful shape through the glass shower recess. Moments later, the offender walked up the lane. He was wearing a suit and carrying a brief case. He stopped next to us. The three of us stood there looking up at her. The offender said, 'I'm late. It wasn't the little light blue nightie was it?'

I said, 'It was the little light blue nightie.'

Moments later she got out, dried herself and left the bathroom.

The offender said, 'See you tomorrow morning.'

I said, 'Sure mate, see ya.'

We went upstairs. She was all wet, wrapped in a towel.

I said, 'We fixed the problem. He won't be coming back.' I lied.

The following day we drove down the lane in the middle of the day, just in case. I noticed she had put a blind on the window, blocking any future views. Bummer.

Later that week I found out why. Darren brought her to dinner at my place.

THE following day Bear went to court and got bail. His associates put up a large surety. I was at my office doing paperwork, but Darren was busting to go out and catch crooks. Eventually, we went to the police station to sign out a couple of firearms. It was 3pm, right on the change of shift.

Tyson had finished work. He walked past me mumbling something under his breath. We signed out our guns and went back out to our car. As we got to our car I heard a muffled sound.

I walked over between some cars and found Tyson lying on the ground, bleeding. He said through a mouthful of fat lips, 'It was Bear.' Tyson was only bashed. He was going to be all right. The good part was he now had two black eyes and a badly bruised face.

He staggered back into the station while we went looking for Bear. Tyson was a dickhead, but you can't bash cops. We searched everywhere but found nothing.

We went to his wife's house, girlfriend's house, all his common hangouts, but came up empty. We found that Bear was bailed out from court at 11am. One of his conditions of bail was that he must report to St Kilda Police Station between 9am to 9pm every day. He had reported to the station on bail just before he bashed Tyson. We couldn't find the Bear anywhere, so we went home.

The following day Darren and I were at our office. It was about 10am and I was telling everyone the story about dickhead Tyson, how he had punched a handcuffed Bear and how the crook had met him on an even playing field and bashed him back.

Meanwhile, back at St Kilda Police Station, the front door opened, and into the watchhouse area walked Bear. He casually walked up to the counter and said, 'Can I have the bail book I have to sign.'

The watchhouse keeper stepped backwards, ignoring his request. In shock he bent down and pushed the intercom button and said in a loud voice, 'Attention all members, attention all members, all members to the watch-house NOW.'

Cool to the end, Bear lifted his pen in his right hand as if to say I still need to sign on. The watchhouse keeper gave him the book, Bear signed on as all the cops in the station arrived. Bear didn't fight. He just got bashed.

At the end of it all someone pulled Tyson off him. Bear lay on the floor, bleeding and cuffed while about fifteen uniform members stood around, looking at him.

Bear became a legend that day. He earned the respect of every cop in the district. Crooks also heard what happened. Bear never had to fight again. Everyone also knew about Tyson – that he was a pretend tough guy who could only beat up a guy when he was handcuffed and backed up by fifteen coppers.

THERE once was a crook named Boyd. He was thirty years

old, tall and ugly. He was a heroin-addicted burglar who had one big advantage. His dad was a locksmith, so he grew up learning how to walk through locked doors.

Anyway, I got some red hot mail that Boyd had stolen a safe in a factory burglary in Northcote. Boyd lived in a big, two-storey house in East St Kilda with three other crooks. We all knew Boyd and his house well because, for different reasons, we had raided it three times in the previous month.

I decided to raid the house as soon as possible rather than wait for the usual 4am start. I held an impromptu briefing. Minutes later, four cars double parked outside the house and we climbed out in a busy side street. We were all fully kitted up with vests, sledge hammer, and a couple of shotguns – the lot. Like the Boy Scouts, we wanted to be prepared.

As we walked onto the footpath, we got into our allotted positions. Paul with one strike of the door made it fall flat into the hallway. It had no hinges. He then stepped back.

Darren stepped into the hall, placed a large portable Disco Robo sound system against the left side wall and pushed the play button.

The landing music from the movie *Apocalypse Now* blasted through the house as we entered. It was sensational. As true professionals, we walked at a controlled steady pace clearing one room at a time. Well, that was the plan. The reality was, we all just ran in all directions screaming and smashing into each other until we got tired. For some reason it's more fun that way.

There was no-one home. The loud music would have had a great effect on anyone that was home but, sadly, they were out on burglar business. On the inside of the back door was a post card with a picture of a pig's face on it.

Under the card was the name of our officer in charge of our CIB office. I walked out the back. About five metres from the back door was a small shed. On the door of the shed there was a big 'Keep Out' sign, so I kicked it. It didn't budge. Paul saw me and said, 'I'll get the key.'

He turned toward the back door, where there was an axe leaning against the wall of the house. He picked it up and hit the middle of the door as hard as he could.

The axe cut the door neatly in half. We pulled it open and walked in. As we started to search the shed I noticed blue and white string hanging either side of the door.

One end of the string was tied to a nail. The other was tied to a small piece of wood that was in the jaws of a clothes peg. The clothes peg had wires attached to it, the wires were attached to a battery, the battery had a wire that went into a small souvenir style liquor bottle labelled Irish Whisky. The bottle was full of white powder.

What I was looking at was a bomb.

I realised that the axe had gone through the door and cut the string, if I had managed to kick it open or hit it with a sledge hammer it would have detonated. Paul was still looking around.

I said, 'Paul, don't move, there's a bomb here.' Paul and I tiptoed out of the shed and warned everyone.

Darren said, 'Where is it, can I have a look?'

I said, 'You want to have a look at a bomb?' Paul wanted to put it in a bucket of water or something because he had seen that in a movie. I had a better idea. I wanted to get right away from it.

We called the SOG. They came down and made it safe, then it was taken out to forensic and detonated. The boffin said it would have killed everyone in the vicinity of the shed and in the back of the house.

The expert also said, 'This bomb has been taken directly from a book called *James Bond's book of Medicine* – an American book written by anarchists.

We searched the house again, this time looking for evidence. There was nothing there. The only other address we could connect to Boyd was his mother's home in Malvern.

We took out a warrant and began leaving the station to execute it on his mum's house. As we were leaving I looked at my partner and said, 'Ah, Darren, I um, don't really think we need that.' He dropped his head and reluctantly turned around and carried the Disco Robo sound system back into our office.

We got to the house, knocked on the door and a lovely old women opened it. She invited us in. We explained we were looking for her son. She understood he had a drug problem. On the television I noticed a collection of small liquor bottles from all over Britain. There was a dustless circle indicating one bottle was missing. We then located the book we were looking for, and the wire etc. The only thing we didn't have was Boyd.

I found several small black canisters with a plastic grip attached to them. They were strange little spray packs.

I said to Paul, 'I'll just test it.'

Paul said, 'You're not going to smell it, are you?'

I said, 'No, don't be stupid.'

I did a little spray toward the doorway and stepped back. I then called out, 'Darren, come in here for a second.' The trusting soul walked into the room. I asked him, 'Can you smell?' Just as I said that Darren grabbed his throat and fell to the ground. I said, 'I thought it was mace ... I was just trying to work out what it was.' Darren didn't look happy, but he couldn't complain. He was too busy choking.

We photographed and video-taped everything. Back in St Kilda Darren and I went looking for the informer that told us about Boyd doing the safe job.

It turned out that Boyd himself had been spouting off to everyone that he'd done a safe job. We could never find out which job it was. That's because there never was a safe job. Boyd just wanted us to raid his house again so he could blow us up. The search for him intensified.

He was nowhere to be seen.

About two weeks later we stopped to get lunch at a take-away shop in The Street. I went to the toilet, Darren was standing in line to be served. The man in front of him had purchased his food, picked it up and turned around. Darren looked at him face to face. It was Boyd.

They instantly recognised each other. Boyd let go of his food and reached for his gun, which was tucked into the front of his pants. Darren reached for his gun in its shoulder holster, but it wasn't there because he didn't have one.

Boyd levelled the gun at his face and pulled the trigger. It went 'click'. Nothing happened.

Boyd stepped forward, slamming his gun into Darren's face with such force it pushed him back two steps into the large glass front window.

It was safety glass and it exploded into a thousand pieces. Boyd followed Darren through the window, falling on top of him. Darren helped break Boyd's fall. While my partner rolled around in the glass trying to get up, Boyd left the scene. Fast.

I came out of the toilet and saw the mayhem. Darren was concussed. I lifted him up out of the glass. By now people were everywhere. He said, 'Boyd tried to kill me. I could have sworn I signed out a gun this morning.'

I said, 'You did.' I lifted the bottom of his jacket and there was his gun in a holster on his belt. I said, 'Remember you forgot your shoulder holster and put on a belt one instead?'

Lesson: When you get used to one thing, stick to it. When an emergency happens and you have to react instinctively you instantly do what you have done time and time again. The moment Darren found his gun was not where his reflexes told him it should be, he decided he had no gun. The simple mistake of forgetting his shoulder holster almost cost him his life.

Everyone searched for Boyd, but we didn't get a sniff. I decided to look for an old girlfriend of his, only because there was nowhere else to look. Darren and I sat off her house. We watched her leave and followed her. She ended up at a restaurant. We sat back. It was hopeless, nothing. All of a sudden a car double parked and a dark figure walked in. I said to Darren that I was going to have a closer look.

The driver's hair was all wrong. It was black and too short. I saw him talking to the old girlfriend. He turned and looked straight at me. It was Boyd. He turned toward the rear door of the restaurant. Darren was standing there. I was just inside the front door. I started to draw my revolver, and he drew his gun from his pants then ran straight at the front window.

As he got to the window he dived head first into it. He hit the window in full flight, head first, CRASH. It held firm, like a brick wall. It barely even flexed when he hit it. Boyd bounced off it like a wet sock, fell to the floor in a crumpled heap and didn't move. It might work in the movies, but not in St Kilda.

The Italian manager of the restaurant screamed, 'What he do, this idiot.' The food wasn't that bad.

Boyd's girlfriend screamed, 'You've killed him, you bastards.'

Covering him with my handgun, I walked up and stood on his wrist, bent down and took his pistol from his hand. I made it safe and tucked it into my pants. I cuffed his lifeless body – nothing like being safe. People in the restaurant were still screaming when I lifted my portable radio and called for an ambulance. Darren walked up, looked me in the eyes and smiled. He was a happy camper.

The manager was a middle-aged, hard-working Italian. He walked up to Boyd's lifeless body and started to abuse him.

He said, 'These idiots my window she break one time, two time so I spend more money and get good quality. This one window even hammer she no break'. She broke Boyd instead.

We charged him with everything: Set explosives, attempted murder of Darren and every other charge we could think of. A month later he died in prison of a heroin overdose while awaiting trial. No great loss.

a cunning stunt

'You have to know The Street and become part
of it ... there was always criminal activity there'

MARIELLE was very attractive. Her good looks distracted
cops and crooks alike. She kept very fit and had a body to
die for. Marielle was a constable about twelve months
junior to me.

We had a gym in the station that nobody used. Our bicep
curls were done in the pub, lifting pots of beer.

That was until Marielle decided to start working out.
From then on the gym was packed. I recall straining to pick
up the hand piece of the telephone after lifting grossly
excessive weights trying to impress her.

While working plainclothes I became aware of a flasher
exposing himself in Alma Park. His modus operandi was to
walk up to female sun bathers and masturbate near them.
At times right above them. He was a real toff.

I knew the park well. It was beautiful, with a large well-
kept grass area in the middle surrounded by huge trees.

It was open enough for women to feel safe, yet enclosed
enough to be private. On any sunny day women could be
seen soaking up the sun. I thought of a cunning plan. My
plan needed bait and Marielle would be perfect. I asked the

sergeant if I could use her for a while, and he agreed. My plan was perfect except that about ten minutes after I hatched it the sun disappeared. It took forever before the sun came out again.

Well, three hours, anyway. By this time Marielle had been able to drive home to collect what she called her 'gear'.

Her gear was in a large sports bag. Darren and I grabbed our stuff and we all left. Several members asked us what we were doing. I mumbled something about us going to a private function. Darren and I decided to keep this one to ourselves. There were times for back-up and this was not one of them.

At the park the three of us walked into a small gable-roofed pergola situated on the south edge of the grass area.

I said, 'We'll have the briefing in here. This will be the command post. Now Darren and I will sit in here pretending to be a couple of pissheads drinking cans and talking shit while you walk out in the middle there and work on your tan.'

Marielle thought it was a great idea. She said, 'Now, he is about thirty-five, Australian, long brown hair with a large pot belly, right?'

I said, 'He'll be the one with his dick out.' I then screwed up my face pushing my lips as close as I could to my nose and said, 'His face will look like this.'

Darren and I both laughed. I qualified that by saying, 'Well, that's what I've been told a bloke looks like when he's masturbating. I wouldn't know.' I was trying to impress her with my wit. It wasn't working.

Marielle said, 'Yeah, right.' She looked bored. She

opened up my esky, took out a cold can of bourbon and coke and walked out into the middle of the park and looked for a nice patch of grass.

As she walked off I called out to her, 'Monitor channel two.' I was trying to impress her with my professionalism. It wasn't working.

I sat back on the bench, cracked open a can and said, 'Right, let's start pretending.' Handing Darren a can, I said: 'My plan is to drink a few of these cans, then fill them up with coke or something and sit here pretending to drink real cans like real yobbos so we don't look like cops. What do you think?'

Darren tuned into the cricket on his little transistor radio, sat back and said, 'Perfect.'

Now this was what I joined the job for. No freezing nights hiding in frontyards trying to catch druggies. Sitting there drinking bourbon and coke in the sun while perving on a near-nude girl was clearly the go. And we got paid for it.

We watched as Marielle stopped, opened her bag and removed a large beach towel. She carefully laid it out on the grass. She dropped her dress to the ground revealing tiny little bikini pants. She then stood there and removed her bra while she still had her T-shirt on.

Darren mumbled, 'That's incredible, how do they do that?'

I said, 'I still have trouble putting my shoulder holster on.' Darren felt his shoulder holster under his shirt, sat forward and tried to work out how to do it.

Back to Marielle. She said down on the towel and started removing about ten bottles and containers. I grabbed our small telescope and zoomed up on them. I said, 'They're sun tan lotions.' Darren said, 'What?' and promptly grabbed the scope from me.

I said, 'I had no idea sun baking was so bloody technical.' She then began to slowly rub the different sun protection stuff onto different parts of her body. Darren and I were entranced. It was as though he had just discovered the meaning of life. He said, 'Oh, I geddit. Those bits must need a higher protection factor.'

I said, 'If she keeps that up we'll get more than just our target.'

Darren said, 'If he doesn't hurry, I'll be out there.'

I said, 'If I have to arrest you, can I borrow your cuffs, mine are back at the office?'

Marielle reached into her bag again and produced an old-fashioned alarm clock. It was the type with the two little bells on top. I said, 'She is a professional, mate.'

I knew it wouldn't take long. Two large blokes struggling with an esky staggered toward us. I looked at them and said, 'Shit, did you tell the CI?' Darren said, 'No way.'

Our CIB had somehow heard of our operation. These two looked like the reconnaissance team. Minutes later several other detectives arrived. They set up camp a few metres behind us. When we needed them for surveillance at night they were nowhere to be found. But when it came to a pretty, half-naked girl they were there in droves. It was obvious that their main aim was not to protect the public as much as it was to observe our bait.

About ten minutes later her little alarm rang out. She re-set it and turned over onto her side moving around on her towel to expose a whole new section of her body to the sun.

A small cheer rang out from the gallery each time she moved. Darren said, 'And to think I thought sun baking was just lying out in the sun.'

Over the next hour numerous boys and men took huge detours to walk past Marielle to have a perve. After an hour we got sick of saying, 'Here he is, I think this is him.' None of them was the offender. Darren crushed his empty can and threw it out onto the lawn in front of us. I said, 'What?'

Darren said, 'I'm a yobbo.' Darren was having a ball. I looked up and noticed a small thin dark-skinned bloke stop and appear to talk to Marielle.

I noticed she had undone the strap of her bikini top. She was lying face down wearing nothing but her tiny bikini bottoms. This unknown male then walked off on his way.

I picked up the radio and said, 'Angus to Muzza, what's his go.' Marielle said, 'His line was, "Would you like to share the sun with me?" I said to him, "I think not" and he walked off.'

I said, 'If you want a break sing out.'

Marielle said, 'I'm okay. I finish work in about half an hour. I suppose I could do some overtime.'

I noticed a bloke was heading straight back toward Marielle. He walked up behind her and was out of her sight. She was reading a book facing away from him.

He undid his pants in a flash and produced a large erection. He looked quite proud of it, actually. He began to sway from side to side pulling on his penis as fast as he could.

I jumped to my feet and began to sprint at him. I first tried not to spill my can, then I realised I didn't need it and threw it aside. I was doing well until I caught the guy's eye.

He looked at me running straight at him. He burst into a sprint after putting the trouser snake away. As he did I screamed, 'Muzza.' She looked up and saw him begin to run. Marielle jumped up and gave chase.

I recall the sight in slow motion. I remember as if it was yesterday.

As a matter of fact I did remember it yesterday.

Marielle had undone the back strap of her bikini top. This gave her breasts no support, so they bounced heavily. She then put her right arm across her right breast and took a firm grip of the left one.

I knew if I was ever to be allowed to do this sort of operation in the future we had to catch the crook, not the lure. It didn't really matter that he wasn't 'our' crook. An arrest would be a bonus.

Cops are like seagulls and sheep. One moves, we all move. I heard the spectating detectives begin to give chase. But they were definitely chasing the bait.

They ran because the bait ran. Our friend the mystery masturbator looked over his shoulder and saw everyone in the whole park chasing him.

He ran straight at Alma Road. By now it was about 5pm, peak hour.

Darren passed me running flat out. The bourbon and cokes were slowing me down. Our tosser ran straight out into traffic. Two cars just missed him.

Marielle stopped just short of the gutter. In doing so, to save her balance, she let go of her breasts. Drivers paused to look, then the cars behind them slammed on their brakes to avoid collision.

As brakes screeched our suspect looked back at Marielle.

The sight of her made him stop. Darren, running at full sprint, poleaxed him to the ground. The arrest was completed. He was stiff to be caught.

I eventually crossed the road and took possession of our catch. He wasn't much, but I suppose he was something. He was that small I should have thrown him back. He appeared to be harmless until he opened his mouth.

I said, 'Listen, sunshine, you're not obliged to say anything but anything ...'

He interrupted: 'Let me go. I am a solicitor.' Funny, to me he looked African. I said, 'I don't give a toss, even if you do. You are busted, now shut up while I'm trying to tell you your rights.'

Sunshine said, 'I have done nothing. I am an Egyptian citizen. I am a solicitor, let me go.'

I asked him what his mummy would think of what he had done. He didn't get it. We charged him with wilful and obscene behavior. He was not a happy man.

Knowing that his career was on the line he fought the charges with everything he had. He was found guilty, suspended from acting as a solicitor and fined $500. It was a good result.

He appealed. At the County Court a jury found him not guilty. He was reinstated as a solicitor and is still practising today.

St Kilda days were great. Incidents like the one with Marielle and our day in the sun made them special. Marielle went on to marry a colourful detective inspector known as The Rocket. He is a very lucky man. They have two lovely kids. Good luck to them.

MY girlfriend and I decided to have a dinner party with

friends. I invited Mark, a bank manager, and Vince, the bricklayer, and their wives. The six of us used to take it in turns to have dinner at each other's houses and it was our turn.

We started talking about the usual stuff people talk to cops about: drugs, crime and how best to stop both. Mark and his wife Nicky lived in St Kilda. They said they never see prostitutes, drug addicts or criminals. None of it.

They said they see some 'bad' types, but not criminals. Mark could not understand what I was on about. I kept telling them that St Kilda was out of control, crime wise.

Vince apparently hadn't seen real crooks anywhere, either, let alone St Kilda, except on TV being led into court. He did say he was offered some stolen stereo equipment at work once.

Vince said he'd punched the bloke in the head and dragged him off the building site.

Vince worked hard for his money and paid tax, so he hated crooks as much as he hated dole bludgers.

Anyway, this night my girlfriend had meticulously prepared a taste sensation – crab quiche. As the guests arrived they commented on the incredible aroma of the fresh crab.

These were big sand crabs or swimmer crabs. I explained how I had risked life and limb catching each crab by hand underwater, scuba diving. How I saw the eyes sticking out of the sand, estimated where the claws would be, then grabbed each claw.

I explained how I'd brought them home, boiled them up, sat in front of the cricket and removed all the crab meat by hand and put it in a bowl ready for my girlfriend 'Harry'

(Harriet). When entree was ready we solved a few more of the world's problems, then made our way to the dinner table.

Harry brought the entree. It was fresh crab mixed with chopped fresh scallops and small pieces of rockling, carefully put in a soup.

I had dived out off Sandringham and collected a heap of scallops then dived off Black Rock and got a large spotted rockling.

I had gone to the Bentleigh Market and bought five large chicken carcasses, simmered them with onions and herbs for four hours and made the stock, reducing it to a couple of litres, then added the fresh crab, scallops and rockling.

When it was almost cooked I added finely sliced egg omelette after slowly dribbling two egg whites through the soup – and, finally, sliced shallots, a bay leaf and assorted spices. The result was to die for. Several fish and crustaceans already had.

While we ate the entree we were consumed by the moment. The atmosphere was warm and close. This is what life is all about, friends talking about everyday family things ... such as one of their young daughters being taken to the toilet by her mum wearing 'in-line' skates and the young girl telling her, 'Be careful mum – don't get poo on my wheels.'

I found myself bragging about why the food was so good, why it was all so fresh and why their tastebuds were overdosing.

I said, 'A lot of people individually select their seafood through the chilled glass window of the local fish shop. My window is my mask.'

Sure, I was showing off, but I got enjoyment from the hunter-gatherer bit. No harm in that, I suppose.

These moments are what life is all about. They gave me perspective.

We were a world away from The Street – and it was a relief. I wallowed in the normality, hoping to wash away the evil that had become part of my daily life. It was a wake-up call to remind me not everyone was a criminal or a crime victim.

Our tastebuds were still recovering when Harry opened the oven. The fresh crab quiche was a perfect light golden brown. The aroma was mouth-watering.

Harry was wearing a small oven glove. She put her hand under the metal tray, gently lifted it off the metal shelf and began to turn toward the kitchen bench. The hot outer metal ring of the quiche dish came away from the pastry and base and fell down onto her inner forearm.

As the soft skin burnt she threw the quiche into the air and squealed with pain. The quiche landed with a splash on the bench and then the floor – face down, of course. Overwhelmed with embarrassment and pain, Harry fell to her knees, crying. Nicky and Sally immediately consoled her.

I mumbled something about two large pizzas and we left. We went in Vincent's beaten-up old Ford Fairlane. I ordered the pizzas on my mobile phone. Vince drove, Mark sat in the front passenger seat and I sat in the back. I told them I would take them on a tour of their precious St Kilda.

We drove down Grey, Acland and Barkly Streets. I pointed out prostitutes, petty crooks and drug dealers, not to mention a few well-known local idiots. I gave them a running commentary while watching two cops who had no idea what they were doing.

The two cops could not see what was going on around them – they were like tourists. Deals were going down in front of them and they couldn't see. I said that to be a cop you have to know The Street and become part of it.

I explained how much fun it was to catch crooks and said there was always criminal activity there. You just had to know where to look.

I directed Vincent to double-park right out the front of the St Kilda Cafe. I held my left hand over my face and told the other two to look inside and when they got eye contact, to nod.

All of a sudden Mark the bank manager screamed, 'Quick go, go! Get out of here. Here comes one! Go, go.' Vincent started to drive off but I told him to stop and learn. A large and very aggressive female walked straight up to the window, looked Mark in the face and said, 'What do ya want – smack?'

I had never seen her before. Her face was about three inches from Mark's. He froze with fear. She then held a foil of heroin up to his face and said, 'Give me $90 and go.'

Mark couldn't breathe. She then said, 'Okay, ya can have two for $160 and that's it.'

Mark said, 'Go.' Vincent accelerated off. As we left, the female trafficker yelled abuse at us.

I sat up in the seat and said, 'There you go, crooks up close and personal.' Mark was in shock. Vincent raved on about how he couldn't believe how she offered us heroin like that.

We stopped down the street a bit to buy smokes. They voted I leave the safety of the vehicle to buy them. I laughed. When we got home they had great stories to tell their wives.

I was happy. I had given them a little peek at my world. But it had also given me a flash of insight into myself ... I realised The Street had hold of me and that if I stayed out there too long I'd rather be with the freaks than with decent people.

Name .... M. CULLOCH L.N. .... Reg. No. ....24205.........

REMARKS BY OFFICER IN CHARGE OF DISTRICT AS TO CONDUCT AND EFFICIENCY, RECOMMENDATIONS, ETC.

(To be entered on transfer, discharge, dismissal or death of member or when Officer in Charge of District transfers, or retires. See Regulations 278 and 279.)

Date	Comment
30.1.86	Appointment confirmed.
22.4.86	A keen, well conducted member with a good work performance. A BOLTON, Chief Superintendent.
17/11/1986	"Commended at District level for observation, initiative and diligence displayed in the detection and apprehension of two offenders for a number of offences, and in the recovery of a substantial amount of stolen property."
23/3/87	"Commended at District Level for initiative, diligence and attention to duty in following up a casual remark which they overheard and which resulted in the detection and arrest of two offenders for a car theft which would otherwise have gone undetected." J. FRAME (Assistant commissioner) File No. 13-3-3841
1987	Passed Theoretical (Law) Examination. P/G 12/11/87
25/10/88	A well conducted, effective member who performed his duty at St.Kilda in a highly satisfactory manner. R. F. GILL Chief Superintendent

CHOPPER 9

The Final Cut

OUT NOW

MARK BRANDON READ

The man who inspired a picture of the underworld.

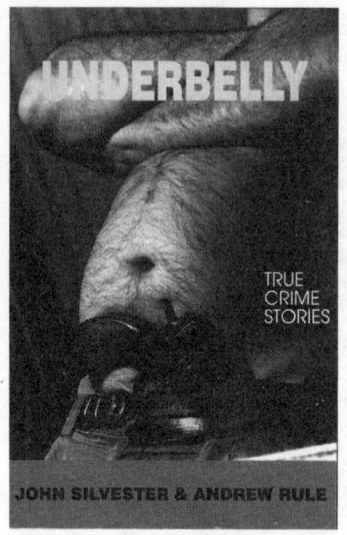

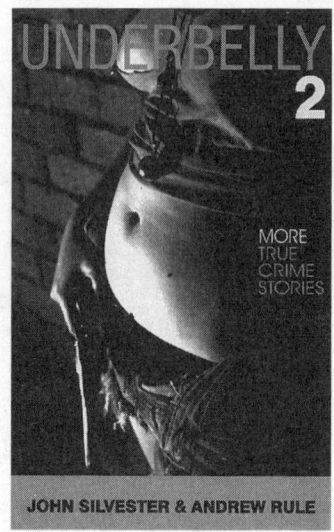

More great crime stories for the discerning psychopath

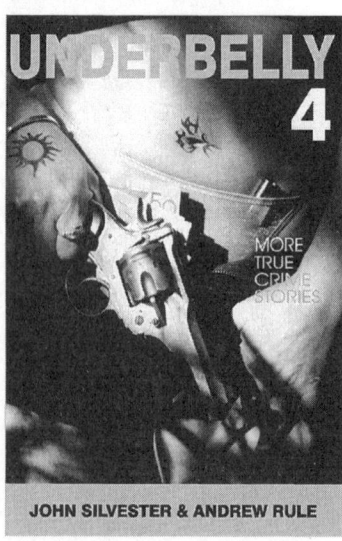

Dedication

To my mother, Jan, who
really did make a difference.

the
street 2
More confessions of
an undercover cop

by LACHLAN McCULLOCH

The Street gives an insider's
account of the black humour
and tragedy of life on the street.

– Victoria Police Journal

McCulloch's infectious enthusiasm
and gung-ho tales of life as an
undercover cop are hard to resist.

– Crime Factory

The Street provides a rare insight
into the way police think, act,
talk and amuse themselves.
It paints a fascinating picture
of the dark side of police life.

– Keith Moor, The Herald Sun

McCulloch has enough stories
to keep the stoniest faces
amused ... or horrified.

– Gareth Malpeli, The West Australian

Contents

Contents

I didn't want to expose corruption.
I just wanted to be another copper.

Prologue

IT WAS March, 2001, when I finally let go. It was Graduation day at the Police Academy. I watched young men and women march past in their brand new uniforms. They had their careers in front of them. Mine was over.

I saw the look in their eyes. They were going to change the world, protect the public and all that. I wished them well.

I didn't know any of them, but I knew them all. Some would prosper – others would be crushed. Some would just cruise; some would make a difference.

I had joined the force in January, 1984. Some of these new coppers were just out of nappies when I first walked into the academy.

I wanted adventure back then and I got it in bucket-loads.

I thought I would be a copper until I was ready to retire, but it was not to be.

When I went to the drug squad one of my investigations was

sold out from within. I found out who did it and for years no-one believed me. In the end, the policeman who sold me out was charged – and convicted. He ended up going to jail for five years, but it took its toll on me, too.

I loved being a copper. I worked in uniform, plain clothes, under-cover, as a suburban detective, the drug squad and the rape squad.

I learned something new every day – and I'm still trying to forget some of it.

I worked undercover against the infamous Pettingill clan – and got the right result. It was dangerous, but incredibly rewarding.

I saw a man shot dead in front of me, which reminded me that this was not a game and we were playing for keeps. I saw big drug deals and I chased rapists, burglars and murderers. I like to think that I made a difference.

I worked on The Street disguised as a vagrant named 'Dean Collie', who became one of my favourite undercover characters. I worked with men and woman who were the bravest and best society can produce. But I also saw some police who were bad and bent. Blokes who betrayed us and you for the price of a second hand car.

When you are a policeman or woman at the sharp end, life is played out on the big screen. Everything is full on. You see the funniest and the bleakest events. Every shift is different and then, suddenly, they all seem the same.

We did things that could have got us locked up, but we always worked to catch the crooks. Most times we won; sometimes we lost.

Every police officer has a brain-load of unbelievable memories. Mostly they share them only with other coppers, believing that the rest of the world would never 'get it'. I started to take notes of what we did and I have invented a policeman, Angus, to be my eyes and ears.

The events that happened to him happened to me and my colleagues. He could be a copper from any city in Australia. He just happens to be based in Melbourne. I have worked with many partners, but in this memoir I have referred to all of them as 'Darren', the name of a trusted mate in the job. To him I say thanks.

Some events have been changed to protect the innocent and the guilty. Some stories had to be disguised.

There is a chapter about a lion in a circus where events have been changed. But there is more than one place where you can find a lion. It won't take too much imagination to work out what really happened.

I knew by 1999 that I was finished in the force. The eight-year battle against corruption had left me exhausted. I didn't want to expose corruption. I just wanted to be another copper. But it just happened and I couldn't look the other way. If I had, I would still be a detective.

I always gave everything to policing because I loved it. It was never a job – it was The Job.

But The Job had consumed me. I was in danger of losing myself. I was changing and I didn't like all that I saw. I had a wife and a family. I owed it to them to try to become human again.

But back to the academy …

I was there to meet the Chief Commissioner, Neil Comrie. He was about to retire and this would be his last graduation parade.

I was there to receive a Chief Commissioner's Certificate for exposing corruption. We shook hands and said goodbye. It was the end of the journey. There is nothing more ex than an ex-copper. I was no longer one of them, I was one of you.

I had left The Brotherhood.

I did a screaming U-turn
and gave chase.

Home sweet home

HOME was an old two-storey mansion. It was double brick and in a bad state of disrepair. It had lovely stained glass windows but always smelt musty. But for the shoulder holsters hanging on the hat stand, the huge poster of a very angry Rambo with a Victoria Police cap glued to his head and the never-ending police radio blaring in the background, you would never know it was a police station for plain clothes coppers.

Early on, just after we moved in, I drove a crook up to the front of our office. The crook looked at the old joint and said, 'You're supposed to take me to a police station – not home.' When the office heard about this comment it was dubbed 'Home', and that's what we called it from that moment on.

It was funny because, after we caught crooks, we would often say things to each other like, 'If you want to finish searching, we'll take the crook home.'

The crook would hear this and think, 'You're letting me go?'

or 'I'm going to a cop's home?' We would have to explain to the crook that our office was a 'home away from home'. For us, anyway. Maybe not for them.

Home sounded a bit too good for the police force to lease, so there had to be a down side. The back wall was about one metre from city-bound trains on the Sandringham line.

In the middle of an official police interview being recorded on audio tape, a slight rumbling could be heard. This would quickly turn to a desk-shaking, tooth-rattling roar that would last about five or six seconds, usually at a serious and vital stage.

After a while, the investigators didn't even notice it. On one occasion I recall, a crook hid under the interview room table with the tape still going.

On another occasion, in the middle of giving evidence under heavy cross-examination, my partner and best friend Darren said, 'I then handcuffed the defendant and took him home.'

In those special days I recall that we all spent more time there than at our real homes. 'Home' was full of keen young cops all trying to become one of the chosen few, to become detectives.

MY best cunning plans came into my head while I'd be lying on my back looking up into the blackness of my bedroom ceiling at 3am. I would lie there thinking of ways to catch crooks, gather evidence and investigate.

I tried to think laterally. Often, when you approach crooks from different angles, you can catch them out.

I was down The Street one day when I turned to Darren and said, 'I'll search Stiffy, you do his mate.'

We gave them a quick pat down in the middle of Fitzroy Street. Nothing found.

Darren and I got back into our car and drove off. I said, 'What do you think they're up to?'

Darren said, 'Selling heroin. They've got a stash somewhere.' I did a U-turn and stopped about 100 metres west of Stiffy and his mate.

I lit up a smoke and said, 'Wouldn't you love to know what they are talking about?' I tuned the car stereo to FM and fiddled around.

At first there was muffled voices but then you could hear two men talking.

I said, 'There you go – the deeper voice is Stiffy.'

Darren couldn't believe his ears. He said, 'What, you what, how?'

I said, 'Dick Smith sells FM band listening devices. It cost me $25.50 and I kept the receipt to claim on tax.'

Darren said, 'But isn't it illegal?'

I said, 'Well, if you want to get technical. We're not going to use it in evidence. It's intelligence gathering. Christ, the FBI, CIA, and KGB all do it.'

Darren said, 'Exactly.' He was always quick to get with the program. I whispered, 'I thought it would be fun, now shut up and listen.'

We started listening intently to their conversations. It was so interesting the illegality of it became irrelevant. Their voices boomed through the stereo speakers.

Darren whispered, 'Where is it?'

I said, 'It's in the little coin pocket in his jacket'. We had to move around and park in a couple of different spots to stay in range but we could hear just about everything.

The whole gist of their conversations revolved around Stiffy trying to telephone a bloke named Teco. Finally Stiffy got onto Teco and they arranged to meet at the Cosmopolitan Motel, Room 209, at 4.30pm.

In the conversation 'Twenty G's' was mentioned. Twenty grams of drugs or 20 grand – whatever it was, it was bound to be criminal.

I rang the office and spoke to the boss. I told him I had received reliable information that a drug deal was to go down at the Cosmo Motel. I asked him if he could get a couple from the office to sit in room 208 or 210 as soon as possible. He agreed. He was a nice man ... sometimes.

I drove flat out and skidded to a halt, double parking in The Street right next to Stiffy. He looked behind him, hoping all this action was not directed at him. He was wrong.

I jumped out of the car and threw him up against the wall. In a loud voice I said, 'Stiff, as long as you sell heroin I am going to harass you.' I searched him fast and rough, and he didn't notice me taking the small 'Tic Tac' size LD (listening device) from his pocket. Stiffy screamed about police harassment and said he was going to report me to the Ombudsman.

I thought, 'Shit, I should put the LD back.'

I said, 'My name is Angus, number 23104. Go for it.'

It was 3.15pm. I had just arrived back at the office when my boss informed me that Stiffy was at the divisional office complaining about harassment by Angus..

The boss said, 'Have a quick word to Inspector Jellyfish.' We called the inspector that because he was spineless. The boss added: 'Piss in his pocket. I told him you've only got a few minutes because you've got a job on.'

I said, 'Thanks, boss.' Then I said to myself, 'I'll give him police harassment.'

I drove down the road and pulled up outside district headquarters. As I was about to put my hand on the front door handle, the door opened. Stiffy pushed me out of the way wearing a big smirky, smart-arse smile, as if he'd had a win. The smile suggested that Stiffy had found a friend in Inspector Jellyfish. I looked into his face, giving him a worried look, until he turned away. Then I gave his back a big smile and entered.

The inspector read me the riot act, explaining that I couldn't treat people like that and that people had rights, blah, blah, blah.

I wore the barrage of abuse and explained that I understood what he was saying but my boss had requested I attend another job.

Tail between my legs I left, picked up Darren and radioed Ross who was in Room 208 at the Cosmo Motel. Ross informed me that there was a single unknown male present in room 209.

We changed cars, disguised ourselves as much as possible and, as we would say in evidence, attended the vicinity of the motel. Ross gave us the all-clear. Darren and I knew the Cosmo well, we entered via the rear door and quickly sneaked into Ross's room.

This is the best time of any job. Tension is high and the adrenalin is pumping. As Sherlock Homes says, 'The game is afoot.'

It's never the catching that's the big rush, it's always the chase, the wait, the expectation of pending success or possible failure.

What will it be? Often the difference between the two is minuscule. Anything you do can't be undone, but this is great stuff. Can you believe we get paid for this?

It was 4.20pm. The phone rang as I was briefing Ross and Sandy. It was the manager informing us that a male in a leather jacket had just asked where Room 209 was. He was heading up. Stiffy walked past our room and knocked on the door of 209.

Stiffy entered … then nothing. We attempted to listen to the conversation through a locked door between the two rooms. But we had a problem.

Was Stiffy doing the deal, or was he just checking the drugs? And did he have to go and get the money or did he bring it with him?

If we hit too early we could end up with nothing and if we were too late we'd end up the same. Ross said, 'Let's hit now.'

I said, 'Wait.' Suddenly the door of 209 opened. Just before it opened I had opened our front door. I heard, 'It's in the car with me mate, I'll be one minute.'

I let Stiffy go back to his car but I started to sweat when he took longer than expected. Just as we started to think the deal had been done and we missed the whole thing, Stiffy came into view and walked back into the room 209.

Tension was at the max. I wondered what we were to do when Stiffy made our decision by walking out of the room again. He closed the door and walked past us. Ross gave me that 'please' sort of look. I nodded, then Ross and Sandy silently left our room. Darren and I paused at the door and watched Ross as he tackled Stiffy from behind.

The carpet muffled the fall and Ross pinned the suspect with his hand over his mouth. Sandy searched him, finding four bags of white powder, then held them up to me and nodded her head. This gave me reasonable grounds to enter the unit under Section 459 of the Crimes Act, no warrant required, no questions asked … unless we found nothing, of course. But that was the risk we had to take.

The unknown male was kneeling at the coffee table counting money. He glanced up in time to see Darren's foot hit him in the middle of the face, knocking him backward. I was impressed; Darren was getting a bit of a taste for this stuff.

The result: we'd caught them red-handed. Stiffy had four ounces of high-quality heroin, and his supplier had Darren's footmark on his head and a legal headache as well. He was a high-level dealer who had been targeted by the Drug Squad, but the Druggies were having trouble catching him. And here we had him with the gear.

It was a top pinch. Interviews and paperwork made it a long day. As the sun was coming up I fell asleep on the mess room table at 'Home', with half a can of beer in my hand. God, it was great to be a copper.

I WAS working a short time later when a job came up to attend a dead body at a house in Elsternwick. We knocked on the front door and were met by a lovely Jewish couple. They informed me they had reported their son missing two weeks ago. They thought he had run away from home.

Now they thought different. They had noticed a bad smell in the back corner of their yard. Their son had hidden in behind the swimming pool, to inject himself with heroin. And he'd died.

It was summer and the stench was overwhelming. There was no wind. Darren and I had to bend down and crawl through some bushes to find his almost liquefied body.

I took a mental note of the type of gold chain he was wearing around his neck. We crawled back. We called all the services and the morgue. Then we described the chain to the mother. It wasn't good news.

It was their son, all right. As soon as possible we left. The smell went with me. The smell of death was stuck inside my nose, then it worked its way into my head. Darren went all quiet.

We had missed lunch. I drove straight to a pizza shop and ordered a pizza with the lot with double anchovies. Turning to Darren, I asked him what he wanted.

He looked at me as if I was from another planet. Darren

couldn't eat. I got the pizza and sat in the car, opening the lid I breathed in deeply through my nose, trying to smell it. I couldn't. I felt like vomiting.

Darren wanted to throw up at the thought of the pizza. He couldn't stand it any longer and had to say something. 'How can you do that?' he demanded.

I took a deep breath and said, 'If I can eat this without seeing it again, I'm coping, I can handle anything. Now, shut up and let me concentrate.'

I then got down to it. Eating that pizza was hard, real hard. Truth be known I wasn't coping at all, but I thought I was and that was what mattered. Darren said, 'You can't eat that pizza.'

I said, 'That's the worst part of this job, mate. After a while you can always eat the pizza.'

I WAS down The Street one lunch time. I asked Darren what he wanted to eat. He said he felt like a hamburger. He was the type who thought Pritikin was a bloke who wrote fairy stories.

I drove up and double-parked outside the St Kilda Cafe. I jumped out and burst into the caf, flinging the multi-coloured tassels apart, stopped and said in a commanding voice, 'Everybody freeze.'

The four small coffee tables full of scruffy undesirables looked at me and froze. Nick, the fat Turk cooking hamburgers behind the jump, just gave me an disinterested glance and continued to flip the burgers and eggs as though I wasn't there. In an attempt to save my questionable authority, I said, 'Nick, you can keep cooking. I'll have a hamburger with the lot, no heroin or onions and I like my egg a little bit runny.'

Nick gave me another half a glance and big sigh. As all this happened I flipped open my police badge, the metal badge fell out and tinkled onto the floor. I chased it, bent down and quickly picked it up, holding it back in place.

I said, 'Everyone put your hands on the table and don't move'. They did what they were told.

At this stage the coloured tassels slowly parted and Darren peeped inside. In a sarcastic yet very serious voice I said, 'I have received reliable information that there are criminals, prostitutes and drugs in this establishment – not necessarily in that order. I must inform you that under the Vagrancy Act of 1958 section four, paragraph three, the three is in Roman numerals, they look like three little i's. Anyway, it is illegal for Nick here to suffer prostitutes and criminals or have them frequent his place of business. Please remain seated whilst my partner and I collect your names and conduct drug searches. Don't move.'

Darren took this as his cue to enter. We started searching each of them, and Darren wrote their names in his official notebook.

Each person was recorded on our files and admitted prior convictions for drugs or prostitution.

They all knew the game – behave and keep your mouth shut. Don't under any circumstances be a smart-arse to police. The third bloke on the second table decided to get lippy while we conducted our lawful search. He said, 'What's this shit? We've got rights, you can't do this.'

I said, 'You're from out of town, mate?'

He said, 'Yeah.'

I said, 'Are you a law professor, numb-nuts?' The moccasins gave him away. 'Where are you from?'

He said, 'I'm from Fornbrey'. I knew straight away he meant Thornbury. It's called being bilingual.

I said, 'You don't want to play the game. That means you've got something to hide, mate.'

He said he was clean. In his pocket was a set of car keys. He told me they were his brother's and that he didn't drive. I gave him the keys back and moved on, searching others.

At the end of the searches I said in a loud authoritarian voice, 'Nick, you have suffered – that means allowed – four prostitutes, three female and one male, on your premises.'

All the blokes looked at each other. That was a joke, but they didn't see the funny side. I kept going ... 'seven common burglars and reputed thieves – reputed means that they would steal if given the chance.' A couple of the crooks nodded their heads as if to agree. That's fair enough, they probably would.

'Two convicted armed robbers and one person that was the victim of a house burglary three years ago. Okay, we'll cross her off. She can't help that. Nick, this is an official warning.'

Nick slapped the burger on the counter and waved his hand indicating that I didn't have to pay for it. I said, 'Thanks Nick.' I slapped a $5 note on the counter and said, 'You owe me 50 cents,' and started walking out. In a strong Turkish accent, Nick said: 'Angus, if you can close me down for one or two week, do it in September – snapper season. My uncle, she has a boat.'

I said, 'I'll try,' and walked out.

Darren came up behind me and said, 'I didn't know you ordered a hamburger.'

I said, 'I thought you wanted a hamburger – I did the search to pass the time.'

Darren shook his head, 'Jesus, I've gone off it. I'll get chicken and chips instead.'

Years before I had done the same thing. I actually took the cafe owner to court after several such searches using the Vagrancy Act. I finally got it to court and a magistrate closed the cafe for two weeks.

It didn't do any good. Once it opened again they were back at work. Darren said it was a waste of time but I pointed out the real value.

'It looks great on your CV. Promotion boards love it when you use obscure sections of obscure Acts.'

I parked down the street and we began our healthy lunch. Just after we parked 'Mr Fornbrey' walked out of the cafe and started walking quickly away from us up Fitzroy Street. Darren said with a mouth and lap full of chicken, 'Can't we have lunch, for Christ's sake?'

I said, 'Fornbrey doesn't want us to see his car for a reason.' We followed him for about two kilometres into Windsor.

At times I would get up ahead of him so he wouldn't see us. He was constantly looking behind and appeared to be making sure he wasn't followed. So I stayed ahead and it was easy – I could have pulled faces at him and he wouldn't have known. He suddenly climbed into a white Commodore sedan.

I accelerated straight at him. I screamed on the brakes heading straight at him as I went the wrong way around a roundabout. He thought he was dead, braked and held his arms up over his face.

We went to jump out but he looked at us and, recognising me, he turned the wheel hard left and accelerated off. As he did he hit the front driver's side of my car, causing serious damage to both our vehicles. I did a screaming U-turn and gave chase.

Darren came up on the air, 'Blue 511 in pursuit' and all the rest of it. This was no time for chicken and chips. After about two minutes he turned into a dead end street.

As we both accelerated up the dead end I realised he was not going to stop in time. I started to brake as he rolled out of his vehicle onto the road like some stunt man. I skidded to a halt just short of running over him, which was probably a mistake.

He got up and started to run as the vehicle smashed through a fence and straight into a house wall. Darren, being young and fit, was right behind him. Thank goodness he didn't have a gutful of fried chook. Darren tackled him to the ground and a short fight ensued. My man subdued him as I ran toward the wreckage.

I checked to see if anyone had been hurt by the car this idiot had jumped from. I was fuming as I walked over to Fornbrey. He had left a large amount of skin from his hands, legs and face on the road. I grabbed him by the hair, turning his face toward mine I said, 'That is a kindergarten! Hear me, a kindergarten.'

Luckily it was empty. I said, 'What is it, car stolen or full of stolen goods and drugs and shit like that?'

He said, 'I'm unlicensed. It's my car.'

I said, 'Bullshit, you idiot.'

Fornbrey was right. The vehicle was registered in his name to his address and he was unlicensed. The car was spotless. I was in shock.

He was a heroin addict but really wanted his licence back soon and couldn't stand being charged with unlicensed driving again.

He later said that had he escaped he would have just said that someone stole his car. I informed him that we had followed him to the car and saw him at the roundabout driving. He looked at me as if to say 'Yeah, that's right.'

Unbelievable.

Our car was a write-off. There was damage from one side of St Kilda to the other and we had a bloke for traffic offences. Unlicensed driving, dangerous driving, speeding, and a few damaging property offences.

Back at our office Darren and I suffered numerous taunts. Something about our suitability for positions at the Traffic Operations Group. It was not a good day.

CHAPTER 2

He stuck the bullet
back into my ear.

Bullets and bad mouths

IT WAS just another day. Darren and I were in plain clothes, driving around the back streets of St Kilda when something caught my eye.

I laughed and turned right. I drove slowly behind a podgy female prostitute named Jackie. She was a chronic heroin junkie with a terrible attitude toward every male on earth, especially male police.

Jackie was riding an outdated large man's bike with high handle bars. On her back was a huge sports bag full of bulky items. Precariously balanced on her handle bars was a late model television set. She was erratically peddling as fast as she safely could. It was a funny, if somewhat sad, sight. It was a cross between *Trainspotting* and Benny Hill.

Before intercepting her, I turned to Darren and said, 'Do you know Jackie?'

Darren said, 'No'.

I said, 'Well, you speak to her. She doesn't like me.'

I drove up next to her, but she was so busy concentrating she found it hard to spare a millisecond to look at us. Darren held up his police badge, indicating her to pull over.

The second she glanced at it while still riding she let loose with, 'You fucking smart-arse, you think you're so clever. Why pick on me, you maggots?' I think it was a rhetorical question.

The wall of abuse hit Darren through his passenger side window. He turned and gave me a bemused look. I said, 'It looks like she doesn't like you either, I thought you'd get on well.' Jackie had obviously been out burgling.

She didn't even attempt to give us some bullshit story about where she got the goods from. She knew the game was up as soon as she saw the badge.

She fell off the bike with a crunch onto a grassy verge. She recognised me and went right off tap. I never said a word and let Darren handle the situation.

While she abused me, Darren opened her large sports bag. It was full of cameras, leather jackets and jewellery. I handcuffed her hands behind her back.

I then started examining the goods for identification numbers. There were also several cheque books in different names. As I did this Darren started to build up a rapport with Jackie. Darren located $700 cash in her pocket.

He politely asked her where she had stolen the goods from. She spat the words, 'Chew me lettuce, pig' into Darren's face. He paused and had to think about that one.

As we started to pack all the stolen gear into our vehicle Jackie continued to abuse Darren. She seemed to pick on him as he was the only one talking to her and she always got a reaction from him.

He continually tried to be nice to her – he was really quite a nice guy. With the big old bike hanging out of the boot, we limped back to our station.

I was driving. I stopped at the next set of traffic lights, pulled my gun out of its holster, opened the breech, dropped two .38 bullets into my hand and stuck them in my ears – that calibre fits perfectly.

This trick effectively nullified her continual foul abuse. As we were in plain clothes in an unmarked car, I got a couple of funny looks at the next set of traffic lights, having about an inch of brass bullet cartridge sticking out each ear. I just smiled at them and drove on.

As I was driving I turned the rear vision mirror to look at Darren, who was sitting next to Jackie in the back seat. I smiled and said, 'Building up a rapport, hey Darren?'

He leant forward, removed the bullet from my right ear and shouted, 'She's horrible.' He stuck the bullet back into my ear. Seconds later I glanced into the mirror again. Darren was smiling. There was a bullet sticking out each ear. He was a quick learner.

Constable Jackson was in charge of the watch house. Everyone called him Jack. He was a very handsome young cop who was also very gay.

His uniform was always immaculate, never a hair out of place. Everyone always gave him a second look as he was the only male cop that wore make-up. He was a classic. Everyone loved his quick wit and jovial personality.

As we entered the watch house area, Jack greeted us. He was jovial about the fact that we had caught a crook. Jack stood in front of us. He was standing tall, with a white piece of paper folded over his left arm, looking exactly like a posh waiter.

He said in his best voice, 'Table for three? Come this way, thankyou. We're very busy today, but I sure we can find you a lovely interview room and table.'

Jackie shouted, 'And I don't need a smiling smartarse fag in me face either.' An offended Jack walked off. Jackie continued, 'Are you bastards being happy just to give me the shits or what?'

Within a couple of hours we found that she had committed five house burglaries, stealing items from each, including the bike.

Several victims telephoned the watch house, reporting burglaries. I got the victims to come to the station. But one of the victims was a 91-year-old Jewish woman who couldn't make it in.

Darren was getting on so well with Jackie, I decided to leave them alone and drive out to see the old dear.

Her house was almost empty. The only item she had of any value had been stolen. I saw a series of faded numbers on her forearm. She saw me look at them and said, 'Auschwitz.'

I showed her the TV. She said it wasn't hers. I was determined to recover her television.

I drove to a nearby secondhand dealer. He had paid a Julie Simmons for a television, video camera and other items. Simmons was the name of one of Jackie's other victims.

The dealer had in fact purchased several items from Jackie just before we picked her up. One of the items was the old lady's TV. The dealer had paid Jackie $100 for it.

I removed a $100 note from the exhibit bag containing the money I had seized from Jackie and gave it to the dealer. I then placed the receipt back into the bag to account for the missing $100.

I proudly returned to the old lady and carried the TV into her home and plugged it in. She was crying with happiness and kissed my hand.

I wish every problem was that easy to solve.

Back at the station I found Jackie was still the same – that is, really pissed off at life in general, the fact that she had been caught and that she hadn't scored and used heroin.

To top all that off she had 'fascist pigs' interviewing her about her misfortunes. She made it impossible for us to conduct a proper police interview.

I actually attempted to talk to her. I said, 'Jackie, we're just trying to sort this shit out. We're trying to conduct an interview so you can explain why you broke into several houses.'

She said, 'I'm sick and tired of "hawking the fork" (prostitution) so I'm having a break. Christ, I stole some stuff – so what, get over it. Now fuck off – which of those two words don't you understand?' I decided to just lock her up in the holding cell.

Darren and I took Jackie to the watch house area. She was screaming, and still had her hands cuffed behind her back. We were met there by Constable Jack.

I was amused at the fact that she could remain so shitty for so long. I tried and tried to find her better side. She was spewing mouthfuls of vile abuse right up until it was time to bin her. I said, 'Your finest cell, please, Jack.'

He said, 'Welcome, welcome to the Copa Copacabana' and launched into a dancing singing imitation of Barry Manilow, but without the big nose.

'At the Copa, Copacabana the music is north of Havana, at the Copa Copacabanaaaaaaa ...'

Jackie fell silent and watched.

Jack danced and twirled, touching his hands on his elbows,

wiggling his bum in rhythm to the imaginary music, leading Jackie toward her cell.

He spun as he opened her cell door and to a crescendo, 'Where music and passion is always in fashion, at the Copa she fell in love, ah.'

Jackie timed her kick to perfection, hitting Jack fair square in the balls.

He fell silently to his knees, the top of his head touching the floor as Jackie quietly said under her breath, 'Dickhead.' She stepped over him, happy to escape. She entered her cell and slammed the door in disgust.

I laughed so hard I could hardly breathe. Neither could Jack. I managed to say, 'That's the nicest thing she's said all day.'

About a month later I was summoned to be interviewed by the Internal Investigations Department. I had no idea why. Just before the interview I was told it was something about the arrest of Jackie.

I attended their offices and was taken to an interview room. An inspector asked me questions about me returning the television to the 91-year-old lady. I was angry about this trivial shit.

It turned out that when I returned the television to the lovely old lady she was so impressed she wrote a letter to the Police Minister's Office explaining what a wonderful thing I had done, hoping my behavior would be recognised.

In the letter she stated that I had paid $100 and got the TV back. Some pencil pusher decided that I must have done something illegal or against departmental instructions and ordered an investigation.

The inspector wanted to know where I had got the $100 to buy back her TV back. I was supposed to hold the TV for a year or so until the court ordered it to be returned.

Because the dealer had paid good money in so-called good faith he now had a legal hold on the TV. I had taken it upon myself to give him his money back and return it immediately.

I said to this pencil-pushing prick, 'Hang me out to dry, you've got me, I'm as guilty as hell of doing the right thing.'

I walked out a short time later. The moral of the story is that pencil pushers can be very dangerous to sensible, sensitive, humans and members of the public that just so happen to be cops. Like me.

I WAS working in uniform years earlier when my turn came to work 'Warrants and Files'. This meant that for one month I had to execute parking warrants on people, issue summonses and, at times, interview and charge people with minor offences.

Working by myself, I attended at an old cheap flat in East St Kilda. An old man answered the door. He was on crutches, as he was missing half his left leg and his whole left arm. He asked me inside.

It was immediately obvious that he was drunk. It was 8.30am so I knew he either had a drinking problem or was an old-style journalist. Possibly both.

I said, 'I'm Constable Angus from the St Kilda Police Station. I'm here to interview you in relation to a file I have received from Vic Rail.

'I have to ask you questions and charge you with placing an object on a railway line in East St Kilda on the tenth of June last year.

"Why did you place an object on the railway line?'

He said, 'Suicide, mate. I put my body on it. Just before it got me the noise and vibrations on the tracks scared the shit out of me. I chickened out and rolled off, but it got me. Now I'm worse off than before.' I looked at him and could not believe I had been sent this file. I ripped it up. He said, 'Trains don't muck around.'

I said, 'The bloody pencil pushers are trying to finish you off, mate.'

He looked at me as though a pencil pusher was some kind of new train.

CHAPTER 3

'I had to bash him for 10 minutes
to get him to let go of the crook's arm. Once
he gets the taste of blood ...'

Reality
bites

IN MY plain clothes days, most of our crooks were caught by
pro-active policing – that is, by us going out and tearing around
like hoons and getting paid for it. But, sometimes, while hunting
we would hear a job come over the radio, respond to it and then
have to remember how to act like real police.

Darren and I were working late one night when an 'Offenders
On' call came over the radio. We called in, stating we would do
the job.

An old woman had rung D-24, reporting an unknown male
person stealing from a nursery and garden supply centre in St
Kilda. We skidded to a halt at the rear of the nursery.

In front of us was an old Holden ute that had been backed up
to a big Cyclone wire fence with a big hole cut in it. The ute's
engine was still running. We looked inside and found the vehicle
had been hot wired. I turned it off. Step one.

Even to brumbies like us, this looked suspicious.

Darren and I jumped out of our car and ran to the fence. It was obvious we had disturbed the crooks in the middle of their job. They had already loaded about 20 pots containing expensive trees into the back of the ute. I shone my torch around, but there were so many places to hide, so many trees, plants, bushes, and big pots that it was impossible to find anyone.

Once the crook lay down or even ducked he would be invisible, but anyone standing would be seen easily. Darren and I could see each other, but nothing else.

We met up and I whispered to him, 'This isn't going to work. The crook could crawl around while we're searching and we wouldn't see them. Let's call for a dog. Dogs are great fun.'

Darren thought that was a great idea. We went back to the car. I spoke softly into the radio so the crooks couldn't hear. I called in and told D24 that we required a dog ASAP.

The D24 operator stated that the two K9 units were tied up at a violent demonstration at the Iranian Embassy and they were unavailable. I requested another unit to assist us as we believed we had an offender or offenders contained in an area.

The D24 operator stated all units were tied up but she would send another unit later. I stepped back out of the car. Darren said, 'What is the ETA (Estimated Time of Arrival) of the dog?'

I said, 'We're it, mate. Dog's tied up in the city.'

Darren said, 'We need to flush them out. I saw it in a National Geographic show. What if we both get an empty rubbish bin each and a big stick and we start down one end and smash and crash our way through the little trees, like I think it was the Amazon jungle – you know the Zulus after lions...?'

I said, 'Mate, that was tigers not lions, and it was India not the Amazon and not the bloody Zulus!' Geography was never Dazza's strong point. Luckily, I suddenly visualised a cunning plan. It just came to me. I tip-toed up to my driver's side door and carefully opened it. I then slammed it shut loudly. Acting as dog handler in a deep voice I said, 'G'day fellas, what's the go.'

I said loudly in my normal voice, 'We got a call, came up and searched the area. We can't find anyone but we thought your police dog might. I reckon there's one still in here.' I quietly opened the door of my car again, sat in the driver's seat, quietly closed the door and wound the window down.

Putting my head out the window as the dog handler I said, 'Angus, I want you to meet Shaka, Shaka Zulu.' I wound the window up leaving a small gap at the top and went berserk barking, growling and smashing the inside of the vehicle.

Darren was onto it like a flash. In a loud voice, he said, 'Christ, it's a Rottweiler! You're not going to let that loose in there, are ya?' Then he said, 'I didn't know you guys had Rottweilers! Rottweiler police dogs.'

I was shaking the car and growling as deeply and loudly as possible. I had to change from a mad German shepherd to an insane rottweiler. I just dropped the German accent. Tired and with a sore throat, I got out of the vehicle.

Playing the dog handler, I said, 'Shaka nearly ripped the last crook's arm off. He found him hiding under a trailer and I couldn't get to him in time. I had to bash him for 10 minutes just to get him to let go of the crook's arm. Once he gets the taste of blood…'

Suddenly there was a voice nearby. 'Okay, okay don't let him go!' A crook had decided the thought and sound of Shaka Zulu, the huge black Rottweiler, was too much. This was instantaneously followed by a second crook surrendering. Darren and I were shocked and not quite ready.

I said, 'Okay, um, just stand there and we won't let Shaka go.'

As Darren and I made our way toward the two crooks the first crook said, 'Hey Dave, they're full of shit, there's no bloody dog. Run!'

They both ran, hitting the fence at the rear of the nursery. They frantically started climbing the fence. We were close behind.

One of them made it over through a large amount of barbed wire at the top of the fence. The other got tangled up in the wire. I grabbed him, of course, and let Darren try to get over the fence.

Naturally, he got all tangled as well. The crook I had was screaming like hell in anger and pain as I kept pulling at him. He wanted to carefully take his time in extricating himself from the barbed wire. I was in a hurry.

I kept pulling at him, causing the barbed wire to rip at his flesh and clothes. He had put himself in this position and it was my job to get him out. My partner was still caught up on the wire. It became obvious that both Darren couldn't and I wouldn't get over the fence. All of a sudden the second offender re-appeared.

From the darkness came, 'You bastards, let him go.'

I screamed through the fence, 'Put your hands on your head and lay face down, you're under arrest.'

The crook paused for a second just in case we knew something he didn't. He then kept on abusing us.

I said, 'Well, come and rescue him then you hero. You're a gutless prick for leaving your mate behind in the first place.'

He said some rude things back to me. We abused each other for a while, then he ran off into the darkness.

We'd caught one. He was all scratched and a bit shitty looking, but I didn't blame him for being scared of a big, black vicious Rottweiler called Shaka Zulu, even if it was imaginary.

CRIMINALS prey on the weak and vulnerable, turning citizens

into victims in an instant. Searching a city for these crooks was hard, requiring huge hours for little result.

I recall fishing with my father as a young boy in outback New South Wales when we came across an old man. He was a professional shooter, driving an old beaten up Holden ute and dragging three burnt kangaroo carcasses tied to a rope.

The old bloke stopped for a chat. As my dad gave him a cold beer, he explained that he was too old to drive around all night shooting with a spotlight, so he dragged the 'roo carcasses along the ground all over the place, then parked and waited for the foxes to follow the trail. He had learnt to get them to come to him. It's no use getting old if you don't get cunning. I never forgot that.

IN THE late 1980s, Alpine car radios were all the rage. They were worth about $2000 each and could be found in all late model Saabs.

That meant crooks could steal them and sell them for about a third of the price, say $650. Crooks love to find heaps of easily accessible vehicles parked under the cover of darkness for long periods; this means they love to work in restaurant areas. St Kilda was (and is) packed full of restaurants and had heaps of luxury cars. Saab drivers get hungry, too. I was working in the plain clothes office with Darren when it became obvious that we had a gang or two of crooks targeting Saab Alpine radios. At one stage, three to six cars were getting done over every Thursday, Friday and Saturday night in our district. Eventually, this problem was made my problem. I was assigned to fix it.

After the first night, driving around trying to catch these crooks on the hop, I realised a more clinical approach was required. Every time we tried to sit back and watch a likely target Saab, it either drove off or there were no car parks nearby to sit back and watch.

The MO (modus operandi, remember?) of the crooks was that between 7.30pm to midnight, Thursday to Saturday, they walked up to the passenger side door on the footpath side, pushed a largescrew driver or similar into the lock and broke it.

Damage was done to the lock and the dashboard as the crooks removed the radio using screwdrivers and cutting wires.

I estimated the whole job would take no more than two minutes. They always wore gloves, and no-one would see a thing.

I hatched a cunning plan.

Surprise, surprise. This plan required a Saab as bait. I drove to Melbourne City Saab and spoke to the manager. He had heard of the Alpine radio thefts, and said it was affecting the insurance of his vehicles.

I asked him for a Saab. He was very pro-police and he gave me a real sexy black convertible with the lot. I assured him we would protect it with Darren's life. I then found out that it was in fact his own company vehicle, his favourite.

I told him that the crooks entered by forcing the passenger side lock and asked if he was able to place an old lock into the door to avoid damaging a new one.

He agreed. His workshop could do it in a minute. They removed both front locks, just in case, replacing them with damaged ones they had in a nearby bin.

I assured him the vehicle would be locked up in our police compound overnight. Darren and I showed off our new car all over town, as boys do. We then got down to business. Protecting the $75,000 car was paramount.

I found a perfect side street. A big gum tree right in between two street lights created a perfect black hole in the target area. I parked the Saab inside this black hole.

It was only 5.30pm so the streets were bare. This parking space was right outside a lovely Edwardian home fronted by a low red brick fence lined by small covering rose bushes.

I knocked on the door of the home. A lovely young couple said that if we wanted to sit in their front bushes all night we were most welcome. So we did. All night – well, until midnight – without a nibble.

On the second night, we were in the middle of freezing our tits off when for the thousandth time we sat still as a vehicle drove up the street. It drove on. Seconds later, the same vehicle returned, driving slowly past our target vehicle.

Suddenly, it stopped. We could not see who was in the car, as we were too busy hiding. Darren and I had practised jumping the fence and attacking imaginary crooks many times. Jump the knee-high fence, take four steps and we were at the vehicle, catching them at or inside, the car.

This vehicle paused, causing us to treat it with great suspicion. We held our breath. The car reversed slowly and stopped exactly adjacent to the driver's side window, so close that their door handles almost touched.

I could not work out what it was doing. But still we couldn't act until they committed an offence. How could they be the crooks when no-one could even get out of the passenger side doors. My thought was interrupted by an explosion.

The passenger had wound down his window, pulled back a high-powered slingshot and fired a steel ball through the driver's side window, shattering the glass – and the silence – with a bang that had to be heard to be believed.

The safety glass fragmented into tiny safe square pieces. In one fluid motion the passenger dropped the slingshot and slid from his window through our Saab's window and into the driver's seat. He was well-practised at this manoeuvre, and was hard at work removing the radio while his legs hung out the vehicle's window.

Darren and I sprang up and forward, heading straight at our crooks. We were asking our tired, cramped and cold calf and thigh muscles to propel 80-odd kilograms apiece, upward and forward at an impossible speed.

As I sprang up, my left hamstring snapped, causing great pain and me to fall onto the rose bush face first. I then fell over the low fence onto the footpath. Darren's muscles held, thrusting him at our target.

As Darren stumbled over me he got to the passenger side door. Opening the door he lunged at the target. The target had removed the radio, the driver of the vehicle grabbed his feet and pulled him back into the getaway car. The crooks sped off as Darren feebly attempted an arrest.

Darren's feet hung out the passenger window as he smashed the driver's side window in disgust. I limped up to Darren's feet as I called frantically on the portable police radio for assistance. We were left high and dry with our now slightly less than $75,000 worth of bait.

The driver's side window was worth nothing compared with the damage the prick caused to the whole front console when he dug the radio out.

The total damage was later estimated at $4250. I made inquiries with nearby districts and found that these same crooks had hit several times in the Prahran area. Unfortunately for us, we were not aware of them and how they operated. They would have to stray into our patch that night, the low-life scum.

Some plans work, some don't. We, and most of all, I lost big time that night. But I never stopped believing there were cunning plans out there that we hadn't even thought of yet.

I had made a big error, thinking that five metres and a low fence was close enough to protect that vehicle.

The crook had entered and exited the vehicle with the Alpine radio and driven off within 10 seconds. I was quietly impressed. I had underestimated the crook's ingenuity. I promised myself it wouldn't happen again.

I WAS up to my old tricks, walking down the middle of the street in my big grey jacket at the start of my shift, searching a few people and making sure everyone saw us.

I would wear something distinctive so when we left all the crooks would know we had left. That way, I figured the crooks thought they knew what to look for. When they couldn't see us, they would feel safe.

All we did was change clothes and enter the shadows. We would then lie in wait and attack the weak and vulnerable. As they preyed on the most vulnerable, so did we.

We were never short of targets because our area attracted the losers of the underworld. Anyway, this particular morning Darren and I were a bit bored, so we searched Bones, a crook I have mentioned before that I particularly despised. He stood over several of the local prostitutes and lived off their hard-earned money. Bones was wearing a leather jacket. As I conducted a drug search on him in the middle of the street, Darren searched his mate. We walked off and searched another couple of crooks. We found nothing and walked off. We climbed to the top of our favourite building, lay down and peeped over the side.

About 10 minutes later, while we had him under surveillance, we watched as he was being cool with his mates outside the St Kilda Cafe.

We watched as he discovered something squishy and squashy in his pocket. He could not work out what it was. Darren had the binoculars on him. Bones produced a bit of egg shell. Darren said, 'It looks like he's got a broken egg in his pocket.'

I was chuckling away under my breath. Darren said, 'Why's he … what the …?'

I started laughing and said, 'He'll work it out. Don't you worry about that.'

Moments later we could see Bones stomping up and down, trying to find me. Sometimes I did stupid, silly things on the spur of the moment without thinking, many of them totally unprofessional.

But I always got over it. I knew I was far too old to stop being silly now.

A day or so later I went to do another drug search of Bones. Just as I was about to search him, he said, 'Hang on a second.' Bones then patted down my sleeves and pockets, searching for another egg. I stood there with a smile and let him search – even if it was the wrong way around.

When he finished, he took a step back, spread his arms and legs out and assumed the search position. He said in a serious voice, 'Right, you're clear to search me.' I asked, 'What are you on about?'

He smiled and said, 'That's two now – the writing on me head, now the egg. You did the writin' didn't ya?'

DEAN Collie was often thirsty and would call into the local pub and have a beer. It was a way of keeping in touch and he also liked the taste. Dean would often meet losers wanting to commit various crimes.

But there was always some sort of problem that prevented them from doing it. Like they never had the money, the car, the partner or the inside knowledge.

One such loser was Phil. He was always crapping on about how he wanted to buy a pound of speed but he was looking for top quality.

He would always say he could find the money if he could buy top gear. He wanted speed.

He would always ask me about my brother. I often told him stories about my fictitious brother named Sebastian. I told him Seb was a top-level dealer who lived in Perth. Seb had his own laboratory.

Phil thought that was great. One day I called in for a beer just to see and be seen when I got cornered by Phil again. Off he went, on and on about how he wanted a pound of speed.

It would set him up for life, make a fortune. But Seb was in Perth. I called his bluff.

I said, 'Hang on, I'll ring him.' I grabbed my mobile – even Dean had a mobile – found the number in my phone and rang. Darren answered his phone. I said, 'G'day Bro, it's Dean, blah, blah, blah … I've got a top mate who wants to meet one whole girlfriend but she's got to be a virgin, you know what I mean?'

I covered the handset and whispered to Phil, 'That means a pound of pure, mate.' Then I went back to the phone call and said, 'Fair dinkum, great. Ring me when you get here.' I hung up.

I told Phil that Seb was doing a delivery to Melbourne in two days. I said, 'Price is $30,000 for a full pound of the best stinky shit you can get.'

Phil was so excited he could hardly speak. He said, 'I, I, I'll see you here tomorrow, same time.' Phil hurried off. There was no way he could come up with that sort of money.

The next day Phil snuck up to me and whispered, 'How much for an ounce'.

I said, '$4500.'

Phil said, 'Tell your brother I'll take two ounces for $8000.' Even scrotes wanted a discount.

I arranged for Phil to meet Seb the following day. Next day Seb (me) met Phil in a nearby park.

Phil loved to talk. He told me how I was nothing like Dean and as usual, everyone bagged Dean. I was beginning to get a complex.

I told Phil that I was hoping to deliver half a pound of gear to Cairns tomorrow, but there was a problem with the lab in Perth and I had to go back.

I said I didn't trust Dean but I could trust him. I told him that I could sell him the two ounces for $8000 and he could double his money immediately by delivering the rest to Cairns for me. I even said I would pay his return air fare. I told him that a mate of mine would take the two ounces off him for $16,000 at Cairns airport.

I said, 'Speed's real expensive up there mate.' I told him that Tom up in Cairns was one of my top customers. Phil thought he had just won Tatts – he wasn't all that bright.

He said, 'If this goes well we could do more business, eh?'

I said, 'Sure, just do a good job.'

I took his mobile phone number and he took mine. I then rang a mate of mine, Tom, who lived in Cairns. He was a plain clothes cop I had met at a drug squad seminar in Melbourne the year before.

I telephoned him on my mobile and introduce Phil to him. Tom thought the whole thing was hilarious and played his role. He was amazed, as they were not allowed to do this sort of stuff in Queensland.

There was no problem getting authorisation from my bosses as we had the drugs and the crook under full control. The following day I (as Seb) met Phil at the airport.

As he was about to step on the plane I handed him his hand luggage containing two ounces of pure speed. He quickly checked the gear, as soon as he smelt it he knew it was top stuff. He gave me the $8000 and I handed him his tickets. Off he left.

We all pissed ourselves laughing as I rang Tom and told him Phil was on the way. Hours later, a laughing Tom rang me saying that the arrest went smoothly. He said, 'The clown just thinks he was unlucky'. He had no idea how unlucky he really was. Several months later, Tom sent me a Cairns newspaper. The front page read: *Victorian Cops have drug scene under control.*

'Philip Dixon of St Kilda, Victoria, was sentenced today in the Cairns County Court to seven years imprisonment. A Melbourne undercover police officer sold him a large quantity of 'speed', Dixon then flew from Melbourne to Cairns and sold the drugs to another undercover police officer.'

How could you live that down? We framed the page and put it on the wall. It all happened because he gave Dean the shits. It was not the right move.

THERE were some lovely places in St Kilda, little hotels, lovely restaurants and groovy nightspots. There were some shit-holes too. It never ceased to amaze how the old world people, the yuppies and the losers could all exist in the same suburb and pretend the others didn't exist.

There were several cheap motels in the area. One was called The Flower. It must have been named after a flower that smelt of four-day old urine and junkie vomit.

It was always full of prostitutes and assorted criminals. The owner was Stella, commonly known as 'The Dragon Lady'. She was horrible and very, very anti-police. We were always in there searching rooms and checking out patrons.

Stella suddenly decided she was going to paint the outside and fully renovate the inside. The plan was to then sell it to some unsuspecting sap.

Anyway, while these renovations were going on, we got information that a local drug dealer called Blackie was buying a large quantity of heroin at 8.30 that night. The deal was apparently going to be done in his motel room. Darren and I got four others from the office to help out. We needed surveillance and an arrest crew. It was our job so we got to do the fun stuff. Darren and I were the arrest team, assisted by the Turk and Paul. Sandy and Dave did surveillance and the outer perimeter.

We were in position at 8pm.

Every other motel enthusiastically assisted and supported · police, so we were used to having an adjacent room. But The Flower was unapproachable on such matters, so the arrest team had to hide in the back of a small van parked out the front. At 8.40pm, a typical drug dealer type nervously entered the motel. Surveillance picked up this person attending at the target address.

I bit the bullet and made the decision to hit. Based on what I was being told by Sandy over the radio I called, 'It's a bust, arrest team entering now.'

I wish we could have calmly flowed out of the van, executing a surgical strike on the target premises and its occupants.

Instead, we burst out of the van, running flat out, bumping into one another.

The Turk was still running as he hit the door of the room. We all ran in. Both targets were sitting at a table on the right-hand side. Blackie had just enough time to grab an ounce bag of heroin and look for a place to throw it.

He threw it into an exposed wall cavity – a hole in the wall where it was being renovated. Rather than close the rooms down, skinflint Stella kept renting out the rooms for a slightly cheaper price. We arrested Blackie and the dealer.

I reached inside and searched the wall cavity, finding the plastic bag containing the ounce. We took him off and charged them. We searched the dealer's car and found two more ounces of heroin hidden under the dashboard. We took them back to the station, interviewed and charged them. They were both remanded in custody.

Two weeks later, after several attempts Blackie was finally bailed. A short time later Darren and I were sitting around our mess room table in the uniform section.

I overheard one of the uniform members state, 'That bitch down at The Flower had her walls kicked in, and she rang us – as if we care … ' I interrupted, 'Where abouts?'

The copper said, 'First floor, room 204, the old couple staying there reckon they didn't do it.' That was the same room we had arrested Blackie in.

I spoke with Darren. We decided to go and check The Flower. Sure enough, the renovations had finished in the vicinity of room 204. Someone had broken in and kicked three large holes in the wall. Darren and I had a chat about that day. I said, 'Mate, after I found that ounce bag Blackie threw into the wall cavity, did you search the rest of the hole in the plaster?'

Darren said, 'I thought you did.' We now knew why Blackie wanted bail so badly.

As we were talking the current occupants of room 204 returned. They told us that they had disturbed a bloke in their room and that he ran off. The description of the bloke matched Blackie.

Darren and I searched the wall cavity – found nothing. Then Stella appeared and abused the hell out of us. Somehow it was all our fault. To her we were responsible for all the damage. She was horrible. She also made official complaints about us to the Ombudsman's Office.

I rang the station and found that Blackie hadn't yet reported on bail that day. I asked the watch-house keeper to arrest Blackie when he reported on bail and telephone us immediately.

Later that day he was arrested reporting on bail. We searched him and his home, nothing. No heroin at all. We spoke to him about the damage to the motel.

We had him identified as the person responsible for the damage to the room. He was off his head on heroin, so I was sure he had in fact recovered his hidden stash.

Darren and I charged him with criminal damage to the motel room wall. This was enough for us to have his bail revoked. He was again remanded in custody, no bail.

Over the next few months or so, numerous criminals kicked and smashed holes in all of Stella's new walls. She was forever calling the police to stop the damage.

It cost her a fortune. The criminal junkies in St Kilda had heard of a mythical stash of heroin hidden in the walls of Stella's motel. I thought, 'When I get back from leave later this month I must ask Dean to stop spreading those rumours'.

CHAPTER 4

I was proud of my designer derelict
clothes – sort of Salvation Armani.

It's not easy being Dean

DARREN and I loved our work in St Kilda. It wasn't really work, it was fun – and we got paid for it. We knew our patch so well we could second guess what the local crooks would do before they did it.

We had been there so long, we were part of The Street. The trouble was, we had become well-known and our quarry would scatter when we arrived. Bummer.

There was only one thing two clean-cut coppers could do. We called on Dean Collie to come out of retirement, yet again.

As you probably know by now, Dean was my alter-ego – a no-hoper destined to spend his life as a vagrant. I had used my disguise as Dean many times to gather information on crimes and trap crooks to be arrested later.

Not one ever tumbled to the fact that the cop that arrested them was the same smelly vag they had run into some time before.

I had a light brown wig and clothes that had been covered in fish guts and blood that even the Salvos wouldn't take. I would fill my cheeks with toilet paper to get that alcoholic, puffy look. The other way to do that was to go to officer's college, but I didn't have the time.

It was the usual routine: pull out my old green japara fishing jacket, stupid pants that were far too big, worn-out snow boots and a big floppy jumper under my jacket. I topped it off with an old canvas bag I used for fishing, filled up with empty bottles and rubbish. I was proud of my designer clothes – sort of Salvation Armani. As usual, I would drink out of a half-empty cordial bottle as I walked down The Street.

I rubbed fat through my wig to make it look like it hadn't seen shampoo for about two years (which it hadn't). The smell didn't do the disguise any harm either. You don't have to look the part, you have to smell it as well. If you see a street derelict and he smells of Gucci aftershave, he's either a fake or he's been drinking the stuff.

We called him Dean Collie because he looked (and smelled) like a wet collie dog – although he wasn't as well house trained and not as intelligent.

It was decided that Dean would target a particular arsehole by the name of Cliffy Calender. Darren drove Dean down to The Street to find his target.

It was like old times. I sat on the footpath at the front of The Cafe, opened up my old fishing bag and took a swig of from the old Cottees cordial bottle.

I winced as I took the mouthful, as I had forgotten that Dean was a piss pot and the cordial was mixed with half a bottle of Vodka. It was quite tasty, really. After a few mouthfuls it became quite drinkable – almost. It was 10am. I heard one local shithead make the comment that I was probably drinking metho. I turned around and looked at my reflection in the cafe window, and yep, Dean looked like shit.

I found an almost empty packet of Drum 'rollie' tobacco and proceeded to make a smoke. Not that I needed one, but it matched my image – I was right into method acting, or was that metho acting? Lighting it almost set fire to the hair in my wig. The fat in the hair helped the image but it almost set me alight like an old chip burner. I made a mental note not to go out on total fire ban days.

Crooks can be like coppers and taxis: there is never one about when you want one. There was no Cliffy Calender when I wanted him. But the beauty of The Street is that if you wait, something will always happen. And, after about five minutes, I noticed a new player in town.

He was full on. His whole demeanor screamed out, 'I'm a crook, I'm over here.'

He had a face that looked as if he had been squinting through a key hole as a child and then the wind changed. It was like a cross between a bulldog and a rat.

He was obviously up to no good, the way he nervously looked out for cops.

Then he proved he was a total loser. He walked up to me and introduced himself, and anyone who wanted to know Dean is not worth knowing. He said to just call him Stiffy. After the small talk he said I could call him Stiff. I thought, 'Good name, clown – you will be, soon.' But, of course, I didn't say it. I just grunted and burped and sort of grinned at him.

He botted a 'rollie' off me. It was then I thought, can this job get any lower? He started the usual crap: 'My gear is the best, mate.'

He went on and on about how great his heroin was and that I should trust him. I thought he should not be allowed to use the word trust.

I went on and on about how I was from Shepparton and that I was looking for my mate. He then made the sweeping statement, 'Stick with me and I'll show ya how to work the cops.'

He was not any smarter than he looked. I would have laughed if he wasn't so serious – and the toilet paper in my cheeks made it difficult anyway. He thought Dean was going to be his mate for life. He was wrong

I agreed to buy heroin from him around the corner in Acland Street, in 10 minutes. I then went and met Darren around the corner to explain that I could not wait for Cliffy any longer and this germ had to be removed from the streets.

Stiffy had said 10 minutes, but deadshits like him only knew day time and night time; the 10 minutes turned out to be an hour. So he managed to piss both of us off even before we had a chance to bust him.

Darren was convinced that he was not going to turn up, but I knew he was a deadshit and was not going to miss our deal.

When he finally fronted, I showed him the money and he showed me the gear. We were at the entrance to an underground car park about 80 metres south of Fitzroy Street.

I handed him my money, $90, and he handed me the foil of heroin. He looked at me as if he knew something was wrong. He looked at Darren and realised Darren was no normal pedestrian about to walk past. I'll give 'Stiffy' one thing, he knew danger when he saw it – but, then again, so do rats. Maybe Stiffy made Darren wait too long and Darren had 'Danger, I'm going to kill you' written across his face. Whatever the reason, Stiffy took off, flat knacker.

I dropped my bag and threw my wig, glasses, jacket and stuff into it as Darren took up the chase. Our target had my money and we needed the arrest. I kicked the bag into a small doorway and took up the chase behind Darren. Stiffy ran into a large group of pissheads coming out of the hotel, slowing him down. Darren was less successful and bowled one completely over, sending himself off course into the front of a parked car.

I was coming up fast from behind. I jumped over Darren and headed straight for Fitzroy Street. Stiffy turned around a slight corner and was about 20 metres in front of me.

He skilfully avoided the first car in the inside lane, then he just touched the rear of a car in the middle lane, but that was not his real problem. The big green tram travelling the other way hit him head on, sending him in the air. The sound was like slapping a steak onto a chopping board.

I did the only reasonable thing possible in the circumstances. I stopped dead, and attempted to whistle a tune through my panting (not easy, you try it) as though I had nothing to do with his current state.

Still gasping for breath and trying to whistle, I casually attempted to walk back the way I'd come. By this time Darren was up and had taken up the chase again. Acting as casually as possible, I stopped Darren.

Darren had not got around the corner so he hadn't seen Stiffy versus the tram. I told Darren that Stiffy had just decided to take public transport – the hard way.

I ran back to my bag and used my phone to call an ambulance, explaining that a poor unfortunate pedestrian had been hit by a tram. A nearby doctor helped our injured suspect until an ambulance arrived.

We were both upset we had been robbed of an arrest and my $90.

After his week in hospital Stiffy was hitch-hiking from the city back to Fitzroy Street when we spotted him. We were both in plain clothes and always picked up hitch-hikers in our unmarked car. Darren and I laughed as Stiffy explained how he got his injuries. Stiffy stated he was looking for a bloke from Shepparton named Dean. He thought that Dean had set him up to rob him. He had no idea we (or Dean) were cops. Maybe he had amnesia.

It wasn't easy being Dean. He was not well-liked by anyone that had ever met him. He was a fuckwit, lagging dog, a police informer and now a robber of drug dealers.

The funny part was that he was never accused of being what he was, a young copper doing his best.

Dean went back in the bag. Until next time.

ST KILDA was full of losers in those days. The characters that lived in and around The Street were amazing to us and we were part of it, so imagine what it must have been like for the population at large.

I used to enjoy watching members of the public when they came into contact with some of the characters that were part of the scenery.

I found one bloke with very short hair. On his forehead was a large capital 'A' with a circle tattooed around it. I asked him what it meant or stood for. He replied 'Amercy.'

I said, 'Amercy? Don't you mean Anarchy?'

He said, 'It's Amercy, isn't it?'

I said, 'You're telling the story, mate.'

Another bloke who lived down The Street was 'Sharky'. He got his name from two large coloured sharks tattooed on his face, on both cheeks. I asked him why. He replied, 'No reason.'

Another classic idiot was known as Skull. He was a big, ugly, bald bastard. He had a hare lip and chunks missing from both ears. His nose was flat and bent across his left cheek.

Skull was always trying to be a big criminal but he found the going hard and wanted a partner. But he also had a bad habit of robbing other crooks after they had committed crimes. No-one trusted him enough to team up with him.

But what he lacked in brains he made up for in brutality. When Skull assaulted someone, they stayed assaulted. He appeared to be very angry at the world all the time and always rambled on and on about how he would one day pull off a big job and get out of St Kilda.

He used to talk of doing one big drug deal that would set him up for life. His favourite comment was, 'One day me and Ronald Biggs will get pissed on the beach together.' He would tell this to crooks and cops alike.

Of course Skull was just another heroin junkie. He would often go to jail for assault and robberies or similar, but never for long enough.

I am the first to admit he was a scary bastard.

One Monday – it was around 10 am – I was working plain clothes with Darren in The Street when I observed another well-known St Kilda identity, known only as 'Jarrod'.

Jarrod was a very small, thin 50-year-old homosexual. He

was out of the closet, out of the cupboard and out on The Street. He always had a hand bag with a long strap and wiggled his bum when he walked. He was without doubt the happiest, friendliest person in St Kilda. He actually pranced, some would say 'ponced', up and down the street, smiling and chatting to anyone that would listen.

He didn't use drugs and never drank alcohol. He didn't need it; he was high on life. I never saw him with a boyfriend and I don't think anyone knew where he lived. He was The Street's self-appointed social worker, always available to help the aged and the wayward youth.

About five minutes after I saw him that day, I heard shouting and screaming. I ran over to find a small circle of on-lookers. In the middle was Skull, punching and kicking little Jarrod. The poor bloke was curled up on the footpath at Skull's feet.

Darren and I brought Skull to the ground and cuffed him. I screamed for someone to call an ambulance while I tried to comfort Jarrod. His feeble little face and body were broken. The long strap on his handbag was tangled around his body. Jarrod's cheek and jaw bones were broken. I could hear the broken bones of his face crunch together as he mumbled, 'He wanted my bag.'

I recall the whole Street was in shock. Shopkeepers, crooks and cops were all disgusted by this attack. People who were used to violence were sickened by what had happened. I stayed until Jarrod was safely in the ambulance.

We then took Skull to our plain clothes covert police station. It was more of a house, really. There was just a very small Victoria Police badge on the front door. Other than that, it was just like any other house in East St Kilda. Anyway, Skull didn't give a flying fuck about what he had done to little Jarrod. Darren and I charged him with serious assaults and attempted robbery. Skull was then remanded in custody. No bail.

I spoke to Darren about getting rid of Skull for a long time.

We knew he would only get a few months jail for the Jarrod attack – not enough in our view.

Most of what we thought of was highly illegal. Then I thought Dean might be able to come up with something. Over the next couple of nights and many, many drinks later a cunning plan was formed.

The problem was how to do it without being bashed and robbed by the bastard. Skull got bail the next day because we wanted him out and about.

In Fitzroy Street there was a line of telephone boxes just outside the post office. Many drug deals were done in and around these boxes, as it gave them some cover. People could pretend to make phone calls or look like they were waiting to make calls. The fact that they were pathetic street junkies and looked like it was supposed to be lost on everyone else.

Two or three people would crowd into a box and pretend to talk to someone on the phone but actually be doing a deal. The box gave you just a hint of privacy. Skull was in the habit of using these boxes to make calls and buy drugs.

The day after Skull got bail, he was seen making a call from one of these very boxes. I told the guys who were in the car with me to stop for a second while I ran into the Commonwealth Bank.

A minute later I came out of the bank with a smile on my face and a small package in my hand. Back in the car I put the package into a sports bag and then turned into Dean Collie.

I opened the bag and put on the wig, jacket, filled my mouth with toilet paper, the lot. Moments later, Dean was seen carrying the sports bag and getting into a phone box right next to Skull.

Dean was wired for sound.

Darren and two other cops sat in an old panel van parked down the road listening and watching the situation. They all started to laugh when they heard Dean shouting into the telephone, 'Listen, I've got a pound of speed here that you said you wanted to buy at 12.30. I am here, you're late and there won't be a next time.'

Darren and the boys could see Skull's ears had pricked up and he was onto the situation. When Dean slammed the phone down, it was all too much for Skull. He couldn't contain himself.

He left his phone box and pushed open the door of Dean's phone box, squashing Dean inside. Skull leaned inside, took hold of the sports bag and ran up the street, full bore.

Dean sat down in the phone box laughing and said to himself 'Go, Skull.' Darren spoke on the radio, 'All units, Thunderbirds are go, Skull has the bag, heading south in Fitzroy Street.'

Darren pulled up next to Dean, who jumped into the back seat. Dean got changed in the back seat and again became a hard-working, plain clothes policeman dedicating himself to guarding the right, or something like that.

Darren and I laughed as we drove in the direction of the fleeing Skull – we knew he wouldn't go far.

We drove up Acland Street. Over the radio came, 'He has stopped inside the underground car park of the Prince of Wales Hotel.'

We knew he wouldn't be able to help himself. As soon as he thought he was safe he would look in the bag and that was what we were waiting for.

We listened and we all jumped as there was a loud sort of 'ka-thump' sound. It sounded like a depth charge in an old submarine movie and it echoed right through the underground concrete carpark. Seconds later Darren called out 'over here.' Our team ran over to a dimly lit corner of the car park and there was Skull, his whole face, hair, shirt and arms were covered in indelible fluorescent green liquid dye. He looked like he had been 'slimed'.

His hair, mouth, eyes and nose were dripping with green shit. For a splash of colour, his nose was bleeding freely. He was in shock. No doubt his ears were ringing – but there was no-one home.

I had got a large dye bomb from the bank and placed it inside the sports bag with the alleged drugs. A small cord acts as the detonator. When it is pulled the bomb explodes. I had attached the cord to the bottom of the bag, knowing Skull would pull it. Later, Skull told me that after he had run off he decided to hide in the corner of the car park to see what he had stolen, but there wasn't much light.

He said he had lifted the bag right up to his face so he could see what was in there. He said he could not work out what the little package was or work out why it was attached to the bottom of the bag.

He said just after he had pulled it out of the bag he held it up to his face and read 'Danger' just as it exploded. He said that as we walked up to him he was still trying to work out if he was dead or alive.

As soon as we found him we argued about who should handcuff him, but then we realised he was barely able to walk, let alone escape.

We led him out to the back of a divisional van. There were a few cheers from a small crowd when they recognised that the dazed, green, bleeding dickhead in our custody was the feared Skull.

Many clapped as we put him into the back of the van and we were congratulated by the uniform members. We took him back to our office, interviewed and charged him. As expected, he made a 'no comment' interview. The remand application at court several hours later was hilarious. There was Skull, covered in fluorescent dye, trying to explain to his solicitor and the court that he was innocent.

Skull thought he had robbed a drug dealer. His green face changed colour when I informed the court that he had in fact robbed me, an undercover police officer, during the course of my duty.

I informed the court that the accused had ruined a large-scale drug operation. The magistrate was not impressed with Skull at all, especially when this same magistrate had only given him bail the day before. He said, 'Bail refused, take him away.'

Skull went away for a long time. He also remained green for months. It was not a good look.

I love it when a cunning plan works.

CHAPTER 5

This skinny little rat had
his face all screwed up
trying to look mean and scary.

Tatts too big
for his body

I ALWAYS found it amusing that the police force requires you to have a plan. In this plan everything always works perfectly. In real life and actual fact, the plan never works.

I always wanted to type, 'The good guys are going to catch the bad guys, for details come to court.' But no, the perfect plan had to be typed. It was called an Operation Order. There was never any order about it, although sometimes the crooks would need the operation afterwards.

Years later, this plan was to be officially named the Briefing Paper. As years went by, the briefing paper got bigger.

The last one that I completed in 1999 was a centimetre thick and included everything from the location of the nearest hospital to the protocol of media releases.

The problem always was that my bosses would never let me give a copy to the target, so they never, ever got it right.

ONE quiet afternoon, I was at my desk when the phone rang. It was a lovely old lady. This made a change from the routine calls from the mentally ill, the sexually perverted and the homicidal – and that was just the other coppers.

Anyway, this old lady stated that one of the uniform police told her to ring the plain clothes boys. She also told me there was a young girl living in a flat next door to her in Milton Street, Elwood. She said everything was fine until a horrible little man moved in with her and there were comings and goings all night. She said, 'I think they are doing silly things with drugs.'

An hour later Darren and I were sitting in her flat conducting surveillance through her front window. We melted off her couch as two local druggies known as Torvil and Dean walked past and knocked on the target's door. We named them after the famous ice skaters because they were so dissimilar.

They were so stupid that I was constantly amazed they could manage to find, steal, beg or borrow enough money on a daily basis to be heroin-addicted in the first place. They took so many stupid risks they were always skating on thin ice. Anyway.

The arrival of Torvil and Dean meant only one thing. Heroin. It had taken us about 20 seconds to establish all the evidence we required to obtain a search warrant. We finished our tea, then had a couple of quick sherries and it was time to go.

The lovely old lady was most upset that we were leaving so soon. I assured her we would be very discreet and that I would return to fill her in on all the gossip after we finished. She couldn't wait. She was updating her friend Mavis as we sneaked out the back door.

We did all checks possible on the flat. It was owned by an old Jewish couple who were renting it out to a clean skin (no priors) named Karen. As it was my job, I got to make the arrest plan.

One member was to sit in the old lady's flat and call in and out the drug buyers. Sandy (our young, blonde plainclothes police-woman) was chosen for this job. Darren, Ross, Paul and my good self were to sit in an unmarked cop car down the street.

We were the 'raiding party'. Paul was the biggest so was logically put in charge of the key (the sledge-hammer).

Sandy identified a druggie called Karen leaving the flat. Karen walked past us on the way to a nearby milk bar. She was 24, Caucasian-Australian, skinny, with shrunken boobs, mousy brown hair and the typical sallow gaunt face of the heroin addicted. Her appearance alone was a cry for help. She looked as if she had just spent 12 months in a prison camp. Heroin must contain the opposite of vitamins, protein and fibre or maybe it just makes everything else less important. Anyway.

Moments later she returned to her flat. Within seconds Sandy called in a buyer. As she called the buyer out, I had another unit intercept them well clear of the address. Once I was advised they had seized a small quantity of heroin, it was time to hit the flat – I mean conduct a controlled search of the premises.

As we moved into position I radioed Sandy to clear her position and join our raiding party. Paul had the key. I nodded, he hit the door. It held. It gave way on the third strike. Paul had a swing like Tiger Woods on speed.

As the door opened, Paul stepped back. I entered, gun drawn and held out in front of me. I screamed, 'Police! Don't move.' That's what we do. It's all right, too.

I entered a small lounge room. As I did this, the sound of smashing glass came from the kitchen to my left. This distracted me for a second as I headed for the bedroom doorway.

I started to move to my right around a large wooden coffee table. All of a sudden, the male target rushed out of the bedroom swinging a large pair of nunchukkas – Chinese fighting sticks joined in the middle by a short steel chain.

The target, a chap named Glen Aumont, was obviously well practised in the art of fighting with these sticks.

Glen screamed, 'Wattahhhhhhhh!' – that strangled chicken sound that Bruce Lee used when he was about to kill 25 bad guys. He swung them hard and fast either side of his head and around his body as he charged towards me like a wild dog. That is if a wild dog watched Bruce Lee movies.

He was a very skinny little bloke covered in heaps of tattoos that were far too large for his skinny little arms. This skinny little rat had his face all screwed up trying to look mean and scary. If he had given us time, we would have laughed.

But no, he was hell-bent on attack. I levelled my .38 revolver at his chest as a precaution. He jumped onto a coffee table. His fighting sticks immediately smashed into the glass light fitting above his head, causing them to explode like a shotgun blast, sending glass and sparks flying. It was a very impressive show and would have been a highlight at a theatre restaurant.

Glen screamed (more like Peggy Lee than Bruce Lee) as pieces of glass entered his eyes, and the heavy wooden nunchukkas hit his forehead just above his right eyebrow. This opened a big gash, causing blood to flow freely down his face. As Glen fell face first off the coffee table toward me, he managed to twist his right knee. He lay on the floor screaming, holding his face with one hand and his knee with the other.

As I started to put my revolver back into my shoulder holster, Glen's de facto, Karen, came screaming out of the kitchen. She was convinced I had just shot her Glen in the face. He rolled around in pain. My pleas of innocence fell on deaf (and stupid) ears as Karen abused us. Almost innocent, for once, and trying not to laugh, I tried to explain to her that he did it to himself. She wouldn't listen. In the end, I screamed, 'All I did was yell, "Police, don't move" and he went, "Wattahhhhhhhh".' I started to imitate him. She loved Big Tatts and was not impressed by me mocking him. He was too busy squirming in pain to worry.

I ordered an ambulance on the police radio. They were used to being called to police raids where the target needed help for self-inflicted wounds – it was no big deal.

They checked his eyes and they were fine. Only his face and ego were bruised and cut. The good news (for him) was that he was going to live and, for us, that he was fit enough to be interviewed.

We searched the flat, finding a few small foils of heroin, a little cash, and a set of scales. I even searched Big Tatts himself, but could not find out why Karen loved him so much.

Anyway, we conveyed our damaged target back to the station. As I held open the swinging glass doors for Glen to limp through, I said, 'It's dangerous to fly around thinking you're an eagle when you are, in fact, a quail, mate. Glen said, 'Yeah.' He didn't seem to get it.

He said, 'I was concentraten on me tekneek, coz I'm highly trained in them weapons.' He continued, 'Yous guys av seen nuffin, if that light hadn't stuffed me timen up.'

Obviously we were all very lucky to have lived through the experience. Especially Glen.

Karen was free, but decided to follow us to the station anyway. She insisted on staying with and supporting her hero. We heard Karen abusing us as we walked into the station. I interviewed and charged him with trafficking in heroin. I could have charged him with being an idiot in possession of a dangerous weapon.

Throughout the interview Karen remained in the public foyer

area of the watch-house loudly protesting Glen's innocence. Glen was a user as well as a trafficker, which helped explain his pitiful appearance. Bail for him was an impossibility as he was in a show cause situation. Glen could not show sufficient cause why he should get bail.

As we walked through the watch-house area I stopped Glen and let him kiss and cuddle Karen for a moment. They said goodbye. Glen was not coming home for quite a while. I did that because us cops always let criminal lovebirds say goodbye. I did that because I am a compassionate, caring, human. Okay, yes, that was bullshit. I did it so Glen would think I was a good bloke and I cared. He then might trust me and become an informer. Even if his tatts were too big, he still had something to offer. Like his heroin supplier, for instance. But, no, he was not an informer. Just an idiot.

In the foyer I noticed a local and very vocal prostitute named Sophie. Sophie was an old 17-year-old. She was bitter, angry and had a foul mouth. She was a product of The Street.

She needed it and it needed her or neither could exist. Sophie was seated next to Karen. I walked up to Karen and said, 'Glen sells heroin and that's illegal, so he won't be coming home. You're free to leave.'

Karen was not impressed. She screamed, 'You're all a bunch of bastards and if he doesn't sell the shit, someone else will. You found nothing. You think you're so fucking smart – you missed $8000 back at the flat.'

She said she would use the money to get the best team of lawyers to get him off. She finished with an oldie but a goodie. 'I'll have your job for this, you bastard.'

Karen left the station. Seconds after that, Sophie followed. I thought of Karen's last words. Crooks often try to portray the fact that they are so smart. They are unemployed because they're unemployable. They get out of bed at 11am, they have no self discipline or sense of self worth, their own mother would not trust them with the milk money, yet they believe they can outsmart us 100 per cent of the time. Give me a break.

As Glen was being put into the cells, he pleaded with me to tell Karen to bring him some decent clothes for his bail application.

Just to shut him up, and because I did feel the slightest twang of pity for the little skinny pathetic dopehead, I agreed. He yelled out the phone number as I walked away. In the watch-house I rang the number. Karen answered. She was crying and not making any sense.

Through the gibberish I made out that she was complaining that police were searching her flat again. She said, 'Listen.'

She held the phone out and I could hear smashing and crashing. Karen was hysterical. She sobbed something about plain clothes cops bashing her and searching her flat.

Something was very wrong with what I was hearing. I knew what she was saying was total crap because we don't bash women. Alarm bells rang. I slammed the phone down and screamed, 'Darren!'

As Darren and I ran to our cop car I told him Karen was in real danger. The problem was, I had no idea why. As I skidded to a stop outside her flat, I heard her crying. We ran inside.

Karen was leaning against a wall bleeding from her nose. She had been bashed, all right. Her front door was off its hinges and the flat was demolished. Even worse than we had left it.

I asked her what had happened. Karen told us that the plain clothes cop who was sitting next to her at the station had done a drug raid on her flat and bashed her. She said a copper named Sophie had bashed her and asked her questions. Karen went on to say that Sophie kept demanding the $8000 and any heroin that was missed in the earlier raid.

Karen sobbed, 'I was just lying.' This time she was telling the truth.

As Darren called for more police and an ambulance, I put my hand on the Karen's bony shoulder and told her, 'Sophie is one of you guys, not one of ours.' Karen then described Sophie's side-kick. It fitted Sophie's boyfriend, Wayne Elms.

Within two days we arrested and charged them with aggravated burglary, assaults, theft of Karen's credit cards, TV and stereo. Of course, there was never any $8000 or extra heroin.

The last and best charge we could lay against Sophie and Wayne was for impersonating members of the Victoria Police Force. They were ultimately convicted of all charges at the Prahran Magistrates Court.

Of all the offences you could give a crook, impersonate a police officer is the worst. One reason is that other crooks might think that you really want to be a copper. That's bad shit. I think it's just bad for your criminal karma.

I handed the lovely old lady who started the job off in the first place a copy of the court story which was published in the old *Truth* newspaper that we knew and loved.

The 'Babe Ruth' knew all about how to wring every drop out of a good court yarn, and didn't let us down this time. I spent a lovely quiet evening explaining all the funny, sad and gory details to the old dear while sipping on a few sherries. Moments like that made it all worthwhile.

CHAPTER 6

I had only seen the
problem – she had lived it.

Outside
looking in

I HAD been in the police force about three years and I had been full time undercover for 18 months when I had a reason to be back in uniform. I was walking down Bourke Street, Melbourne, in full uniform on a lovely sunny day.

All of a sudden a middle-aged man wearing a suit walked right in front of me. I attempted to walk around him, but he moved right in front of me. I stopped dead and gave him a look that said, 'How dare you stop me'.

I was offended that this person thought he could stop 'me'. I walked right around him. This man said, 'Excuse me.' I turned and again gave him the, 'Fuck off, you idiot' look. I walked on, I could hear his voice getting more upset as it thankfully became fainter. I thought, 'Who the fuck does he think he is?'

Shit! I stopped suddenly. I looked down at my tie, gun and the police badge on my shoulder as it dawned on me. I wasn't just a cop – I was dressed like one. I was supposed to help and serve the public. The poor bastard probably wanted directions or something. I quickly walked on and tried to lose myself in the crowd. How embarrassing. Can you imagine what he would have thought of me? I had spent so long not being a cop, I found that I had to put conscious effort into being one again.

Cops and robbers are at times actually civilians. I love the fact that I get to play all three. I remember walking on mumbling, 'We're playing Angus the cop today, you fucking idiot. You're a cop for Christ's sake. No wonder people think we're arseholes.'

I found myself all self-conscious, as people were looking at me. Everyone notices you when you wear the 'superman suit'. You just can't hide. I recall how you can't just cross the road wherever you like. You're supposed to use the lights. When you go to the lights you find that nobody walks against the 'red man' sign, especially you.

I WAS working the St Kilda divisional van for two weeks just before becoming a detective. It was a lovely, warm Sunday afternoon.

Things were quiet when we got a call to attend at a house in East St Kilda. Meals on Wheels were concerned about the welfare of an old man at a particular address.

We attended a house that was very clean and neat, and found an old man deceased. He was well dressed and had only died in the past couple of hours or so. I called for an ambulance, as you do, then a doctor and Tobin Brothers to remove the body. That's the sad part of the story. The better part was the fact that downstairs was a television featuring the second day of the Test between England and Australia. There was a large couch in front of the TV.

We had to wait for an hour or so for all the services to arrive, so my partner went and got a heap of McDonald's. We had a great time relaxing, eating, drinking and watching the Test.

The Tobin Brothers boys arrived and walked in the front door and found three of us sitting in front of the TV cheering on the Aussies.

One of the Tobin Brothers asked me where the body was and I said it was upstairs. The cricket was very interesting and we didn't want to be disturbed. They both went upstairs. A while later they came down and said they couldn't find him.

I looked at our mate sitting between us in front of the TV and said, 'Time to go, Digger.'

One of the Tobin Brothers said, 'You're sick.' He proceeded to lift up the old bloke and place him on the floor. As rigor mortis had set in, they started to break his arms and legs to get him from a sitting position to a position that would fit into their body bag.

The sound of bones and tendons breaking was terrible – almost enough to put you off your Big Mac.

My partner and I went back to work.

I FOUND myself back in uniform working the van another day – it was real policing. Working the divisional van, attending to shoplifters, drunks, stolen cars, burglaries – all the uniform police shit.

Then there were always the domestics. The best domestics were on Sundays. I think it was because the couple had spent all of Saturday and Sunday morning together. Then, bang, they were at each other by Sunday afternoon. Of course, some domestics were caused for specific reasons.

I was driving the marked van in uniform with my young

partner when we got a call to a domestic in a flat in East St Kilda.

I parked out the front and we both started walking toward the flat. It was an expensive, pastel-coloured complex built for the yuppies who were flooding the area. There was a courtyard in the middle, surrounded by six flats on the ground floor and another six on the first floor. There was one large staircase leading up to the top floor.

As we walked into the courtyard we didn't need to ask directions. We could hear where we had to go and we started up the staircase. As we got to the top, I motioned my partner to stop and listen. After hearing a couple of sentences it was obvious that a young guy wanted a young women to stop using heroin because it was destroying her life.

I whispered to my partner, 'Go around the back of the flat and stand under the kitchen window. Stay there for one minute after I knock on the door then come back here.'

I waited for him to get around the back, then knocked on the door. A female voice said, 'Who is it?'

I said, 'It's the police, can we have a chat?'

She said, 'One moment, please.'

Seconds later the door opened. A young, well-dressed woman of about 25 stood in front of me.

She said, 'Hello officer,' in a well-spoken and confident voice. She attempted as best she could to present as a 'straight head', but her sallow, gaunt face and penetrating eyes told the real story.

She said, 'I'm sorry, officer, it's just an argument.'

I said, 'Your heroin addiction seems to be impacting on your neighbors. They probably have enough of their own problems without being subjected to yours.'

She realised I had interpreted their domestic as being drug related. My partner walked up the stairs and handed me a small make-up bag. I opened it and pushed a small syringe to one side, removing a small silver foil containing white powder. I smiled in the knowledge that I was right again. I had caught another crook.

Her face changed. She no longer wanted to hide her real self. Her words spewed out like venom. She said, 'You think you're so smart, you have no idea what it's like to try to get off heroin.'

I said, 'You're wrong. I've been working St Kilda for more than three years. I've dealt with thousands of heroin addicts. I know exactly.'

She had found the wrong cop to start this, 'You have no idea' crap. If anyone knew about heroin it was me. She had cut me off mid-speech. She moved her face slightly closer to mine and said, 'When did you last use heroin?'

I realised that this was serious shit. I struggled to respond. 'Come on, Angus, where is the answer?' I said to myself. I stepped backwards at the thought that I had no answer. There was none. It was like she just put a knife in my stomach. She twisted it by saying, 'When did you last try to stop using?'

I looked into her eyes and it hit me. I was shocked to realise she had me. I had only seen the problem, she had lived it. I wasn't even qualified to comment. I knew absolutely nothing. In fact, how could I ever have thought I did know what is was like to be addicted to heroin? I realised I was totally out of my depth. Humbled.

I said the only words possible, 'You're right.' I opened the small silver foil and blew the white powder into the air, screwing up the empty foil. My partner reached forward in an attempt to stop me.

He said, 'Don't.' He had no idea either.

I leant forward into the flat and said to the unknown male, 'Good luck mate, keep trying, but try quietly, would you?'

He just said, 'Thanks.'

I handed the make-up bag back to the women. She looked just about as shocked at my actions as my partner did. I was trying to leave with as much dignity as I could.

I said, 'I hope you can get off the merry-go-round.' I pointed toward her boyfriend inside the flat and said, 'It sounds like he's trying to help.'

She nodded her head. She now looked fragile and vulnerable. Her boyfriend was crying seated on a couch. She leant back against the outside wall of the flat. She sobbed, 'I was a nurse.'

Heroin had obviously put an end to that. With a voice on the verge of cracking, I whispered 'Good luck' and truly meant it. But, deep down I knew she had no chance.

I knew that for some unknown reason heroin was bigger and stronger than all of us. Heroin must be able to give you something people can't. I didn't know the answer then and I don't now.

As my partner and I started to walk back to the car he said, 'What do you think you're doing? That was heroin. It kills people. She threw it straight out the window and I caught it. I saw her do it.'

My partner kept on and on at me. He said, 'It's not like a traffic offence and you can give a warning. It's a serious indictable offence and carries a penalty of up to five years imprisonment.' The young man had read his Crimes Act. 'If it's the paperwork, I would have done it,' he said.

I said, 'Did you learn anything from all that?'

He said, 'Heroin disappears when you blow it?'

I said, 'Close.'

All my partner wanted was the arrest. I suppose that's what cops are meant to do. I thought that maybe he was right and I was wrong. It would be so much easier for me to just arrest and process the problem rather than attempt to understand or solve it.

ONE day while working in Fitzroy Street, St Kilda, I came across a young guy about 20 with a tattoo on his forehead. The tattoo looked like it was Chinese writing. I stopped him and identified myself. I asked what the writing meant.

He said, 'I got stoned one night and tattooed the words 'FISH and CHIPS' across me head.'

I said, 'That doesn't say FISH and CHIPS.'

He said, 'Yes it does, it's just back to front 'cos I did it in the mirror.' Silly me for not realising straight away.

IT WAS around the same time at St Kilda when Darren and I decided to check out an old, derelict building. As we walked through the underground carpark we heard a loud, uneven snoring sound. Right down the back there was a little alcove. In the middle of this small open area was Bones, a crook we knew all too well. He was an angry little shithead who had a big dose of small man's syndrome. He thought that being a bad arse would make up for being a short arse, but he was wrong. It just made him an arse.

Bones lived off prostitutes – he stood over them, bashed them, robbed them and used them. He had heaps of tattoos, very short, cropped hair and a high hair line. He would often rob drunks and commit shit armed robberies ... in other words, a would-be-if-he-could-be crook.

When you eat a bad oyster the experience can put you off oysters for life. Well, I reckon Bones must have had a bad experience with a copper, because he really hated us. Unless it was just me, but I doubt that.

There he was, lying on his back on a large, concrete slab. His whole body was supported by the slab up to his shoulders, but his neck and head were falling off the edge in what looked a very dangerous position.

This caused him to have great difficulty breathing. There was a freshly-used syringe next to him. He had ripped the bottom of a Coke can apart and mixed his heroin in it, then placed the filter of a cigarette into the liquid and used it as the filter.

As Darren walked off to check the rest of the building, I walked forward, grabbed Bones and pulled him back onto the concrete slab so his head was supported.

I rolled him onto his right side and lifted his left leg forward placing him into the coma position. His breathing sounded normal, so I left him there.

We went about our business. A couple of hours later Darren said, 'Do you think Bones is all right?'

I said, 'Only the good die young.'

Darren said, 'If he dies our footprints and shit are all over the place. Maybe we should have called an ambulance or something.' He might have been young, but he was not stupid. I decided to drive back to check on Bones. I got to Grey Street and there he was, walking with his back to us on our side of the road headed toward The Street.

I pulled the police car over next to him. Darren was in the passenger seat. I tooted the horn. Bones reluctantly walked over and looked in the passenger side window at Darren. I smiled, Darren laughed out loud and turned to look at me. I shrugged my shoulders. Written in black texta in the middle of his forehead was a large bullseye target and written underneath it were the words 'I HATE COPS.'

We both laughed.

Bones looked bewildered as we drove off. He then walked back onto the footpath and continued towards The Street. Darren looked at me and said, 'I can't leave you alone for one minute.'

In a mock serious voice I said, 'Stop laughing. Policing is a very serious business.'

CHAPTER 7

'Why don't you kiss him better
while you're at it?'

A slippery
customer

IT was a lovely sunny day and we were in plain clothes. I was driving our new unmarked car, a Commodore, and we were crapping on about how some crook had just got a lenient sentence or something when I stopped at a set of traffic lights. As I stopped the car I noticed a hotted-up car had stopped next to us, with two heads (people) on board. What are known in the game as young shitheads.

Any normal person would have said they were just average rough young blokes, but we were cops and they weren't, so shitheads they were.

I said to Darren, 'Ever been in a police chase?'

He shook his head. He thought I must have found a stolen car. I pulled back the vehicle's windscreen wiper lever, activating the windscreen washers. The driver's side washer squirted water onto the windscreen in front of me, the passenger side washer squirted water directly into the face of the young buck driver parked next to us. I had earlier turned the windscreen washer squirter thing on a right angle in case exactly this opportunity came up.

As I kept squirting I leant forward and laughed at him. Both bucks immediately started abusing me. The lights turned green and I accelerated away. They, of course, gave chase. As we accelerated off up the street, I said, 'This is your first chase, mate.' Darren said, 'But … '

I said, 'That's enough. Put the blue light on the roof. It's time to catch them. They're doing a 100 in a 60 zone – that's breaking the law.'

Darren said, 'But …' again, a little weakly. I was beginning to worry about his lack of chattiness. He put the magnetic blue light on the roof but he was reluctant about it. The young shitheads chasing us slammed on the brakes. The driver almost died.

I pulled over in front of them with the blue light still flashing. I got out and walked up to the driver. Darren held his head with his hands, thinking this was all wrong.

Darren walked up behind me as I spoke to the driver. I showed him my police badge and said, 'Please produce your driver's licence.'

The driver had an agonised look. He said, 'But …' I wondered if he was related to Darren.

I said, 'What is your reason for doing 100kph in a 60kph zone?'

He said, 'You, um, but you, um, squirted me in the face and dragged me off and I, um … '

I said, 'Is that any reason to exceed the speed limit?'

He said, 'Well, um, no.'

I said, 'Exactly. If I wasn't a policeman you would probably be still dragging me up the road right now, endangering lives. The traffic operations group would throw the book at you, but I'm going to let you off with a warning this time. I hope you have learnt your lesson. Drive carefully.'

I handed him back his licence. The young driver looked deeply bewildered.

Darren and I got back into our car. Darren said, 'You've given him something to talk about over a beer.'

I said with a straight face, 'Hopefully, he will learn to slow down and be sensible.'

Darren said, 'Exactly.' He nodded to himself, as if he knew there would be a moral to the story somewhere, but he just wasn't sure where it was.

To me, it was pro-active policing at its finest.

JIM was a gentle, quietly-spoken man. He was also a cowboy. He had real snakeskin boots, a big belt buckle and the biggest Stetson hat this side of Texas. He was always pleasant to arrest. He never cracked the shits. Nothing ruffled his feathers. He was cool. He walked like John Wayne.

If you got him with stolen goods just after he did a burglary he would quietly explain how all the goods belonged to his grandmother and he was selling them so she could get a hip replacement.

He was, of course, a low-life, lying junkie. The sort of low-life bastard that would sell his mother if he hadn't already sold her. Being a junkie meant he was also a low-life lagging dog. He lived burglary to burglary, heroin injection to heroin injection, lag to lag, day to day.

Jim was like so many in The Street. He was caught in the never-ending circle of needing to use heroin, doing a burglary, using heroin, getting arrested, giving information to police (being a give up) thus getting bail, around and around until he would finally go to jail for a month or so. Then out he comes and off he goes again.

One good thing about him was that he was always happy. I always made time to drive past his latest home, which would be more like a squat, knock on his door for a quick chat. He would often tell me how to find the latest drug dealer, car thief, burglar. We had a very good rapport.

When you add it all up, he was a nice heroin-addicted low-life, burglar scumbag cowboy.

One day I was working when a job came over the radio. 'A man has shot a burglar in Redan Street, St Kilda.' Darren and I answered the call. We pulled up out the front of an average house in an average street. Cops everywhere. We were all busting to see who it was. It was Jim the Cowboy. He was a clumsy bastard. He was a burglar, but not a good one.

I found him lying down in a puddle of broken glass outside what used to be large French windows. A cop was standing above him, one foot on him, trying to hold him still without getting blood on his shoes.

As I arrived I could hear Jim moaning. I pushed the cop's foot out of the way, bent down and told him it was me. Jim's eyes were closed in pain. I told him to lie still and he would be all right. It's hard to show compassion to a junkie and failed burglar, but I did my best.

Jim said, 'The owner shot me. It's my fault, I shouldn't have been there. Tell him I'm sorry.'

I said, 'Where did he get you, partner?'

He said, 'I'm not sure, everything hurts.'

The front of his shirt was covered in blood. I carefully peeled back his shirt and saw a bullet hole. I said, 'You'll be okay, but I'm sorry to say that he's killed John Wayne, shot him right in the head. His face is gone.'

Jim said, 'What a bastard.'

The bullet had hit Jim in the upper right side of the chest … right on a tattoo of The Duke.

I showed Jim some kindness that day and from that moment on he always thought he owed me. Later, in hospital as he was recovering, I charged him with the burglary. Any pinch is a good one.

It turned out that the Cowboy had knocked on the door of the house several times and no-one answered. It looked like a perfect job, but Jimbo was out of luck, big-time. The house was occupied by an old, deaf, war veteran.

Jim jemmied open the door and was in the process of unplugging the video when he was shot in the upper chest. Luckily the old gun jammed after the first shot.

As the old digger was unjamming it, Jim managed to dive through the French windows. Just like in the Westerns.

ONE day Darren and I called into the uniform police station to attend the 'read out' that was held about once a week. The sergeants and the officer in charge get to tell all the uniform members that everyone is leaving the cars dirty at the end of each shift, not wearing their hats, getting too many complaints. Not to mention the fact there are always more new forms for the poor bloody coppers to fill out, regarding statistics.

After all that crap, we would be updated by the station crime analysts as to where all the latest crime was being reported – all the hot spots.

We were there to pretend that we plain clothes blokes cared

what the uniform cops did. 'Waving the flag' we called it. Actually, we were there because the uniform boss rang our boss and demanded more interaction. That was the real reason Darren and I attended the next read out.

During the meeting, the sergeant spoke about all the latest crimes. The officer in charge of the station then told everyone he was sick and tired of members doing 'whammies' in the cop cars.

A 'whammy' is when the driver turns the vehicle off, pumps the accelerator causing extra fuel to flood the manifold or something, then you turn the ignition on again and 'Bang!' – it backfires with an explosion louder than a shotgun blast.

The boss said it was destroying the exhaust systems or something. It was fun, though.

The officer in charge of the CIB addressed the read out and said, 'As you're all aware, the Shadow Rapist is still at large and active in our patch. The taskforce want to hear from anyone that knows any crook that wears this type of runner.'

He held up a picture of a very distinctive late model men's runner. All the members in the room mumbled to the negative. I looked at the shoe and thought 'Fuck.'

Darren whispered, 'What?'

That was the end of the meeting. We all left. At our vehicle I said to Darren, 'It can't be. Could you see the Cowboy doing that shit?'

Darren said, 'The Cowboy? What?'

I said, 'What does the Cowboy wear?'

Darren said, 'Cowboy gear and boots.'

I said, 'When he was shot?'

Darren thought for a second, 'He was in plain clothes. Christ, he had runners on.'

I couldn't believe that everything was pointing to the fact that nice, calm, cool Jim the Cowboy might be the Shadow Rapist.

I said to Darren, 'He had those runners. He's been doing house entry rapes for more than two years. Finds that a single female lives in the flat, collects tape, rope, a hood and a knife, puts them all on the bed and waits for them to come home. He's a burglar, but Christ.'

Darren said, 'That's not in him, no way.'

I said, 'We'll find out.'

I drove straight to Jim's house. His wife answered the door. I said, 'G'day Shirley, Jim home?'

She said he was out getting medicine for one of his kids. I said, 'I need his runners urgently.'

I followed Shirley into the laundry. Jim's runners were on the floor. They were exactly the runners we were looking for. I picked them up and said, 'Thanks Shirl, I'm playing basketball this afternoon.' She was ecstatic at the fact that she could help me out. The fact that Jim and I had different size feet didn't seem to worry her. Then again, she wasn't the sharpest tool in the shed, or else she would have married a bit better.

As we were about to leave I grabbed Darren's official note book from his back pocket. I wrote, 'Received two REEBOK RUN TECH Blue/White Runners 3.56pm March 21 at 12 Shore Street, St Kilda, from Shirley blah, blah.'

She said, 'All the best, Angus, see you soon.' If she only knew.

I handed the runners to the taskforce. It was him. When shoes are made at the factory they are all the same. Once they are worn they become individualistic. The tiny marks, cuts and wearing are like fingerprints to an expert. And everything on those runners indicated that Jim was the rapist. No doubt.

Months later the taskforce asked us to a briefing. They had compiled a 'Life Line' including every detail of Jim's life. This Life Line had him living in the vicinity of all the attacks.

Jim had since been sentenced to eight months for burglaries. They had to wait until he got out. He had denied all allegations. The taskforce needed his DNA for comparison. This was to be the very first DNA case in Australia's history. Jim was the chief suspect for 26 house entry rapes. On three occasions, he raped the same woman twice.

On the evening before his release from jail, the taskforce gave us our jobs. We were all working when surveillance called, 'He's out and free, cuddling his de facto, into a car and off.' Surveillance followed as he drove to Coburg and purchased heroin. He then drove out east to his home. We all sat back and waited as he had sex with his de facto.

In those days we believed we needed sperm from our suspect to match the sperm he left at the crime scenes. The officer in charge of the job waited 25 minutes before he gave the order to execute the warrant.

Sure enough, Jim had just lit a cigarette, signalling it was all over. We collected the samples, but it would take three months for them to be analysed in England. Meanwhile, both Shirley and Jim were conveyed to the police station.

He made total denials about everything. His shoe impressions were put to him. He just agreed that he probably did the burg, but not any rape.

The ace had to be played. The main investigator sat down in an interview room and explained in detail how Jim likes to have sex, the investigators described every little touch, every whisper, what he liked and disliked.

After a few sentences Shirley burst into tears and sobbed. She knew. Only she could know that it must be Jim. She sobbed the words, 'Can I speak to him?'

She was put in the interview room with Jim. The video recorder rolled. She said words like, 'If you love me and your children, please talk to them. I know it's you. Talk now and you'll get out one day. They'll have a father, how … why … '

He cried and made full admissions to two and a half years of rapes. I felt I had to say something to him. During a coffee break I walked into the interview room and looked at him. He looked at me and cried. I felt nothing and said nothing. I turned around and left. The more you think you know about people, the less you know.

HE was known as The Drain Pipe Burglar, and in our plain clothes office we regarded him as a persistent pain in the arse crook. That's because we couldn't catch him. All we knew was that he was a little bastard who could climb like a monkey.

This might come as a shock, but he got his name by the mode of entry he used, not because he was knocking off drain pipes. Everyone who lived in a building with a window near a drain was fair game.

Drain Pipe would disappear for a week or so then, bang, he would strike again. Everyone wanted to catch him. Everyone had their own theories how he could be caught, but no-one got him. This went on for months. Unfortunately, our office was given the task of catching him.

At one stage he became very active. He started to specialise in blocks of flats. I found that anyone who lived in a flat above the ground floor believed it was safe to leave their bathroom window open all day and night. I also realised every bathroom window has a drain pipe leading right up to it, which makes sense when you think about it. I continued to harass heroin traffickers. Several members could not understand why I was not interested in catching the burglar.

My first thought was how in the hell do you cover such a huge area trying to catch him 'on the hop', so to speak? That is, until the superintendent of the district offered five days extra holiday to be taken whenever you liked for anyone who could put an end to the Drain Pipe Burglar.

I decided he had to be stopped. I then planned a fishing trip to Lake Jindabyne in NSW for five days, starting soon after. Everyone in the office laughed.

I found a print of a pencil drawing by a well-known artist made many years ago. It was framed. I hung it directly above my desk. It was a perfect picture of a piece of pipe. Under the pipe were the words 'This is not a pipe'. People in the office would look at it, look puzzled and walk away.

I called Darren into the collator's office. I informed him that we had to get serious. I showed Darren how to go through all the crime reports. I found a folder containing more than 80 home burglaries. The collator had placed red pins in a large map of the East St Kilda-Prahran area in the inner suburbs where the burglaries had been committed.

I found that he mostly targeted flats late on Friday and Saturday nights. I 'borrowed' the folder and directed Darren to drive to several of Drain Pipe's latest crime scenes. Reading the details of the victims and seeing each of the flats, it was obvious they were the young 'yuppie' types that infested St Kilda.

I stopped outside a large block of flats. He had burgled four of the 10 flats in the block. We got out of the car. I said, 'We need a cunning plan and we have to understand our target to catch him.'

I stood and looked at one of the long, high, thin drain pipes he had climbed to gain entry. I said, 'To do such a difficult climb he must check it out during daylight hours.'

I turned and walked back to the front of the flats. I said, 'It's about midnight, I walk up to here, I've got a vehicle parked somewhere nearby because of the items I have to carry and distances travelled.'

Darren said, 'You have to select a flat, so check if there are any lights on.'

I said, 'Yeah, but first I must check the car park; each park has a corresponding flat number written on it.' We walk to the car park. I stopped and said, 'If I was the Drain Pipe I would want to do flat seven, they own a blood red RX7 with mags, sunroof and car phone. Nine looks good, with a nice convertible white BMW including sports pack. It's midnight and I would check the carpark and they would have gone night-clubbing. Then I would walk up to the front door, stop and listen. Nothing, check the power meter, and it's only just ticking over – probably only the fridge and alarm clock. I would knock on the door just to check, then I would be right to do it.'

Looking back at the MOs (modus operandi) I found that some of the bathroom windows were locked and he had to force them open with a small jemmy or screw driver.

I said, 'So our target has a breaker's kit – screwdriver, probably a torch, other bits and pieces for car thefts. Gloves etc. He probably has a bum bag or back pack. Look at this report, entry via toilet window, second floor, front door deadlocked, not forced by offender, exit via same entry point. Goods stolen, two cameras, high-tech stereo system, jewellery, cash. Let's add a long rope to his kit to lower the stuff down.'

I thought for a second then said, 'Darren, I just thought of something.' As we walked to the front of the property I said, 'Always gloves and no foot prints or shoe impressions.'

Opposite was a large building site. I walked up to one of the builders and flashed him my badge and asked if I could use one of his long ladders.

I carried it back to one of the drain pipes that the crook had climbed only three days earlier. Climbing the ladder, I looked carefully at the drain pipe. I found what appeared to be small dimple-type shoe impressions. I told Darren and asked him to get the Instamatic camera from our car. I took a couple of instant photos of the impression.

Darren and I drove to a large shoe shop in Prahran. The manager told me that he didn't sell anything similar to the impressions. We went to a specialised mountain-climbing store in the city.

Sure enough, they matched a small, high-tech climbing shoe. This type of shoe is only for climbing. It fits the foot like a glove.

The shop assistant said to me, 'Your foot becomes like a hand, you can use your toes, unlike with a conventional shoe, to give you maximum grip.' I thought about it and realised this is a serious little bastard. It was that moment that I also thought of a cunning plan, but I wasn't going to tell Darren. Not yet.

This was not a pipe.

For the next week or so Darren kept on and on at me to work a night shift like everyone else trying to catch Drain Pipe. The whole office was on permanent night shift.

I told Darren, 'We'll catch him, but we're not going to catch him walking down the street hot on a job. The little bastard sneaks around in the dark, hiding every time a car comes down the road. He would be in all black or dark blue. Once he keeps still, you'll never see him. We won't catch him at his own game; he's at home in the dark sneaking around.'

Darren said, 'Find him through his stolen property?'

I said, 'No, none of his stuff has surfaced, so he must be getting rid of it interstate or whoever buys it takes it interstate or something. We just have to wait.'

I paused and added: 'You want to do a night shift – do it. Good experience sneaking around out there.' Darren joined in on a few night shifts and then agreed to do it my way.

Darren thought I was working on my four-wheel-drive or hanging around fishing tackle stores. I was not. Everyone in the office continued to try to catch the pain in the arse burglar, while I continued to catch other crooks, mostly heroin traffickers.

Several times Darren asked me why I was not trying to get Drain Pipe Man. I told him that I was, and to be patient.

Darren and I were on an afternoon shift on a Friday night. I came in late for work. Darren heard me on the phone. I had telephoned Mr Daley, the officer in charge of the local ambulance department.

I asked him if he could telephone me immediately on my mobile phone if any ambulance calls came involving a person falling in the East St Kilda area. He was most helpful and agreed to call me as a matter of priority. I hung up. Darren said, 'That would be handy if it ever happens.'

Later that night, while I was driving home about 11.45, my mobile phone rang. It was Mr Daley. He said, 'Angus, you might be interested a call that just came in from a Mrs Cummins at Landsdowne Street, East St Kilda. She reports a person has fallen off his bike outside her flat and requires an ambulance.' I asked which hospital would he go to and he said, 'The Alfred'.

I thanked him. Then I rang Darren on his mobile. We met at the office minutes later and drove straight to the scene.

We found the ambulance about to drive off. Ross and Sandra had beaten us there. I was surprised to see them as there had been no police call and we cops don't monitor the ambulance channel.

Ross told me that he was in the next street when he heard an ambulance pull up nearby and came to check it out. Ross said, 'It's not our man, he had just hit a cat on his pushbike and fallen off.'

Darren said, 'Where's his bike?'

Ross said, 'He lives in the flats down the road and his brother took it home when he called an ambulance so it wouldn't get stolen.' Darren went to say something else, but I kicked him. He got the message, and finally shut up.

I said, 'G'day, what's his injuries?' to the ambulance bloke as I leant over the injured man. The ambo said, 'Broken right arm, compound fracture, right leg seems broken in two places.'

His eyes were closed as he writhed in pain.

His tracksuit pants and windcheater had been cut open. I grabbed both his hands and said, 'You'll be right, mate.'

He opened his eyes and said, 'Fuck off, get him away.' He wasn't in the mood to chat.

Ross said, 'Why don't you kiss him better while you're at it?' I stepped back as the ambulance drove off.

I called out, 'Oh well, good luck, catch you later.' I don't think he heard me. Ross was going crook about not catching the Drain Pipe Burglar. 'For his sake, I hope I don't catch him first,' he mumbled as he got back into his car. 'Trying to sleep all day, working all night in the freezing cold – if I catch him I'm going to … '

Darren and I got back into our car. Darren said, 'Didn't you say it was a woman that rang in?'

I ignored him and said, 'The Drain Pipe Burglar just told me to fuck off.' I waved to Ross and Sandy as they drove off.

Darren said, 'You think that might have been him?'

I said, 'No, I know it's him. Open my bag down at your feet.'

Darren opened it and removed an industrial size jar of Vaseline petroleum jelly. I held up my hand and said, 'Look.' I then wiped Vaseline onto the back of his hand.' I said, 'His hands were covered in Vas.'

There were times for a team effort, but with a few days off as the incentive, this was not one of them. With Ross and Sandy safely out of the way, I got back out of our car and Darren followed. We knew his equipment had to be somewhere near.

I told Darren, 'This morning I greased up this drain pipe here and he fell from here. I put Vaseline at the top of this one just below the window and it got him.'

But Darren was busy, fishing out a backpack from under a bush nearby. I took several photographs of it 'in situ'. Darren opened it. Sure enough, there were gloves, several tools, a long thin cord nicely tied up, the mandatory mobile phone turned off, a thin pencil torch – and the climbing shoes we were looking for.

I stopped taking photos and stood there, smiling. Darren said, 'You could have killed the bastard.'

I said, 'He knew how to climb so I figured he should know how to fall. After he fell it must have almost killed him taking those climbing shoes off and crawling out onto the roadway.'

We gathered the gear and left for the hospital. At the hospital I had him placed under guard. I informed him he was under arrest for numerous burglaries in the St Kilda area. He was in so much pain that the charges were the least of his problems. He had a wash board stomach and rippling muscles. He was just about the fittest bloke I had ever seen.

Darren commented later that he would have been a bastard to catch if we ever did see him on a job. I telephoned Ross and Sandy to tell them of our investigations. They couldn't believe it – Ross was spewing he had let the crook go. They went back and found his car parked down the road.

I telephoned the boss and said, 'Boss, sorry it's so late but Darren and I would like next week off, starting Sunday. Oh, and yeah, we just caught the Drain Pipe Burglar.'

The boss was impressed, and not wanting to know how we caught him. He said he was going to phone the superintendent immediately, as well as all the press. Bosses love headlines.

We executed a warrant on the burglar's home in Malvern where he lived with his mum. The house was full of stolen gear.

His garage had something like a blacksmith's forge he used to melt down all the gold he stole so it was untraceable. We also found several of his contacts interstate where he used to get rid of some of his gear.

The whole office complained how Darren and I were really 'arsey' catching the Drain Pipe Burglar. I kept the methodology secret. I just told them he was a slippery crook, so you had to think slippery. If you go fishing, think like a fish.

Darren later said, 'How did you know he was going to burg there?'

I said, 'Mate, that's my third jar of Vas. I got some funny looks buying it at the supermarket. I've been putting Vaseline on pipes for the past week. With an extension ladder, I found I could Vas around 30 pipes every hour. It had to get him eventually.'

Finally, the boss walked up and congratulated us in front of the whole office. After that he was about to walk away but stopped. He said, 'Angus, what's the go with that picture?'

The boss indicated the picture of the pipe above my desk. He said, 'That says "This is not a pipe", but it is a pipe.'

I said, 'No, it's not, boss – it's a picture of a pipe.'

Sometimes you have to look beyond the obvious, and sometimes you have to look right at it. The trick is in picking the difference.

I HAD been in the job for about 12 months. I was working with a sergeant on afternoon shift. We got called to a 'violent domestic' between mother and son. The sergeant and I got out of the car and walked up to the front door.

The sergeant was a skinny pain-in-the-arse sort of bloke with red hair and glasses. He was not tough, so he thought he had to act it. He was president of some sort of pistol-shooting club and spoke of velocities and penetration power, that sort of stuff. A skinny gun-nut. I think you can picture him.

The mother explained that her son lived in the bungalow in her backyard. He had been threatening to bash her and the mother wanted him removed from her property.

The sergeant led the way. We knocked on the bungalow door and it opened. A fat young bloke of about 25 opened the door. He was really pissed off at the whole world. He ranted and raved about killing the world. He then realised we were cops and decided he wanted to kill us first and then his mother.

He said to the sergeant, 'Mum called the Jacks, so I have to bash her. Get out of my way.'

The sergeant said, 'Please calm down, just relax. Take a deep breath.'

The son had a better idea – he swung a huge punch straight at the sergeant's head. He ducked and the punch whizzed through the top of his hair, just missing its target. I leapt forward to arrest him, but my senior partner put his arm out and stopped me. The son stood there.

My sergeant said, 'That was very, very stupid. You do that again and you'll be in big trouble. I mean it.'

The son learned his lesson. This time he aimed lower. The punch hit my sergeant right in the side of his head as he ducked. He was unconscious before he hit the ground. I jumped on the son, wrestling him for about 10 minutes before help arrived. The cavalry walked in as I had him in a reverse upside down sleeper hold. An ambulance came and revived my sergeant.

Some people are 'yes' men. Others are 'maybe' people that just need a little more talking to and they will obey. And there are 'No' people. The moral of the story is that you don't try to persuade a 'No' person. You can end up with a nasty headache.

CHAPTER 8

He was good – but so were we.

Rolling on a big wheel

DEAN COLLIE was out and about one quiet afternoon. He decided to sit on his arse on the footpath near the St Kilda Cafe. Then Derek came along and wanted to befriend Dean. I didn't want to know anyone that wanted Dean as a friend. But Derek was in my face and I couldn't get rid of him.

He went on and on about what a good crook he was. Dean was impressed. All of a sudden Derek caught me by surprise by saying something of interest. 'But me best bit is drivin,' he said. 'I'm mostly hired as a driver.'

Dean said, 'Like a racing car driver?'

He said, 'Nah, getaway driver. I'm a specialist, V8 Commodore is me go. No cop has caught me – well, not on a job driving a Commodore. I got done in a Ford and a Toyota and a yellow Volvo. Mate, don't pinch a Volvo, they're shit.' I had to interrupt him or I would be listening to this shit all day.

I said, 'You can drive?' I was amazed.

He said, 'I reckon I can trust ya. You can call me Wheels.'

He said, 'Arks me anyfin about drivin', mate.' He was obviously better in front of a wheel than in front of a dictionary.

I felt like saying 'It's 'ask' not arks,' but I was supposed to be a dero, not Professor Henry Higgins.

He wouldn't shut up. 'Me mate escaped from jail up in Sydney and is comin' down 'ere. 'E's really smart, 'e wants me to drive for 'im.' Ignoring his bullshit, I offered him an old stale rollie cigarette. He helped himself.

I said, 'What does he do?'

He said, 'His burgs are special. The targets, the entry, special. Do one job wiff 'im and you're right for a week,' meaning you could afford a whole week's supply of heroin.

I said, 'Fuck, he must be good,' but my new mate replied, 'No, mate, he's special.' He said it like the word 'special' was the biggest and best word in the world. The way he used it, it was.

I said, 'You're like a taxi driver without a licence. You pick him up from home and drive him to where he works.'

He said, 'No mate, I drive. I know what cars can and can't do, mate, you hit a corner too fast, all over mate. I know the angles, power on, power off, cornering, shit like that.' He was making all the movements as he was telling me the story, his feet were accelerating and braking, his arms were steering.

I thought, 'Thank Christ I'm not in a car with this idiot. I'd prefer to run from the crime scene. This bloke couldn't drive a nail.' I saw a bit of an opening and said, 'If you ever need good wheels, me brother works in the Dunlop warehouse, he gets anything you want cheap, real cheap.'

He said, 'Good, mate. Sometimes I put special wheels on for a big job, give me your number so I can ring ya.'

I gave him my mobile phone number. Every shithead has a

mobile phone – even deros like Dean. I would have given him my e-mail address, but it hadn't been invented yet.

I said, 'This is me brother's mobile number. Just ask for Dean. I'm with him all the time.' He saw someone he wanted to talk to and drove his imaginary car off up the footpath. I said to myself out loud, 'Networking. I think this is Dean's way of networking.'

Some time later my mobile phone rang. I picked it up and said, 'What?' I loved that bit. The best bit about being an undercover cop is being able to be rude when you answer the phone. Sometimes it's my mum and I have to explain, but anyway.

The voice said, 'I want Dean.' I called out, 'Dean! Dean! It's for you.'

I made him wait, changed my voice to a stupid low monotone. 'What?'

The voice said, 'It's Wheels, we gotta meet.'

I said, 'Talk to me, the phone's safe.'

He said, 'I got a job, me mate from Sydney is here, but someone stole me car.'

I said, 'Someone stole your car? Your stolen car?'

He said, 'Yeah, bastards. St Kilda's bad, eh.'

I said, 'How can I help ya?'

He said, 'You got a car?'

I said, 'Yeah, but it's a shit 1973 Toyota Corona.'

We arranged to meet.

I told Darren about this loser. We had to be very careful with this guy. Under the Drugs Act, you can play all sorts of games because you're covered by indemnities. You can get away with murder (at least in NSW). But once you start talking burglaries and stolen cars we, as police, can't allow such crimes to be committed. So we have to think of cunning plans, and I was good at that.

I became Dean and drove off to meet Wheels in the 1973 Corona. Darren covered me in an unmarked cop car.

I drove up to Wheels and he got in. He explained that he had stolen a top-of-the-line V8 Commodore with low profile mags, the lot, but someone else had stolen it. He needed to steal another vehicle by the following night as he had a big job on.

The story was that his mate, Jam, from Sydney, had organised a big burg. I struck a deal with Wheels. I told him that if I could get him a car, I wanted a cut of the profits. He agreed and we went to a pub for a few beers.

Dean was up-market on this day, wearing a leather bomber jacket worth about $500. Dean had got it from the property office at work. It had been stolen in a 'smash and grab'. Wheels loved it so much I sold it to him for $80 cash. I sold it cheap after telling him I had stolen it. I then had to leave. I left via the rear door of the pub and met Darren out the back.

I changed clothes and Dean became Angus. I told Darren that I knew a bloke who was wearing a stolen leather jacket. My loyal partner just shook his head. We re-entered and shook down Wheels.

He whinged and whined. I told him that I knew the jacket was stolen. Wheels thought he was very unlucky, which he probably was. He was on parole. A handle stolen goods charge breached it and it would mean he'd go straight to jail for six months.

After 'special' interrogation by both Darren and Angus, Wheels finally decided to come clean. He said he knew we had been following him for the past month. He was a bright lad.

He went on to explain that he knew a well-organised criminal named Dean. Wheels said, 'Look at the surveillance photographs of me and you'll see him.' He stated Dean was the head of a well-organised stolen car and stolen car parts gang. He said that Dean

Not a drug dealer ... just pretending to be one.

Arresting Mr Big … a Maori with size 15 thongs.

A police video surveillance shot
of me as a yuppie drug dealer

Undercover work … mean and Dean and mighty unclean.

Above: Me (front left) with a team of hand-picked detectives about to be set loose on the streets.
Below: Me and the real Darren.

Graduation day ... and (below) Independence Day.

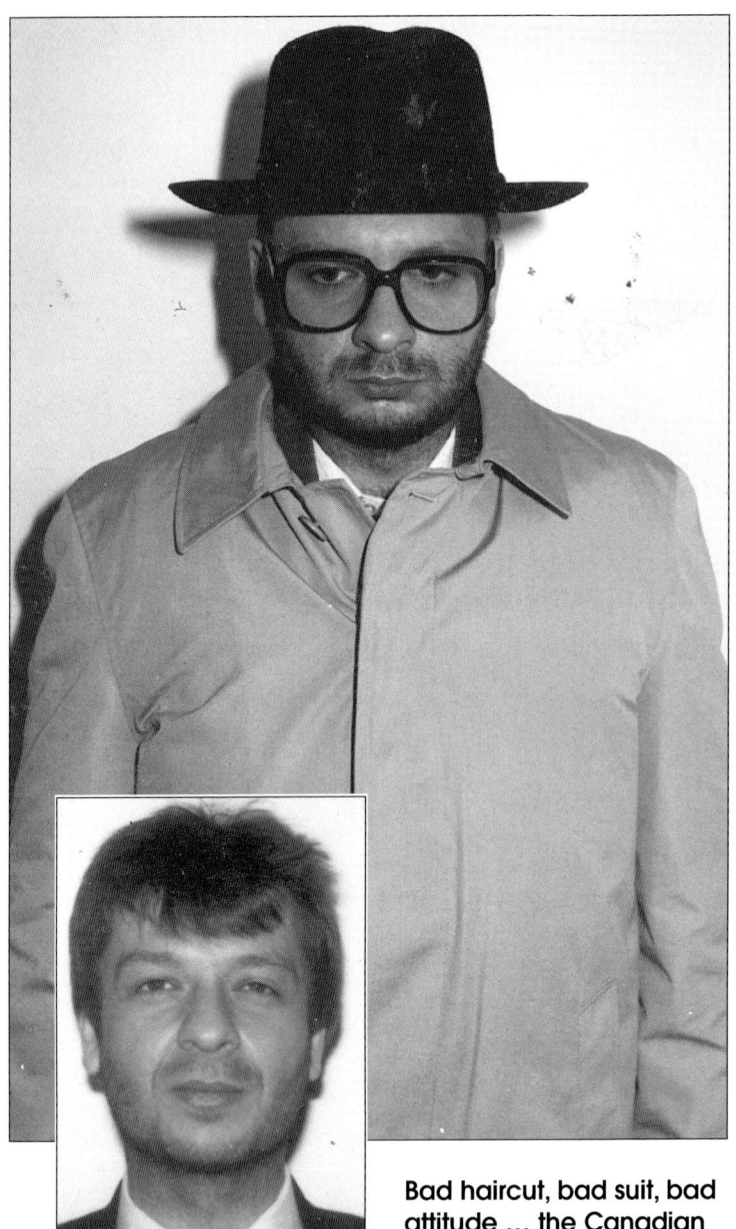

Bad haircut, bad suit, bad attitude ... the Canadian chef with no name.

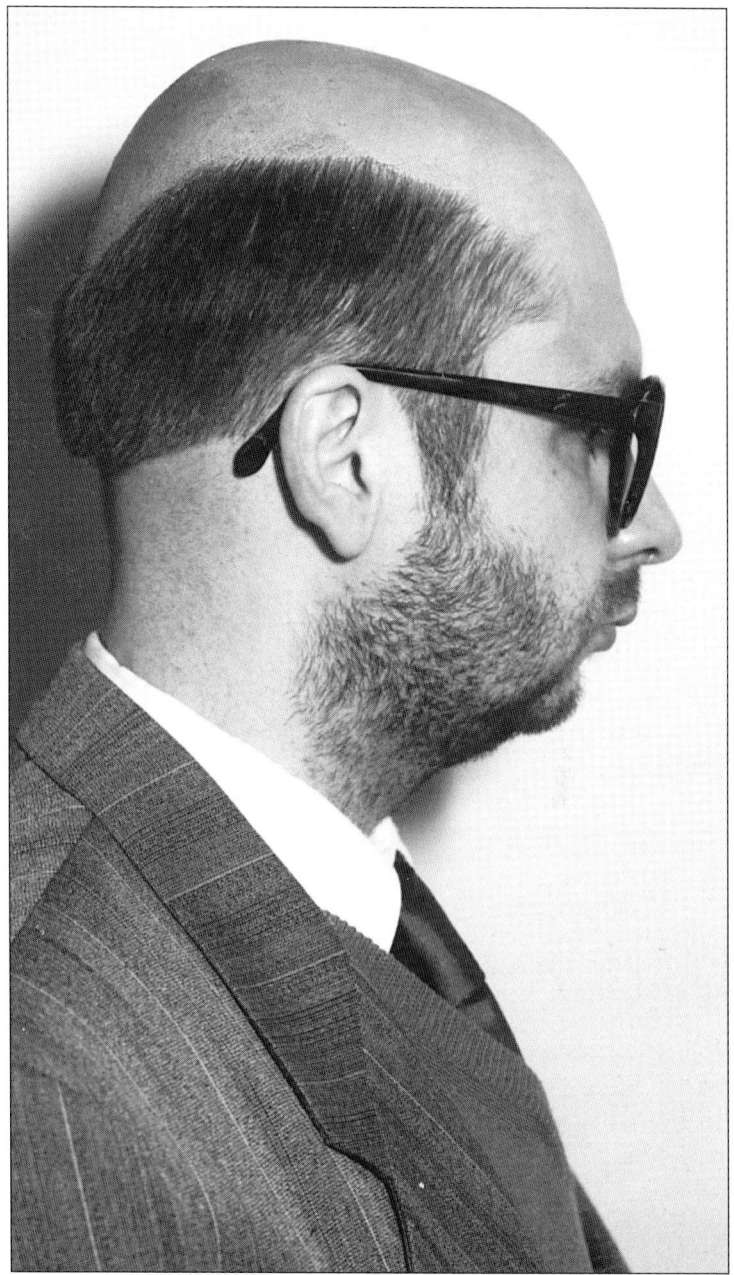

Hear no evil, see no evil ... my sergeant trying to ignore our interview technique.

Smoking can be harmful to your health.

Kids, don't try this at home: No wise man takes
photographs of himself with an armful of loot.

I was
destined
to be a
copper ...
even
kindergarten
was thirsty
work!

I didn't see crabs like this until I went to St Kilda.

Rites of passage … a Fosters at Lords.

You can
catch
anything
with the
right bait.

Prime suspect ... helping our
line of inquiry.

Right: Blackbelt for Cucu ...
dental floss for the lion.

also sold guns and smack. Wheels stated that if we gave him the chance, he would 'set Dean up'. He then proudly handed me Dean's mobile phone number. As you can imagine, we were ecstatic. We walked out of the room. Darren said to me, 'Well, I love it when a plan comes together.'

I said, 'Let's get this Dean bloke. I know where he lives.'

Darren and I went back to the station for a chat. We left Wheels spinning in an interview room while we talked tactics. Sipping coffee, Darren reviewed our situation. He said, 'Wheels wants a stolen car and we can't – Dean can't – give him one. We want to know where he and his mate Jam are going to do the big burg but he won't tell us.'

I said, 'I've got it.'

Darren said, 'We're in enough shit. I don't want to hear you've got it.' He was too late. I set Wheels free after instructing him that I wanted him to set Dean up as soon as possible. Darren gave Wheels his mobile phone number. He was hardly out the door when Dean's phone rang. As expected, it was Wheels.

I told him I was trying to go straight and that I didn't want to steal another car, but he could use mine. Wheels said, 'What, you own a car?'

I said, 'Yeah, it's my stolen car but you can use it.'

Darren said, 'I'm sure Wheels can understand that logic.'

We arranged to meet. I had gone to Ugly Duckling Car Rentals and Fred gave me a car for nothing for two days. I hoped, in fact prayed, that Wheels wanted to do the burg more than set up Dean. I knew there was no danger as I figured I would know in advance whatever it was that he decided.

I gave Wheels my car. He was very happy as I had stolen the keys with it. All we had to do now was follow him to the prospective job. Surveillance followed him away. We just had to wait.

Darren and I couldn't identify Jam. There was no escapee from NSW with that name or any name similar. Surveillance ('the Dogs') watched him pick up a male from Fitzroy Street, St Kilda, and drive him to Chapel Street, Prahran.

They started to case the same video camera store that Felix had knocked off a couple of months earlier. They cased the front and back. From their actions it was obvious this was their target.

When they left, they were happy and I was happy. Surveillance took a heap of photographs of the as yet unidentified male that Wheels called Jam.

I started to take things seriously when the Dogs observed Jam making very detailed notes regarding the video shop. He spent 25 minutes mapping out the front, rear and side streets. Jam looked much more professional and serious than your average scrote.

The store was one of a group of four. The rear of all four shops led into a large storage area that had one very large, heavy roller door. As Jam looked at and made notes of this area, I said to Darren, 'This is the entry point, how the hell does he get through that?'

Darren said, 'Use the front door, or drive through for a smash and grab.'

I said, 'Jam's taking notes. He doesn't just want to grab a few items, mate – he wants the lot. The only way is to get a vehicle in there, fix all alarms and take his time. But how?'

I rang my office and got Sandy to contact a mate of mine at the Sydney city detectives office and run a check on 'Jam'.

I gave her a full description and informed her that photographs would follow. It was imperative we find out everything about our new player.

This was an exciting time. I turned to Darren and said, 'The game stops here, mate. Piss-ant Wheels has done well.'

Darren said, 'Jam must be an idiot to work with Wheels.'

I said, 'Blokes like Jam need people like Wheels to take all the risks. Notice Wheels didn't lag on Jam.'

Darren said, 'Have a look at him (Jam). If he did lag on him it would be would be the last thing Wheels ever did.' We watched Jam finish his notes, say goodbye to Wheels and disappear into the crowd. I instructed surveillance to stay with Jam but they soon lost him. Wheels drove off.

I told Darren to keep a look out for Jam and Wheels while I went to speak to the store manager. You could see from the entrance what was so attractive to crooks ... hi-tech TVs, videos, cameras, the lot.

I was in seventh heaven, standing in my next big crime scene. To catch crooks on the job when their adrenalin – and ours – is pumping to the max – well, it was going to be fun.

I was thinking about all this when, all of a sudden, a bloke pushed past me. He turned and said, 'Excuse me. Sorry, mate.'

It was Jam. He was dressed in a Telstra uniform, carrying a small tool box.

I casually started looking at a display of TVs. Jam told the manager that he had to check the phones. I knew that alarm systems use the phone lines. He got to do close-up reconnaissance and fix the alarm system at the same time – he was good.

But so were we.

I walked out of the store across the road to Darren. Darren said, 'How did you go?'

I said, 'Oh, real good. I ran into Jam, shit myself and came back here, you idiot. Look over my shoulder into the store – that's Jam, talking to the manager.'

We watched as Jam went up into the roof, out the back, the lot. Unbelievable. We left and briefed the boss. Jam was ready to do the burg – no worries. I organised a full crew to start surveillance overnight for the next two nights.

We were short on manpower and we had the usual problems of our boss wanting to arrest them before they committed the offence, but where was the fun in that?

I convinced the boss we needed more evidence. So, for the next two days, we sat around ready for them to do the job.

I had spoken to the owner of the target premises who was very happy to assist us any way he could. On the first night, expectations were high. There were four of us inside the rear of the store and four members outside to call in when the crooks arrived, so they could help make the arrests.

By the second night, I had four members in total. Still nothing happened. By the third night, everyone was pissed off and didn't want to play again. I must agree it is a lot easier talking about doing surveillance all night in the cold than actually doing it. Especially when we started to think the crook might be planning to do it next month.

On the third night, it was just Darren and me, sitting in the rear of the store next to the back door. We spent most of the night planning to do terrible things to Wheels when we got our hands on him.

We had to keep our heads down so no-one could see us from the front windows of the store. It would spoil things a bit if some public-minded citizen saw us, assumed we were burglars and hollered for the marshal.

I had opened the back door so we could see across the storeroom to the roller door. We were ready so we could close the door quickly in case the crooks entered via the roller door. Everything was dead quiet – and boring.

I thought I heard a car. There was a scratch of metal, then a rhythmic, 'click click click – click click click – click click click,' then the sound of crunching metal as the heavy steel roller door was forced upward from the middle. The steel folded like tin foil under the pressure of a big high lift jack. Jam had welded two steel plates to an industrial jack, slid them under the door and started jacking the door up.

It was very effective and reasonably quiet. I pushed Darren back inside the rear door of the store. I quietly lifted a large piece of wood to lock the door, then snibbed one of the large bolts closed, being very careful not to make a sound.

I couldn't make it too easy for them. We then heard a truck back into the store room near the rear door of the store. Our hearts were racing. This was it.

Darren picked up the police radio and whispered, 'Blue 407 to VKC'. Footsteps could be heard outside. I told Darren to shut up. I carefully took the radio from him and disconnected the battery, placing it on the ground all in one motion. We held our breath to help us hear what was going on.

I had placed a large Dolphin torch onto a high stool facing the rear door. This was so I could push the button of the torch, sending a bright beam of light into their eyes, dazzling them as they entered.

We stood there with our heavy baton torches, which hold five large 'D' size batteries and so tough you can drive a truck over them. We stood there poised for action. I then started to get a bit worried so, instead of pointing my baton torch at the rear door, I turned it around so I held it back to front. It was now a blunt but lethal weapon. In the dim light Darren saw what I had done and copied me. Then ... nothing.

We could not hear a thing. I thought the crooks might be breaking into one of the other shops. I stepped forward and listened to the door. Then SMASH! A sledge hammer hit the door. I jumped backwards, knocking over Darren, the stool holding the torch and several other items from the shelves.

We made as much noise as the crash of the hammer. Darren and I winced as we froze. For the first time one of the crooks spoke, in a low voice: 'What the fuck was that?'

'I don't know,' came the answer. 'There must have been stock against the door.' Then the smashing continued. Each crash was short and sharp. We had to remain perfectly still in our painful crash positions. This meant we were not in the perfect arrest positions when the door finally gave way. As the door flew open, the crooks stepped inside between us. One was a crook I had not seen before, but the other was Jam.

He stood and looked down at me, for an instant he froze in fright. I hit him with a wall of screams: 'Police, police.! Don't move!' It was as though we'd all got a fright.

Darren and I let fly with the batons. The crooks tried to take cover but we had the element of surprise. At the end of all the tenderising process we lay on top of our catch.

The crooks were bleeding, Darren was bleeding, I was bleeding. I had hit myself in the face with a back stroke. Darren said I had hit him several times and the crooks never said a word. They just bled. It was a text-book operation. I reached over and touched Darren's hand, it was a feeble attempt at a high five. It was all we could muster. We'd won.

I notified D24 and requested an ambulance to check us all out. I rang the boss at home. It was a great pinch.

Where was Wheels? Who cared, except that he had the car I'd borrowed. Anyway.

CHAPTER 9

He was handcuffed and we still looked
as if we were going to get flogged.

A Tex message

DARREN and I were working plain clothes one night when we arrested a half-baked yuppie off his head on ecstasy. We found four tablets in his pocket. He told us he bought them from a bouncer named Tex at a nightclub. I told my boss this and he agreed we could work on this bouncer the following Saturday.

I enlisted four others from the office to assist and at 8.30pm we gathered in the mess room for a briefing.

I had drawn a map of the club and the area around it. I detailed everyone's duty. Of course, I gave myself the best job.

My job was to 'covertly infiltrate the target's inner perimeter, thus closely observing Tex and his associates'. Ross wasn't impressed. He said, 'So you're going to drink free piss and chase sluts while we freeze to death outside.'

I said, 'Exactly. Any questions?' It was the burden of command. There were lots of mumbles.

By 9pm I entered the club. Tex seemed to be the head of the

bouncers. He looked like the Chesty Bond guy but a lot bigger. His arms stuck out at the sides due to excessive muscle growth.

I heard him speak with an American accent. I settled down to drinking and … well, surveillance. Time flew by. The short version is that I got really pissed. I recall someone had put a piece of lemon in the top of my Corona beer bottle.

I thought I was drinking Scotches and Coke, but anyway. I was drinking everything I could get my hands on.

I sort of recall someone bumping into me. I tapped him on the shoulder and he turned around. I poked him in the chest several times and said, 'Wath doth u think you thdoing.'

Even in my befuddled state I dimly realised the chest was extremely hard. It belonged to Tex.

He grabbed my right ear and started to drag me out. I wondered why I couldn't speak properly. Then I found that I had placed the slice of lemon skin under my top lip covering my teeth. I think it was an attempt at humour but Big Tex was obviously not in a funny mood. I was launched into the street. I checked, and my ear was still there. Good.

I staggered down the street. Then I remembered I had a crew out here somewhere. I stood about 10 metres down from the club screaming, 'Fellas, I'm here! Fellas, oh FELLAS!'

A car sped up and extracted me from the target area.

The boys all laughed their heads off at the fact that I had been thrown out of the club by the target and had no evidence.

I had seen Tex talking to lots of people but I suppose bouncers do that. There was one thing that I recalled him doing a lot. I remembered he would always shake people's hands with both his hands. I started to think that it may be how he was doing deals. All this thinking made me tired and I fell asleep in the car.

An ecstasy tablet is only small and the $60 payment could be rolled up tight and easily concealed within a hand. During the next few days I copped a lot of ribbing. Another cunning plan was needed.

There was not enough evidence to warrant spending more money or time to investigate the possibility that Tex was a drug dealer. I decided to cut the manpower down a bit.

As usual, it would be up to Batman and Robin – or, more accurately, Darren and me. The following Saturday night I double-parked my unmarked vehicle directly outside the club.

There was a long line of suckers waiting to get in. Tex was in command of the area, assisted by two other bouncers.

I jumped out of the car and strode up to Tex. The fact I ignored the queue caused a couple of people to comment. As I walked up to Tex he recognised me. Another bouncer told me to go to the back of the queue, but Tex said, 'Don't bother, you're banned.'

I stepped over a low black rope at the entrance and held my badge up to Tex's face. I said, 'Tex, Senior Constable Angus, St Kilda police. Please walk over here with me – we have to talk.'

Tex said, 'If it's about throwing you out, I … '

I said, 'No, it's not. I would like to search you – for drugs.'

Tex became instantly angry. 'I know my rights and you ain't got no probable cause – you need probable cause.' He spoke with a heavy Yank accent. I didn't like it. He should have sold fried chicken, not drugs to our great Aussie youth.

I said, 'I believe that you possess a drug of dependence, namely ecstasy. I am going to search you – understand?'

I looked up at the surveillance camera above us. I said, 'You cause trouble and your mates might destroy this video but they can't destroy our camera hidden over the road.

It's been filming you for the past two weeks. We've got you surrounded – now step over here.' I grabbed him by the arm and walked him over to the footpath. He thought it must be true, as surely these little twerp cops would not be alone. While he was still very unsure of the whole thing, looking for cameras and our back-up, I patted him down quickly. In his jacket pocket was a packet of smokes. Which was strange. I said, 'In all this time I haven't seen you smoke.'

In the packet was a plastic bag containing 40 ecstasy tablets. I held the bag up to the imaginary camera across the road. I even had to move Darren aside for the camera to get a clear view. My partner looked into the night, trying to find the camera.

I said, 'Right Darren, tell all the boys to come out of that truck there.' I pointed to a large truck nearby. Darren and Tex looked at the truck.

I could see Tex's mind going a million miles an hour, examining options. Just as he was making a decision I quickly cuffed his hands behind his back. That was it, he went right off tap.

He kicked at me and missed, but caused me to fall over as I dodged. He then kicked out at Darren, missing again. Darren stepped forward and punched Tex as hard as he could in the stomach. This had no effect other than damaging his fist.

Tex side-kicked Darren to the ground. As I got up Tex spun and kicked me in the chest, knocking me onto a parked car. We outnumbered him, he was handcuffed and we still looked as if we were going to get flogged.

As Tex started to run off, Darren gave chase. I screamed, 'Jump on to his back'. Darren jumped on his back. He was a good listener. Tex turned and ran backwards, slamming Darren into a parked car.

He then stopped and started straining, flexing his huge muscles in an attempt to break the cuffs. For a second, I thought he would. It would have been a great circus trick.

I ran forward with great difficulty as I was still winded. Darren was wiggling around on his back trying to tip him over. Then Darren started screaming out in pain.

I then realised Darren's balls were sitting in Tex's cuffed hands and Tex was squeezing them. Now, this guy looked like he could squeeze milk out of a coconut, so my partner was in serious bother. Tex then sprinted straight up the street with Darren screaming on his back.

I ran along behind screaming to Darren, 'Hang on.' I don't think he had much of a choice. He had his right arm wrapped around Tex's neck trying to choke him. Darren poked his fingers into the big Yank's eyes, blinding him. Tex still ran flat out but started to drift off course. He ran straight into a parked car. They both crashed to the ground. Tex didn't move, but Darren did. He rolled around the ground holding his crotch. I caught up, patted Darren on the back and said, 'Great stuff, I got him.'

Through gritted teeth he said, 'You got him? You got him?'

I said, 'And we got it all on film. Lucky we had that hidden camera and all that back-up.' Darren got to his feet. He then dragged a very sore and sorry Tex up onto his feet. Tex was bleeding from the nose and from some facial scratches Darren had inflicted upon him.

As we all walked back toward the club, Darren mumbled away, 'Fair dinkum, Angus, you live in another world. No wonder you've got the crooks fucked, you speak so much shit.'

His voice took a bitter and rather mocking tone as he continued: 'Darren, jump on his back … hidden cameras here, we've got you surrounded. What a load of shit.'

Tex said, 'What? Is that shit?' Tex had still been looking for them. Darren stopped Tex, pointed to me and said, 'Well, it came out of his mouth didn't it?'

I said, 'I think Tex is the biggest crook I've ever caught and Darren, you helped.'

Darren said, 'Helped? Helped?' Clearly the pain in his pants had made him lose his sense of humour.

He stopped our prisoner again and said, 'Righto, Tex, who caught you? Come on, who caught you? You can say. It's okay – you'd be half way to Sydney if it was up to him.'

Darren pointed to me. Tex just rolled his eyes. Our prisoner then said, 'Where's my Miranda?'

Darren asked, 'Your girlfriend?'

Tex said, 'No, Miranda. You got yourselves a wrongful arrest.'

I said, 'Okay, I'll give it to you, Aussie style ... Shut up, Yank.'

He said, 'Shut up? That's it? Shut up? It's supposed to be something like, 'You have the right to be silent, if you don't have an attorney one will be appointed to you,' shit like that, not just 'shut up'.' Ignoring him, Darren and I just kept arguing. We argued because it gave Tex the shits. He kept asking to see our police badges because he said he could not believe we were cops. I'm sure he was just trying to have a go at us.

Just as we pulled up at our office Darren tapped me on the arm, wearing a huge smile.

He said, 'And we get paid for this shit.' A big cheeky grin slowly grew over my face as I realised catching crooks really had Darren hooked.

It was no longer just a job. It was adrenalin-pumping fun and he was addicted. I turned to Darren and nodded. We punched each other on the arm – but not too hard. We were still sore from wrestling with Tex.

I look back at moments like these and realise that Darren and I were as close to each other as two blokes could ever get. But I wasn't going to massage his arrest wounds.

CHAPTER 10

I knelt on his chest as
I squeezed his throat – I'm
sure I got his attention.

Flying
the flag

DARREN and I were 'sitting off' a drug dealer in St Kilda late on an afternoon shift when a young bloke rode his bike past us. He was riding a Malvern Star or something, balancing a milk crate on the handle bars, and the crate was full of power tools.

On top of the milk crate was an axe. Not a little tomahawk, a full-size axe. We looked at each other and decided to have a little chat to this idiot.

He immediately told us the truth. Which was that he had stolen all of these items from various vehicles and houses. Even the milk crate was stolen.

Anyway, he started to tell us where he had stolen each and every item. One item I was interested in was a large Australian flag. He showed us the way back to the house where he'd stolen it.

It was about 11.30pm when we got there. I stopped the unmarked police car at the front of a very nice house in middle

St Kilda. In front of it was a large, flagless flag pole. I knocked on the door while Darren remained in our car with the crook.

Knock, knock. The door opened, and the very attractive face of a very attractive young woman peeped around it. She was modestly hiding herself as she peered at me with her sleepy eyes.

I identified myself as a police officer in the most polite way. She instantly relaxed at the sight of my badge and the door opened.

She stood before me in a short dressing gown sort of arrangement – and what a fine sight it was.

I was most impressed. Her body was pert, firm, and instantly made me forget why I was there. She said, 'What is it? How can I help you?' I thought it was a trick question. I found the Australian flag in my hand and said, 'Um, ah, um ... do you own this?'

All of a sudden a hand shot from behind the door and grabbed her left arm, and she was jerked out of the doorway. She squealed. Then there was a loud 'slap' sound and another squeal.

A male voice said, 'Don't you ever answer the door like that.'

I stepped through the doorway and found someone who was obviously her husband pinning her against the wall. He was trying to slap and hit her across the face. I reached out and grabbed him by the throat. As I did this I tripped him, forcing him onto his back on the floor.

I knelt on his chest as I squeezed his throat – I'm sure I got his full attention. He appeared in shock, but was still trying to speak although no noise was coming out of his gob. He was a skinny little yuppie prick in designer pyjamas, trying to be a tough guy.

As I held him down with my right hand firmly wrapped around his wind pipe, I stuffed my police badge in his face and I said, 'Good evening, sir. I am Constable Angus from the St Kilda

Police. Sorry to wake you up. I was just explaining to your wife that we arrested a young male who told us he stole your Australian flag from your flag pole.'

I reached over and picked up the flag I had dropped and held it up to the yuppie.

I said, 'Is this your flag?' He managed to nod under my weight. I said, 'Good, you can have it back.'

About this time I realised Darren was standing inside the doorway watching me. He had a very puzzled look on his face.

I said, 'Thanks anyway, but we can't stay. We have to go out and protect the public.'

I then let go of his throat. He took in a deep breath. I stood up and quickly wrote down my name and telephone number on a piece of paper. I handed it to the shocked and semi-naked women and said, 'If you have any problems please call me and I'll come over for another chat.'

She smiled and said, 'Thank you.' The yuppie didn't say anything, he seemed to have lost interest in proceedings.

He just lay on his back in shock, holding his throat.

We left. As we walked away Darren smiled and said, 'Protecting the public. That's us.'

THE drug problem in St Kilda was massive. There were several people particularly outspoken about how heroin was destroying the community and causing deaths, burglaries, armed robberies, assaults and the like.

No-one who was outspoken about the problem seemed to address issues such as drug education. They demanded more police patrols, more visual police presence and more arrests. They wanted instant results. It was in that environment that Neighbourhood Watch evolved.

A well-known saying is, 'Never go on leave because when you

get back you might be out of a job.' Well, this was very true, but, in my case, it was worse because I didn't lose one, I got a worse one.

When I got back from leave I found that I had been elected the officer in charge of St Kilda Neighbourhood Watch Area 34. I had to do it for three months. There were 39 areas, and I got the worst. This meant I had to attend the area 34 meeting every Wednesday from 7pm to 8pm. It became my unhappy hour.

I looked at the Neighbourhood Watch area map and found that it encompassed an area police called The Bird Cage. It was called the Bird Cage, not because it was filled with glamours like at the Flemington Races, but because it was full of shit. The main street in our Bird Cage was Blackbird Street.

I attempted to get out of Neighbourhood Watch duties, but it was a directive from the local detective inspector.

In my area most of the residents were average Joe Citizens, but there were several blocks where every second house was a rental property intermingled with large boarding houses. These were originally old Victorian manors, but had fallen on hard times. During World War II, ships delivered a huge influx of sailors on shore leave, most of whom required the services of 'the ladies of the night,' and a lot of them lived in those old joints.

Most of these houses had fallen into disrepair and really should have been bulldozed.

Unfortunately, one such manor was still in great condition. It was palatial. The owner was a wealthy local councillor, owner of the largest restaurant in Fitzroy Street and, worst of all, head of 'my' Neighbourhood Watch committee. On The Street he was known as The Ponce.

The Ponce was a tall, skinny, loud-mouth and a real pain. It was obvious to everyone that all he wanted was to get the drug dealers and pushers out of Fitzroy Street because they were bad for business and costing him money.

He wanted St Kilda to be a safe, trendy night spot. The evening came when I had to attend my first Neighbourhood Watch meeting.

It was in a small local hall. I came in late and my heart sank when I found the place quite packed.

I tried to find a hiding place, but one of the residents recognised me and showed me to the front, where there was a large table with six chairs behind it. I wish I had come as Dean Collie.

The Ponce had a microphone and was the only one at the table. He was on his feet, and had already started raving on about syringes on beaches or something.

He eventually introduced me to the audience. I thanked him and excused my appearance, stating I was a plain-clothes police officer.

I said, 'I would now like to talk to you about home and personal security. Before I do so, I notice there is someone in the hall I know quite well, a Mr Phillips.'

I had charged 'Fingers' Phillips with numerous burglaries and thefts the week before. Fingers was sitting very low in his seat, trying to hide his face.

I continued. 'Mr Phillips, I saw your dog wandering out near the road, I suggest you go and save it.'

Fingers looked up, very happy to be given the chance to escape. He smiled and awkwardly thanked me and left.

As he was leaving I suggested to another citizen, 'Spider – sorry, Mr Smythe, you're a fast runner, maybe you could help him.' Spider scraped himself off the floor and left, mumbling under his breath.

There were a few puzzled faces as they left but I felt I was in reasonably safe company. I continued to explain to them how to report crime, how to be good Neighbourhood Watch members.

I was interrupted by a very serious old woman who said, 'I watched a man wearing a funny mask thing. He smashed Beryl's window climbed in and stole lots of things, climbed out and drove off and no police came or anything. Why, why is that.'

I said, 'We need you to telephone us.'

She said, 'But people already say I'm a busybody – why should I always be the one to call?'

At the end of my lecture I held up a computer face image and said, 'This is a computer face image of a man responsible for sexually attacking a woman in Blackbird Street last Wednesday. If anyone knows a person who looks similar to this, could you please see me after the meeting. Are there any questions?'

One old women said, 'If you tell me his name I might know him.' Another women said, 'I think he would be a single man living alone.' She turned to the person sitting next to her and said, 'They get terribly frustrated you know. They just don't know what to do with it. It's disgusting.'

One old retired gentleman added helpfully, 'If you can get his tax file number you'll be right onto him.' An elderly woman suggested, 'A Leo, definitely a Leo. My first husband was a Leo and he wouldn't leave it alone.'

Another would-be Sherlock Holmes said, 'Maybe he is a woman?'

I had to go. I'd prevented enough crime for one night.

As I was trying to leave, a lovely old dear explained that my advice was most helpful, but I was a little bit late, as Mr Phillips had come through her house and advised her the best way to make it secure. I said, 'Well, he should know. Do you still have a house?'

She said, 'Oh, it's a lovely house.'

I made a mental note to have a chat to 'Fingers'.

I WAS undercover in The Street and looking for a particular shithead named Vince. He was the red-hot suspect for an assault and robbery of a young woman who was taking her shop's money to the bank.

In these sort of cases you usually didn't need to be a rocket scientist to get your first lead. As a copper, the first place you looked was The Street to see if they had gone there to score and the first place you stopped at on The Street was The Caf. Immediately after the robbery I drove the unmarked car, screamed up and double parked right outside The Caf with Darren. We jumped out and strode straight inside. It was obvious to all that we were undercover cops on a mission and we were not fucking around. It sort of defeated the purpose of being undercover but I'm sure it looked good. Well, it felt good, anyway.

I burst in and stopped, scanning all the occupants, looking for Vince. Several locals sensed extreme danger and turned away. One tourist didn't. He stood up and said, 'Mate, you looking for something? It's top gear, can't do better.'

I looked at him and realised he was not from my planet. He was from the planet Moron (close – Queenstown, Tasmania, actually). He misread all my signals and was trying to sell me heroin. He was also going to pay for the mistake. He was the weakest link and it was time to say goodbye to freedom.

As soon as Darren saw the Moron approach me, he turned and moved the car then sat back to wait for the arrest. In a nearby shop front Moron sold me a deal of heroin. I bought it with one hand and put him in a head lock with the other, while giving him some well-meaning career advice that he was in the wrong game. While being charged with trafficking heroin the Moron started to bleed and moan.

He explained that these new charges would breach his parole, as he still owed four years jail for armed robbery charges. He had been sentenced to 12 years, had only served eight and was paroled only a month earlier.

He had priors for assaults, thefts, drugs and heaps of burgs. His record suggested he was a good burglar – well, okay, he had done some burgs and been caught. But you know what I mean.

When it came to cops he knew the system and said nothing. At the end of the interview, 'no comment' of course, for the first time Moron suggested making a deal. Well it was more than a suggestion – he said, 'Give me bail and I give you some info.'

I said, 'No mate, you're getting locked up. The reason I haven't asked you for info is that I have nothing to deal with. Jail, no bail. That's it.'

He became more serious and said, 'I'm not fuckin around – if I you give me bail I'll give you sumfin real good.'

I said, 'Listen, I understand your problem but I can't help you. No bail, that's it. Let's go.'

He became desperate. 'You must be able to do sumfin, put in a good word or sumfin. The parole board will fuck me.' It wouldn't be the only one.

I said, 'Give me what you've got and I'll see what I can do.'

He said, 'Bail first.'

Now he was in no position to be making up the rules. It was our game, not his. The watch-house keeper smiled. Moron was desperate.

I passed over the custody of Moron to the watch-house keeper and started to walk away. As I left the room, I heard him blurt out,

'Zarb brought me here to do a job.' I kept walking. He yelled, 'A job on the Ponce.' (You will remember he was the pain from Neighbourhood Watch).

That stopped me. Zarb was the biggest drug dealer come stolen goods merchant in The Street. I walked back, took custody of Moron and walked him to a small interview room. It was time to play that favourite gameshow – Let's Make A Deal.

I immediately knew that Zarb would want much of the paintings, jewellery, antiques and stuff that was in the Ponce's magnificent manor.

I closed the door and sat opposite him. I lit his smoke, then mine and said, 'Give me what you've got and I'll tell you what I can do, that's it.' He thought about that. He was silent.

I said, 'Do you know how Zarb's planning to get rid of the gear? Is he going to melt the jewellery?'

His face looked puzzled. He said, 'Gear? He wants me to baseball bat him across the face.'

Now this was a twist. 'Baseball bat him?'

'Zarb's given me travel tickets and a two grand deposit, another three grand once the job's done,' said Moron.

I said, 'Why?'

He said, 'Do I give a flying fuck? I don't think so.'

I knew that Zarb hated the Ponce because he was always wining and dining the most senior cops in the district, and always lagging on drug dealers outside his restaurant. I found out later that Zarb blamed the Ponce for the big police crackdown in the area. He thought a couple of free lamb chops and a cheap bottle of red was all it cost to get coppers to do what you wanted.

I was shocked and appalled.

It took a hell of a lot more than that. Senior cops know their worth.

ZARB knew it was the Ponce who was bringing down all the heat. He considered The Street his, and that it did not belong to the Ponce. It was all a pointless power struggle, because I knew The Street belonged to me, and neither of them.

I asked, 'When and where?'

He said, 'I was gunna do a practice run today – then tomorrow, 'Whack! Home run.' He motioned with both arms as if he was Babe Ruth.

I said, 'Where were you going to do it?'

He said, 'Only one place. It has to be in the middle of The Street for everyone to see. It has to be a spectacle. That's what he said, a spectacle.'

He went on to say that it had to be done tomorrow or Zarb would give the job to someone else. It was now time to do business. I told him that the more he helped us, the more I could help him with his problems.

That's how it worked. He scratched my back and I would try to stop some dirty big drag queen scratching his in the remand yard shower block.

He went on to tell me about what Zarb had planned. He told me he had been given a photograph of the Ponce, his car and registration number. I locked him in the interview room while I thought of a cunning plan.

After updating Darren, we updated the boss. We had to be very careful who we told so the word wouldn't get out, if you get my drift. You never knew who might overhear something in a busy police station is one way of putting it.

The other problem was that we had to make sure Zarb didn't know Moron had been arrested. If Zarb knew that, he would probably think Moron would sell the information to police to save his arse. Zarb may well have been shower scum but he wasn't stupid about matters of a criminal nature. I had my cunning plan and was keen to run with it.

Ponce drove a large gold Merc sedan and always parked it directly outside his restaurant. If there wasn't a parking space there, he watched and waited. As soon as one appeared the Ponce would pounce.

The following day, as usual, the Ponce drove his car up to the front of his restaurant and, as luck would have it, just as he approached a vehicle conveniently left, leaving him his space. Ponce backed his vehicle in. Wearing a coat and hat, he stepped out of the driver's side.

As he was locking the door a motorbike with no number plates came screaming up. The passenger on the back of the bike jumped off wearing a black full face helmet.

He strode up, the Ponce turned to look at the attacker just as the bat hit him the first time. The Ponce dropped to his knees, the attacker hit him three more blows.

The Ponce lay face down on the road and blood flowed freely from his head. The attacker jumped back on the bike and they were out of sight in seconds.

As it was lunch time, there were people everywhere. Several of them ran to assist Ponce. Two carried him off the roadway onto the footpath. Blood flowed onto the concrete. Seconds later an ambulance arrived, quickly placing the Ponce in the back and left, sirens blasting away. Cop cars appeared from everywhere, crime scene tape was everywhere. It was one with the lot.

As the ambulance screamed off with its lights and bells, the driver said, 'Shit these things have some go don't they?' The driver was Paul, one of our team. Darren, lying in a puddle of blood said, 'This fake blood crap tastes terrible. You said it was strawberry flavoured.'

Darren opened his shirt front and pulled out two almost empty clear plastic blood filled pack cells he got from the hospital. As the ambulance turned into a side street the motor bike appeared doing a wheelie in front of them.

Then the car that had so conveniently given the Merc his spot stopped nearby. Sandy was behind the wheel. The front wheel of our bike touched the road and it came to a skidding stop. I jumped off the back, happy to be alive. After surviving the motorbike ride I said, 'I knew I should have driven the ambulance.' We all celebrated our debuts as method actors.

My mobile phone rang. It was the boss, telling me to hurry as he had to do a press conference in one hour. I phoned the Ponce at his home and told him he was badly beaten up and in hospital. I told him to stay there and not answer the door or the phone.

Paul was telling us how he met this really nice nurse when he picked up the ambulance uniforms. Darren needed a shower and a stiff drink – or a stiff shower and a cool drink. We got changed, got rid of the ambulance and thanked everyone. We knew it wouldn't be long before the game was up. We had to work fast.

Back at our station I told Moron that the whole thing worked really well. He now had to meet with Zarb and get the rest of the money and some admissions on tape. We drove Moron down to The Street, wiring him for sound as we went. I got dressed up with Darren and started walking Moron toward The Caf.

As we walked up and around the crime scene Moron stopped to look at the huge quantity of blood everywhere – it looked like the St Valentine's Day Massacre.

Moron looked shocked: 'Christ, what did you do? Take his fuckin head off?' Now he'd become a pacifist. I sat a very reluctant Moron down at a table, handed him my mobile phone and told him to ring Zarb.

Darren and I found a position where we couldn't be spotted by our target We were old enemies and he knew my face. I had tried and failed to catch him several times. I didn't like that.

When Moron rang Zarb he was just walking up to the crime scene. Zarb wore a large smile as he watched the blood being hosed off the footpath. As Paul was filming Zarb's smile using a long lens video camera, he telephoned me, 'He's happy and on the way'.

I thought a judge would love to see that smile while listening to the defence plead that the accused was 'filled with remorse for his acts.'

That smile was going to get him big years inside. Then I would be laughing.

Zarb walked into the cafe with that goofy smile on his face. He shook Moron's hand like he was a long lost brother. Moron just wanted Zarb to sit down and keep a low profile.

Moron was scared, really scared, but Zarb thought he was nervous about his magnificent attack on the Ponce. Zarb whispered, 'Tell me, what did it sound like? Was it his face or head that cracked open? Tell me.'

Moron said, 'I did it. Just give me the money. I want to get out of here.' But Zarb said, 'Let's celebrate. Come, we drink. Ponce was like an infected boil on my arse. You lanced it and I am healed, I pay you, come with me.'

Zarb was a big, fat bloke who demanded obedience. He reached over and put his arm around Moron picking him up from his seat and almost carrying him to the door.

Moron was strongly protesting. There was a metallic click, as Moron's handcuffs stretched and became taut. I had handcuffed Moron's left hand to the leg of the table. It was my little insurance policy.

Zarb wondered why he could not walk his new best friend out into The Street. Zarb's smile melted as he looked at the cuffs, but he didn't catch on for a few seconds. He even gave Moron another little pull to make sure they were real – just like a fisherman tries to unhook a snag.

I spun around. Zarb looked at me and let out a big angry growl. Darren and I had a huge wrestle with the fat bear and ended up flowing out onto The Street. It was like trying to grab a grizzly bear covered in olive oil and garlic. Zarb was arrested. I grabbed Moron and ripped the tape recording off him and returned him to the watch-house at the police station.

The boss spoke to the media and told them it was a highly-planned operation that resulted in the arrest of a well-known criminal, blah, blah, blah.

I sat down, fired up the computer and typed, 'Chairman of the Tasmanian Parole Board'. Sticking to the facts, I detailed what Moron had done. It didn't get him off, but it knocked off some of the hard time he owed.

I'd made a 'friend', or so he seemed to think. I don't think anyone had ever done anything for him before. Moron turned out to be a bit of a laugh, a down-to-earth sort of shit head. I found out that he could never have gone through with the Zarb job. It was never in him.

Despite that, I still nicknamed him 'The Babe' (after Babe Ruth, not the pig in the movie).

When no-one was looking, I even bought him a beer. I probably hated the Ponce more than Zarb, but it's hard to imagine a more despicable crime than to hit someone across the face with a baseball bat.

Unless, of course, it is a case of good versus evil. Then the rules are different.

CHAPTER 11

I really thought I had been
stabbed, so did Darren.

No winners

IT WAS at the end of my shift and I was getting a cup of coffee when I saw a young woman crying at the counter of the police station.

I looked over and saw that the uniform watch-house keeper was busy with another customer. I stopped, removed my badge from my back pocket and identified myself.

She was quite plain, about 22, a little plump and deeply distressed.

I said, 'How can I help you?' She was sobbing and trying to speak. It was immediately obvious she had a very serious speech impediment.

She tried and tried to speak to me, but her stutter was so bad it was impossible. I tried to calm her down, knowing that her stutter was made worse by her emotional condition.

I asked her to follow me and we sat in an interview room. I went and got her a cup of coffee. When I got back she handed me a piece of paper. It said, 'My name is Susan Wide. I have a speech impediment. I am a make-up artist working for myself. I parked my car at the Elwood Beach carpark and went for a walk to a photo shoot. When I got back to get my gear, someone had forced the lock on my car and stolen four large carry boxes of make-up.'

She was still crying. I sat with her while she eventually explained to me that the make-up was worth about $4000, and that she had borrowed money to buy it.

She had great difficulty in life due to her stutter and she was on top of the world when she had obtained a contract with Crawford Productions as a make-up artist. She had no insurance. She was devastated. I was on the verge of tears myself when I made the vow that my partner and I would do everything we could to get her property back.

I wrote out a crime report and exchanged phone numbers. I went and got Darren and introduced him to Susan. I did this so he could get a taste – a taste of the victim. I could never explain to him in words what the victim explained to him in a moment. We walked her to her car. I examined the mode of entry to her vehicle and then she left.

As she drove off Darren said, 'Were you doing anything this afternoon? I don't mind if we work back. We could check all the dealers and ask around the street, go to the scene, maybe …'

It didn't take much. She had touched him. He was hooked. I said to Darren, 'We'll put all our jobs aside. This one's personal.'

It was just a pissy 'Theft from Motor Car', but we treated it like a murder. Everyone else was leaving when Darren and I walked up to a white board in the muster room. I drew a quick sketch of the area. I sketched where she said her car was parked, the beach and bay, the Life Saving Club, Beach Road – the lot. I then started a list. Darren sat on the back of a chair and watched.

I wrote, 'Jobs to be done – collator checks for similar jobs, door-knock the area, speak to all the crows (prostitutes) to see if they've been offered make-up.'

Darren said 'And the trannies.' I wrote 'trannies' on the list.

I kept writing. 'Speak to all informers, call in the favours, attend the read-outs and see if any of the uniforms know anything. Speak to all CIB.'

I said, 'If he is local, The Street will know.'

Darren said, 'If he's a tourist, we should check the motels.'

I said, 'Good stuff. Crooks love cheap motels. We have to look for witnesses because at the moment we have nothing.'

I circled 'Witnesses' and 'Door knock'. I said, 'Mate, you can be victim liaison officer. Can you pick her up tomorrow and she can take us to the crime scene. We need photographs of the boxes. If no photos we'll take her to the police artist and she can help him draw them. We need a detailed list of all make-up and distinctive features.'

We went to the collator's office and started going through all the theft from motor car reports committed during the past two months.

There were heaps, so we restricted it to the foreshore areas. I made phone calls to the next district south and found several similar offences. They were all happening along beachside car parks. In the middle of our intensive and highly complicated investigations we were interrupted by an announcement over the station PA. 'Would Senior Constable Angus please contact the watch-house?'

I rang the watch-house and explained that I was very busy.

The watch-house keeper said he had a witness at the counter that claims he saw the person who stole the make-up. We dropped tools and hurried there, hoping for a breakthrough.

An attractive young blonde girl about 20 stood at the counter. She was stunning, really.

I introduced myself, pretending Darren wasn't there but he pushed straight in anyway and introduced himself to the new witness. Occasionally he showed initiative. After the introductions were over, she explained that she was looking out her window when she saw a vehicle drive around the carpark.

She then saw a man get out of the driver's side door and fiddle with the lock of the other car. She then said he stole four boxes and placed them in his car.

Apparently he then got back into his car and drove off. She said that a few minutes later she saw a girl who appeared to be the owner of the car that was broken into. She appeared to be crying.

She went on to say that she had been thinking about it and she thought she would come to the police. I asked her several questions. She stated the criminal was driving a large red four-wheel-drive, but she had no idea what make. She said it was 'squarish'.

She said the crook looked about 35, with fuzzy dirty hair, jeans and a light green windcheater. She said that she saw all this from the 11th floor of a building about a kilometre from the offender.

It was obvious we had learnt all we were going to learn from this witness. I had decided she was making some of this stuff up. Why would she be able to remember all that? I thought she was trying too hard.

We had perved enough and it was getting late. I took down all her details and explained that we may need a statement in due course. We said goodbye.

One thing was for sure – the description of the car was a big help.

We had an approximate age for the suspect and a red four-wheel-drive to look for. As we walked away I heard, 'Excuse me.' Our witness was back. 'My girlfriend said that I could make like a face image on a computer or a drawing or something.'

I said, 'Yes, of course, if you could recognise him again or something.' I stopped just short of mocking her. With some people, I might have been even ruder.

She said, 'Well, I could recognise him.' There was a disbelieving pause from both of us. She insisted, 'Well, I could.'

She was getting shitty now, and she kept talking. 'At first I had trouble seeing him, but when I focused in it was like I could touch him. Dad's scope is like four feet long and about a foot around.' She went on to explain that the crook had used a pair of scissors to force the door open, and he had a pimple on the left side of his chin.

After much furious note-taking on our part, she left. As we walked down the hall Darren said, 'I missed the telescope part.'

He pointed to his chest and said, 'It must have been those pert little ski jump boobs.'

I said, 'Yep, I missed it too.'

We were so busy staring at her chest we'd missed the breakthrough. We were the boobs.

The following day she made what she said was a very good computer image of the offender. The crook's vehicle had been side-on so she missed the rego.

I bought a four-wheel-drive market magazine that was full of pictures of four-wheel-drives. She found the vehicle – it was a red 1980-84 Nissan Patrol, short wheelbase.

She said it had a black bull-bar and paint was peeling off the bonnet. Darren and I photocopied the picture and made a poster.

During the next couple of days we investigated every avenue, leaving our posters wherever we went. Other blokes in our office found it amusing that we were working so hard to try to catch a crook for a theft from motor car.

One of the blokes said, 'Why don't you put an information caravan at the crime scene and dress up a dummy? We could all block off Beach Road at peak hours and appeal for witnesses.' This crack was considered the height of cop humour because, of course, caravans and dummies and roadblocks are reserved for homicides and rapes.

Another wit picked up the phone and said, 'Operator, patch me through to NASA. I want all satellites in the southern hemisphere to check immediately for a little red dot near a big, blue, bay-shaped speck.' We would have done all that if it would have helped.

In the midst of our intensive patrolling and investigating, we had a breakthrough ... the station divvy van caught the same crook breaking into another car near St Kilda Pier. What a letdown.

We returned to the station and found the red four-wheel-drive parked out the front. We then saw our man in an interview room. The description of both the vehicle and the man's face were spot on. The blonde witness was a star in more ways than one. The cops on the van interviewed and charged him with the theft they caught him for and then handed him over to us.

In his possession was a small pair of surgical stainless steel scissors, the type used in operating theatres. I said to Darren, 'Christ, that telescope must be powerful.'

He said, 'It is.'

I asked, 'How do you know?'

Darren said, 'Well, I called in and saw her yesterday. She showed me her telescope, and you can see people on the beach in Portarlington right across the other side of the bay.'

'That's good,' I said. 'Did you show her your telescope?'

GEORGE was being a real prick. He was just under six feet tall and quite solid, considering that he was a chronic junkie using heroin about three to four times a day.

He was a Romanian gypsy who came to Australia as a refugee. He said he had been living in the car and had no address. He was sitting at the interview room table uncuffed. His smart-arse attitude was appalling.

I grabbed his left hand and turned it toward me. He had the five small tattooed blue dots on the back of his hand. These five dots are in the shape of a five on a dice.

The four dots on the outside signifies the four walls of a prison, the dot in the middle represents him. All prisoners in Romania give themselves this tattoo.

They wear it with pride because it proves they were able to survive the experience. For some of these gypsies, being a criminal is expected and part of their culture. I don't understand it, but what I do know is that they can be bad bastards. This was not going to be easy.

We asked him about the make-up. He laughed at us and smiled as he repeated, 'In this country, I am innocent. You must prove with evidence. This is a wonderful country. You have nothing.' It was very difficult to speak with him. He had a head that required immediate punching. While we were preparing paperwork and getting ready for the interview I was sitting opposite him, with my head down, filling out the attendance register. All of a sudden he screamed out 'Boo!' causing me to jump in fright.

I looked up at him. He smiled and said, 'You scare too easily – you should relax, like me.' Christ, he needed punching, if only just to make me feel better. I smiled and shook my head and kept on writing.

When it came to the formal interview he said, 'No comment' to everything. He was well schooled. He would not say a word about the stolen make-up. At the end of the interview, George sat back in his chair and smiled. As I was removing the tapes from the tape machine he casually leant forward. He then screamed, 'I have a knife and I'm going to kill you!'

He jumped out of his chair and thrust a silver object that was in his hand straight into my stomach. I fell backwards off my chair clutching my stomach. Darren sprang out of his chair, grabbing the hand that held the object with one hand and George's throat with the other.

As I started to get up I felt for the stab wound, then I got smashed in the back of the head by Ross, who had burst into the interview room after hearing the scream.

Ross (known as 'the Turk') stepped on me as he leapt over the desk and hit George on the side of the face. I couldn't find my stab wound. Looking at George's hand I saw that he had a watch with a metal silver band in his hand. He had laid it flat in his hand, pretending it was a knife. It worked, because it scared the hell out of me. I really thought I had been stabbed, and so did Darren.

Anyway, after we bashed him, he was handcuffed. I sat George up in the interview room chair again.

I sat there and said, 'Now, I feel much better.'

He said, 'You know now I no care about me, so do what you like. My heart it die in Romania.'

I said, 'George, a young woman had four boxes of make-up stolen from her car. She could lose her job, she was crying, she had no insurance, you could help her … '

I gave George the whole sad story. I appealed to his conscience, but found he had none. I asked him if he would go in an identification parade. He refused. We left him in the room.

Darren and I searched his vehicle again. Under the passenger seat was a receipt to a motel in Prahran. It was a motel we hadn't checked.

We went and grabbed George and took him for a drive. At the motel I found that he had stayed there for two weeks, but had left two days before, owing money. Why did that not surprise us?

The manager had put all his belongings into a garage out the back. We took George, still cuffed, to the garage to examine his belongings.

There was heaps of stolen gear, video cameras, TVs etc. There were also several tennis racquets. George said he loved tennis and they were all his. I opened one of the racquet covers and found the name Steven Gibbs and a phone number.

George smiled and said, 'He's a friend of mine.' On the way back to the station we called into the Prince of Wales Hotel. I uncuffed George, walked him into the main bar and bought him a beer.

He was halfway through his beer, and I was standing at the door when our lovely girl witness walked in. She walked among all the drinkers. She walked straight up to George. He had never seen her before.

She tapped him on the shoulder and said, 'This is the bloke.'

I cuffed him, but it wasn't the pinch we wanted. It was the make-up.

Back at the station in just a few minutes we located seven separate owners. All their property had been stolen from cars in the vicinity of the beach.

Now armed with mountains of evidence implicating George in numerous offences we had to interview him again. Just before this I said, 'You're on bail for other offences. After charging you with nine theft from motor cars you will be remanded until you're sentenced. You won't get out for at least 12 months with your prior convictions.

'All I want is to know is where you sold the four boxes of make-up. George, I am prepared to drop all charges. I promise I'll undo the cuffs and you can walk now if you tell me where I can recover the boxes of make-up.'

He looked into my eyes. He knew I was serious. He took a deep breath and finally answered. 'I put the boxes in the car and drove off. I look in them and there was just shit, no value. I just dump out the shit, leave all on side of road.'

I said, 'Where?'

He said, 'Near beach. But I see later someone must take because it was gone.'

That was it. We never did get the make-up. George ended up going inside for the next 10 months. We went and visited Susan at home. I told her the story. We were all losers.

CHAPTER 12

'Can you find out how much
he weighed and how fat he was, he's
completely stuffed Sheba's diet.'

Home on
the mange

WE were working early one morning. Darren and I drove to the top of the Esplanade to watched the sun rise as we drank our take away cappuccinos. Sitting on the bonnet of our unmarked cop car, we looked through the palm trees over to the St Kilda Pier and surrounding beaches. It looked so clean and pure, so different from the shit we normally had to deal with. I wanted to say something profound, but my head was empty, so we sipped in silence.

But the silence was broken by the eerie screams of exotic animals, lions, tigers, elephants and chimpanzees were telling The Street that the circus had come to town.

The great day had come at last. After living with signs all over town for the past month the circus had arrived. It brought over 100 workers, most of them rough, tough nomadic knockabouts. Then it brought the tourists. The huge tents were set up in open parklands next to the beach. The Street came alive. Even junkies like the circus. A short time later, around 7.30am, Darren and I arrived back at work. We started early so we could finish early. Some would think this was due to selfless dedication. Sorry, this was Melbourne and we wanted to knock off to watch the St Kilda v Essendon match at the MCG. Soon after we got back at our office the phone rang. It was Stewie from the CIB. He said, 'Listen mate, we're tied up at a rape scene, you're the only bodies in the district available. Can you go to the circus immediately?

'The manager, a Mr Magnus, wants the police now, something about his lions.'

I said, 'Yeah mate, I'm flat out interviewing the occupants of a spaceship, their intergalactic passports look a bit bodgie,' and hung up.

Seconds later, ring ring, ring ring goes the phone. It was Stewie and he was serious. The natives and the wildlife were getting restless and we had to get on the trail.

We headed off to the circus to meet Mr Magnus, who was the owner and manager – and he didn't even wear a top-hat.

Magnus greeted us with 'I am very upset, lions are worth big bucks, $10,000 to $20,000 each. My lions can get very sick. If he has hepatitis A, B, C or HIV so will my lions. We must check immediately.'

I had no idea what he was talking about. If I'd had a tranquiliser gun, I would have shot him. It must have been obvious to him from the looks on our faces we didn't have a clue what he was talking about.

Magnus said, 'Didn't the other detective tell you? The keeper found the lion eating a body in the enclosure and when the lion saw the keeper he dragged the body back into his den. He's still in there with it.'

I said, 'What sort of body?' It was the best I could think of at the time. I hadn't done this line of investigation before.

He said, 'Male, looks like male.'

I said, 'Human?' hoping he would say no.

He said, 'Of course', as though it was a stupid question. I was new at this sort of thing and it wasn't covered at the academy.

As soon as he indicated the death of a person, I thought, 'That bastard Stewie deliberately left out the important part of the story'. I immediately started being a 'real' detective, opening up my notebook and taking notes, drawing diagrams and doing all those cop things we do.

We walked up to the enclosure. I said, 'Are you sure the person is dead?' I have always been an optimist. The lion keeper introduced himself and said, 'Lions don't eat the hands, feet or the head. The head looks like a male.' I wrote in my little note book 'One male – dead.'

It seemed the thing to do.

The keeper said, 'I've separated the lioness, but the male won't give up the body. The trainer is just trying to get him away from the body now.' We could hear the crack of the whip.

I bent down and looked through the cage into the doorway of the den. It was grotesque.

The lion had the man's head sitting on top of his front paws, and he licked the face with a huge pink tongue. The lion appeared to be very proud of himself. He seemed to smile a lion smile when he ran his tongue around his own blood-smeared face. I heard, 'Oh Christ.' Darren, who had bent down with me, spun around, revolted. The lion just casually looked at the lion trainer and let out a deep roar as if to say, 'Get your own human, he's mine.' I left them to it.

Outside the enclosure lay a pile of clothes neatly folded.

There was a full tracksuit, a black T-shirt with 'TAO MI KARATE SCHOOL' printed on it, a folded black karate belt made of cloth and a pair of runners.

Inside the tracksuit pants was a wallet containing personal papers. The name in the wallet was Ilie Cucu (I found our later it is pronounced Cuckoo) who was born 12/4/1969 and lived at Flack St, Springvale. Above the clothes was a hole cut in the roof of the enclosure. A pair of wire-cutters lay next to the hole on the roof of the enclosure.

MAGNUS called us over just as they managed to get the lion away from his kill. The floor of the enclosure was covered in hay. We walked inside to the body, or what was left of it.

The face, hands and feet were clean. Every other piece of the body was gone. Every piece of skin and flesh was missing, including all entrails and groin. All you could see were a few little bits of red meat sticking to some bones and white tendons holding it all together. There was a sickly fresh meaty smell in the air. All the blood was missing, drunk and licked up, no doubt.

Off to one side was a little pile of blue material. I bent down to get a better look, it was a pair of torn men's briefs covered in blood and tooth marks. I said, 'Look his jocks, the lion must have ripped them off to get to the good bits, he probably left them until last like we save the crackling.'

Darren cut me off and said, 'All right, all right, I get it.' He didn't look well.

We called photographics, video operations and the morgue. The morgue won't take bodies until a doctor had pronounced life extinct. We called a doctor. When he arrived later, his job was very easy. As Darren and I left the enclosure I said, 'Look at my shoes.' They were covered in blood. All the straw had little bits of blood on it, as we walked around we collected it on our shoes. It's a terrible feeling, having another person's blood on you. We had no idea where he had been. The lion keeper offered to hose our feet. We washed our shoes under a nearby tap.

IT appeared that this person had broken into the circus area late at night, taken off all his clothes, placed them neatly on the ground, climbed onto the roof of the cage, cut his way in and climbed into the cage wearing nothing but his jocks. He was then eaten.

Darren said, 'Jump off a high building, take poison, shoot yourself in the head, or do all three at once, but why would you climb into a lion's cage?'

I said, 'Detectives detect. There's no evidence at all that someone else has killed him and shoved him inside, besides it would take half a dozen blokes to drag a dead body up onto the roof of this enclosure. Murder is out.'

I then asked the obvious, 'Why would he take his clothes off?' Heaps of photographs were taken of the crime scene, clothes etc. I told the photographer that I wanted some photos of the lions. The lion keeper took Darren, the photographer and me to where the lions were being kept. We walked up to a big cage. The big male lion looked at us. We looked back.

His face was covered in fresh blood. He was trying to clean it off with his huge paw. I said, 'You're not obliged to roar at anything and anything you roar will be recorded and given in evidence.' He just lay there full and content.

The lion keeper said, 'No, no, he is not the offender – he just ate some of the evidence. The lioness does the killing.' With great relish the keeper continued, 'See him, see the blood is just smeared around his mouth? The intruder was dead when he fed. Come over here.'

We followed the keeper over to the lioness. The keeper said, 'See how she has big thick lines of blood running from her mouth across her face and onto her back and sides. She's the killer. He just pushes in and eats the kill.'

He enthusiastically continued, 'Veins full of blood just flow from a dead body, it just drains away. She has arterial spray marks that means that her prey, the intruder, was alive and kicking when she started to feed.' The way he said feed was disgusting. I was starting think of cancelling the barbecue I was planning for the weekend.

Darren said, 'You're kidding, don't they kill first? I've seen them bite the neck of a zebra until it's dead, then they eat.'

The keeper said, 'I've had Sheba for 12 years. She's caught a couple of blackbirds, but that's it. She was born in captivity, never taught to kill. I looked at the intruder's neck and no bite mark. His heart was still pumping when she started to feed ...'

I cut him off, 'We get the picture. At a later date I will need to take a statement from you regarding the circumstances as to how this person died.'

The keeper said, 'But then the lion would have pushed in.' I cut him off again and said, 'Okay, thanks.' It was a case of too much information, but the keeper was oblivious to our concerns. He continued, 'The male just mates, eats, fights and sleeps.' Sounded like an armed robbery squad detective to me.

We had to go. As we walked away, the keeper called, 'Can you give me a full breakdown regarding his medical history – if he had hepatitis A-B or C, HIV or used drugs?' I agreed. I would have agreed to anything at that point.

As an afterthought he added, 'Can you find out how much he weighed and how fat he was? He's completely stuffed Sheba's diet, she's already overweight.' We laughed.

Referring to the deceased I said, 'What an inconsiderate bastard.' I said to Darren, 'How many calories in an Ilie Cucu?'

He said, 'I suppose he tasted like a cross between chicken and fish.'

We had finished with the scene of the death. Darren said, 'What now?'

I said, 'How about some ribs?' He didn't laugh. He mustn't have been hungry. I then started some serious cop-speak. 'Mate we have to do the 83s, the coroner's reports. We have to explain what happened here. What caused this person to climb into a lion's cage and get eaten?'

Darren said, 'It's crazy suicide, simple suicide.'

I said, 'No more important task will ever be given to a police officer than the task of investigating the death of a person. You want the job?'

Darren said, 'Of course, I know the offenders, the ID of the victim. Case solved, what more do I need?'

I said patiently, 'You need to know why, mate.'

A short time later we arrived at the Tao Mi karate school. We walked up a narrow flight of stairs to the first floor of a grotty little building. We walked into the middle of 20 little kids in a karate lesson.

Sing was a younger version of the martial arts bloke in the movie The Karate Kid. He looked and sounded very traditional. At the end of his lesson we had a chat. We introduced ourselves. I said, 'Did or do you have a student named Ilie Cucu?'

He said, 'Oh yes, he is a fine student. Is something wrong?'

Here it was: death message time. I said, 'I'm sorry to inform you but Ilie has died. Last night he climbed into a lion enclosure and was eaten by lions.'

Sing became upset. I said, 'Did he appear depressed lately, or do you have any idea at all why he might have committed suicide?'

Sing said, 'Definitely not. He was very happy – just yesterday he obtained his black belt in karate. He was very proud. He was not the suicide type. Ilie was very spiritual, he believed in our teachings.'

I asked, 'What teachings? Do you have teachings about lions?'

He said, 'One of our teachings is that when you are content, that is when you are highly trained and have come to terms with your own inner strength, you have truly found yourself. One teaching is if you were to meet a lion, that lion would look at you and appreciate your strength, you would look at it and appreciate its strength, therefore you and the lion would just look at each other respecting each other's strength. Therefore there would be no conflict, no danger.'

It was a good theory. But, sadly, no-one had bothered to tell the lions about it.

I said, 'Well, you got it all wrong, because the lion wasn't his problem. It was the lioness – she showed him no respect.'

Sing looked puzzled and said, 'Our teachings just say lion, I never thought there was a difference, like lion and a lioness.'

I said, 'Well, can you stop teaching that shit because people are full of germs and diseases and are very bad for a lion's health.'

Darren added, 'Not to mention its diet.'

Sing was trying to work us out, without success.

I said, 'Was Ilie fat?'

Sing said, 'Ilie was one of my finest students. He would be maybe only be five per cent to seven per cent fat, and he was very fit and strong.'

I said, 'He went into the cage in just his jocks. Why would he do that?'

Sing said, 'That would be so the lion could see his strength.'

I nodded. 'Of course, what a stupid question.'

Darren took a statement from Sing.

Our next quest was to find a relative. Ilie had a brother named George who lived in Kew. We had to inform George as he was the only member of his family we could find. On the way there, we called into our office and found Sandy. She wanted to know the whole story so I asked her to come along on the death message.

We walked up to George's door. We were laughing at the name Cucu, when I knocked on it. George lived in a boarding house in a small room at the end of a long corridor.

A happy smiling face answered the door. I introduced Sandy, Darren and myself. I was having big trouble trying to speak because I had the giggles. It can happen at the worst times and then you can't stop.

I tried to speak and cover my smile at the same time. Darren and Sandy started to nearly wet themselves. They laughed so hard they had to walk backwards down the hallway to hide so that George couldn't hear or see them collapsing. I just wanted to run away but it was too late.

George's next door neighbour, hearing all the commotion, opened his door. He asked Sandy and Darren what the matter was. They ducked inside his room to hide. I heard a second muffled burst of laughter as the neighbour was told the Ilie Cucu story. The neighbour thought it was hilarious.

Sandy told me later that Darren had held his hand over the neighbour's mouth to try and muffle the laughter. It didn't work – it was amplified in the long empty corridor.

With my hand over my mouth I gathered every fake ounce of sorrow and grief I could muster and said, 'I'm very sorry, Mr Cucu, but your brother has been killed by a lion.'

George said, 'Line?'

I noticed that Darren and Sandy had crept back out of the other room.

'Line?' George repeated as he drew an imaginary line through the air with his finger. 'Line? How can a line kill someone? Don't be stupid. A line?'

Well, that was it. We all cracked up laughing. It was all too much.

The Police Academy instructors didn't mention anything about not laughing during a death message. But it was funny, and the academy brains trust evidently hadn't thought of that possibility. Darren decided to help. He pushed me out the way and said, 'Not line, a LION.'

George looked back blankly so Darren went 'ROARRRRRRRR' like a lion with an angry face and opening his mouth and scratching the air with his bent fingers and open hands.

All of a sudden George got with the program and said, 'No, no, no, there are no lions in Australia.' It was all too much for Sandy, who collapsed on the floor unable to breathe because of her laughing. I managed to say, 'In the zoo, the zoo, I mean the circus there is.'

We ultimately convinced George that his brother had been eaten by a lion. We explained that Ilie wanted the lion to appreciate his strength and him to appreciate the lion's strength and that they would then be at peace and never have to fight. Even George laughed. George said, 'Ilie was a show-bag.'

I said, 'Show-bag?'

George said, 'You know – looks okay on the outside but full of shit. Him think he so bloody special, special karate man, him black belt karate bullshit.'

As we walked away, I said, 'Well, he's just about lion shit now.' We were trained to show compassion.

On the way back from the successful death message we called into the circus to take the final statement from the lion keeper. He raved on and on about how he had kept lions for 15 years. He was a true expert and loved his job.

Our final report went something like this: 'The intruder approached the enclosure and started to undress. At this moment both the lion and lioness would have become aware of his presence. Dressed in only jockettes the intruder climbed up the wall onto the roof. This action would have caused the lions to take notice. The lioness would have crept forward, her instincts causing her to commence the hunt. A hole was cut and the intruder commenced to climb into the enclosure.

This action would have caused the lioness to spring up in the air and take the intruder as he entered. The lioness being 220 kilograms would have held the intruder on the ground with her front paws. The lioness, being Sheba, would have then commenced to eat the intruder. As there was no bite mark on the back of the neck and Sheba has no idea how to kill, I believe the lioness began to eat him whilst he was still alive. The arterial spray marks across the face of the lioness corroborate this hypothesis.'

Mr Cucu was a student of karate and intended to test his strength. The lions would not have allowed this test to occur.'

The inquest found that Ilie Cucu's intention was such that his cause of death was, 'Death by misadventure'. Suicide was closer to the mark.

I WAS getting bored in the special duties office at St Kilda, so I said in a loud voice, 'You guys can just sit around waiting for someone to surrender, Darren and I are going out to protect the public.'

Darren just rolled his eyes. I always made this or similar comments when leaving the office. It was always met with snide remarks, cat-calls and a touch of laughter.

Minutes later as we walked down The Street I saw something that could have spoiled my day. It was a crook named Billy. It seemed like only yesterday that he got eight years for armed robberies and assaults. I thought I must be getting old.

Billy was a nasty dumb thug. But he probably had one more brain cell than his mate Skull. Between armed robberies he lived by bashing and robbing prostitutes and street traffickers. I said to Darren, 'He was a skinny bastard when he went in, now look at him.' He had obviously been doing some serious weightlifting. You could always pick a crook who was just out of jail. They looked fit and mean. Three meals a day and access to a gym helped turn them from skinny junkies into muscled-up junkies.

We walked over to him. He stood there trying to give me a dirty look. I ignored it and waved at him to follow me. He knew exactly what I was on about. I wanted to have a chat in a nearby laneway.

I noticed he hadn't done what I requested so I stopped and started to walk toward him. He reluctantly walked toward me. I turned and let him follow. In the lane I lit a smoke and offered him one. He looked around to make sure no one was looking, and took one. With a smile he said, 'Hello Mr Angus,' as though we were long lost friends, which we weren't.

I lit his smoke and said, 'You know how I was before; now I'm a lot older I put up with less.'

Billy smiled and said, 'I have rights, I know me rights.' I knew then that while Billy may have built up his biceps while inside he hadn't improved his brain box.

Why would a crook say to a copper 'I know my rights.' And why would he say it in a lonely laneway. What he was really saying was, 'I am tired of having my own teeth and would like some dentures, but I don't have private health insurance and can't afford to get a dentist to pull them out. Would you mind removing them with your fist or the butt of your gun if it isn't too much trouble?'

But, with great self-control, I didn't touch him. With my teeth clenched and seething with anger, I stepped forward up to his face. In a calm, most serious voice, I said, 'Don't hurt anyone, don't hurt anyone at all or I will. Do you understand?'

In self-defence Billy said, 'Yeah.' Turning my back on him I walked off. Billy and Darren stood there thinking about my statement. They were the most serious words I had ever uttered.

Billy suddenly realised I had threatened him and the threat was real. He called out, 'Ay, you can't fretten or frighten me – well, you can but you shouldn't. I'll have your job for that … well I don't want to be a cop or nuffin but.'

All that thinking would have made his brain hurt. As I walked off, I realised how incredibly angry I was.

My stomach was all tight and knotted up, my heart was pounding. I took a few deep breaths in an attempt to control myself. I stopped and waited for Darren to catch up. As he got up to me he said, 'I've never seen you like that?' As we walked on, long forgotten images of sleepless nights flooded back. I was rewinding a video tape in my mind trying to get to the bit about my past dealings with Billy.

I had blocked it out so I knew it was bad and I probably shouldn't go there but I wanted to know. I remembered arresting Billy then I went back a little bit further. As I found the memory I quietly said, 'Shit' and stopped walking. Now I remembered why I hated Billy. Darren stopped next to me.

With a voice full of emotion I said, 'Years ago, while he was on the run, he did a burg on a house in Albert Park. He knocked on the front door. No-one answered. He threw a brick through the middle of the glass door hitting a little girl in the face as she was reaching up to open it. Her little face was shredded by the broken glass. When we charged him, he laughed, saying "How was I suppose to know she was there. How could it be my fault?" It came to court and he beat it, we couldn't prove intent. He was right, we couldn't prove a thing. He walked on the assault charges and went down on the burg. He got two months inside.'

Darren was silent. I wasn't. I kept talking. 'You know, I'd blocked that out, I only thought of it when I wondered why I was so angry. The mind must have a place it hides things, especially horrible things.' A couple of days later there was a vicious aggravated burglary committed on a palatial house in East St Kilda. The two elderly occupants were bashed and taped up. They were then burnt with a cigarette lighter until they disclosed the combination of their safe. A large amount of jewellery and cash was stolen.

That was the strange thing about St Kilda. There were the remains of old-world charm and gentleness living next to the worst types on this planet. Sometimes their worlds collided and it was always the decent people who ended up losing.

The St Kilda CIB were in charge, then the Special Response Squad took over. Our boss asked us to speak to all of our informers as this would be a good one to solve. I immediately thought Billy was a top suspect. But I had to be sure. I got a list of everything that was stolen and walked out of the office. Alone I drove to an old people's home.

I visited a very old and very wise Jewish man. He was 88. In his day he'd been the largest handler of stolen goods in the southern hemisphere. Years ago I warned him that he was about to get robbed by a well-organised gang.

I had him leave his house shortly before he was invaded by two crooks with shotguns. The crooks got away as I was unable to get surveillance in time, but I had made a friend. Since then, on special occasions, he helped me.

I never abused the privilege. As I approached his bed he smiled as he saw me. We spoke about old times. Suddenly he grabbed my hand and said, 'What is it, what do you want?'

I smiled and placed a piece of paper in his hand. Through his thick glasses he read the paper. He said, 'Bad one, eh.' I said, 'Home invasion and an elderly Jewish couple was left badly injured. That's their name and a list of all the property stolen. My number is on the top', indicating the piece of paper.

He said, 'Say nothing more. Take care.' I squeezed his hand and left.

The next day, my mobile rang. It was the old man. He said, 'Angus, walk outside to the driver's door of the black Toyota. Next time you come you come just for friendship, agreed?'

I said, 'Agreed.'

The old man hung up. I knew that the crooks had to sell the

stolen goods. I knew that one of the many secondhand dealers in Melbourne must have answered the old man's call. Even from the old person's home, he could reach out a bony hand to his old contacts.

I walked out into the street. Directly across the road was a brand new black Toyota Land Cruiser. It had black tinted windows. As I approached the driver's door, the side window lowered two inches. A small piece of paper appeared between two fingers.

I took the paper. As I did, the vehicle drove off. I stood on the roadway and looked at the paper. It said, Billy Squire, Lansdowne Road, East St Kilda. There was also a phone number.

Back at my desk I rang the number. The house manager answered. I asked for Billy. I said I was Dave. (Everyone knows a Dave or two). He told me he was in his room. I said, 'Sweet' and hung up. I made the house manager the police informer on the search warrant. We worked flat out on the warrant, obtaining it in about an hour. I organised a raiding crew to meet near the address at 6am the next day

I had informed the Special Response Squad because it was officially their case. They sent four members to assist in the raid and search. We all met down the street from the target address.

I ran through the briefing and we did it. We hit the door of the one-room flat and ran in screaming but our aggression quickly dissolved. We all stopped and laughed. Billy was lying face down on the bed. His hands and feet were bound with gaffer tape.

Two big pieces of tape were wrapped around his head and mouth. He looked at us all and shook his head in disbelief. I walked up to him, putting on rubber gloves and quickly ripped the tape off his mouth. He winced in agony as though I had just torn off half his face. Laughing, I said, 'Police to the rescue. Are you going to thank me? You won't have to shave today. Who did it?'

He said, 'Me girlfriend did it as a joke, but I haven't laughed yet, bitch.'

We replaced the tape around his wrists with handcuffs. I said, 'The cuffs give you a bit of a Johnny Roger, do they?' He ignored me. Seven of us searched his tiny room. Nothing.

Billy just sat there as though he was in shock. He lived in a ground floor room. Outside his window was a large old rose garden. Ten yards past that was the main road. Two detectives started searching the garden outside his window, and found nothing. I then asked everyone to swap places and have another go. Fresh eyes can see things differently.

Not this time. Again nothing.

I found a shovel and started digging. I got nothing but tennis elbow so another member of the raiding party took over. A few minutes later he yelled, 'Over here, it's a container.'

I bent Billy over the window sill holding the back of his neck so he could see the find. A large blue plastic waterproof container with a screw top was removed from the ground. A police photographer snapped away. As the lid was removed Billy closed his eyes.

Inside were all the goods from the home invasion and more. It was as if we had just struck gold. Later a fingerprint expert located 17 of Billy's fingerprints on the items and we didn't even put them there.

As it was my pinch, Special Response allowed us to process him back at our office. We were very happy at the fact that Billy said, 'No comment' to all questions in the interview.

Truth be known, I had told him if he didn't I would bash him. All detectives prefer 'no comment' answers when we have all the evidence, as it makes the crook look like an arsehole.

Throughout the day, while Billy was in our custody, he appeared shy and scared. It was most unlike him. He gave us no cheek and did everything he was told. At the end of it all I asked Darren to take him to the watch-house and remand him in custody as I had the happy task of calling the old couple and asking them if they were up to identifying the property. They were ecstatic as they had no insurance and many of the items had a lot of sentimental value. It was a lifetime of memories to them. To a scrote like Billy it was just something to fence for a few bucks. As Darren took Billy to the watch-house they spoke. Darren said: 'Why are you so scared about going back to jail?'

Billy said, 'Lock me up, I'm safer in there.'

Billy wanted to stay silent, but he found it was seriously impossible. With venom Billy said through his teeth, 'What would you do? At four this morning I woke up with a pistol shoved down my throat. A bloke in a balaclava whispered, "Where's your stash?" With the pistol still in my throat he put a pillow over my face and pulled the trigger – "Click".

'Then he said, "The next thing you're going to hear is your brains coming out your ears." The trigger had got caught in the pillow case causing a misfire. He cleared it and again started to pull the trigger. So I told him where the container was buried. Wouldn't you? He taped me up and left. I looked death in the eye, mate, and lived, so lock me the fuck up for Christ's sake.'

Billy was too stupid or too frightened to wonder why the intruder left the container behind.

Darren put him in the cell. Then had a long think. He came to a conclusion. He found me in the mess room, grabbed me by the arm and dragged me outside. In the most serious voice Darren had ever used he said, 'Billy told me it was no bloody girlfriend. He had a visitor. Billy told me he told the intruder where the stash was. A crook would have taken it. But this bloke didn't. It was you, wasn't it? You left it there.'

He was certain. I had been through enough shit with him to know when the game was up. With a disgusted disappointed voice he said, 'You think you're so bloody ethical. It's criminal for Christ's sake. It was you.'

I said in a most dignified voice, 'That's a big call'. Which it was.

But my longtime partner couldn't be put off. 'Let's look at the facts. It was the occupants of the black four-wheel drive or it was you … it was you, wasn't it?' I ignored him. Darren then screamed, 'It was you, wasn't it?' I wanted to answer but I couldn't.

I said, 'Sorry mate, I've only got questions.'

As I walked away I stopped, turned toward my best friend in The Job and said, 'I can feel a fishing trip coming on.' I opened my car door and drove off.

He just stood there. He grabbed his mobile and pushed a couple of buttons. My mobile phone rang. It was Darren. I said, 'Yeah, I've got bait mate, okay. I'll pick you up at six. Bye.'

After all, as everybody knows, it's the early bird that catches the worm.

CORONERS REGULATIONS 1986

Form 1

STATE
CORONER
VICTORIA

RECORD OF INVESTIGATION

I, HAL HALLENSTEIN   Coroner, having investigated the death

of   ILIE CUCU

* WITHOUT HOLDING AN INQUEST;

On The   day(s) of   19

FIND THAT the identity of the deceased was   ILIE CUCU
and that the death occurred on   25/3/89   at

from (state cause of death)
I(a) MULTIPLE INJURIES

I(b)

I(c)

II

In the following circumstances
THE DECEASED WAS FOUND IN THE LION ENCLOSURE AT ▮▮▮▮▮▮
HAVING BEEN MAULED BY A NUMBER OF LIONS WITHIN THAT ENCLOSURE.
ON INVESTIGATING THE CIRCUMSTANCES IT IS APPARENT THAT THE
DECEASED FOR UNKNOWN REASONS HAS ENTERED THE ENCLOSURE BY SCALING
A 18 FOOT FENCE SURROUNDING THE ENCLOSURE AND HAS THEN DIED AS A
RESULT OF THE INJURIES INFLICTED BY THE LIONS.
A NEATLY FOLDED PILE OF CLOTHES WAS FOUND IN CLOSE PROXIMITY TO
WHERE IT IS APPARENT HE SCALED THE FENCE.
THE DECEASED HAD RECEIVED PSYCHIATRIC CARE WHILST A RESIDENT IN
SYDNEY IN 1986 FOLLOWING AN ATTEMPT TO TAKE HIS LIFE AND WAS
DIAGNOSED AS SUFFERING FROM PARANOID SCHIZOPHRENIA. THE DECEASED
LIVED A VAGRANT LIFESTYLE AND LITTLE IS KNOWN OF HIS CURRENT
ACTIVITIES PRIOR TO HIS DEATH. I FURTHER FIND THE DECEASED
CONTRIBUTED TO THE CAUSE OF DEATH.

CHAPTER 13

I had a lump on the back of
my head the size of an orange.

Carlton blues

FINALLY, after almost four years in The Job, the big day came
when I became a detective. It was like a dream for me. While
some of the others at the academy wanted to be traffic cops or
drive a desk, I always wanted to be in the Criminal
Investigation Branch.

What was the point of getting the uniform if you couldn't put
it in the cupboard and work in plain clothes? I wanted to be
involved in catching heavy crims and the fantastic time at St
Kilda special duties had confirmed what I thought. Now I had
passed all the exams and promotion boards so I could apply for
vacancies as a detective.

I wanted a change from St Kilda. I had had enough of the
druggie dropkicks. They were fun but it was time to broaden
my horizons. I didn't want to be typecast and it was time for a
change of postcode.

The word was that there were lots of real non-drug-affected

crooks in Carlton, so I set my sights in moving across town. It took me six months. I arrived at the Carlton CIB in October, 1988.

I remember being like a kid with a new toy when I answered the phone. 'Detective Angus speaking, can I help you?' I had to say 'Detective Angus' as I was a detective constable for several months before I was promoted and could finally say the magic words, 'Senior Detective.' I was, of course, actually a detective senior constable, but 'Senior Detective' sounded so much better. Many detectives get business cards made with Senior Detective printed on them. I know I did.

One afternoon I was at the scene of a big burglary when a call came over the radio that a man was at St Vincent's Hospital with a stab wound in his chest. The local uniform cops wanted a detective there as soon as possible. I left my partner at the scene of the burglary and drove to the hospital alone, or 'one up', as we like to say.

Wearing my new black suit and Dick Tracy style overcoat and holding the mandatory dark blue folder I purposefully walked up to the nurses' station. I produced my badge to the nurse and asked to see the doctor in charge of the stab victim.

The doctor said the victim was a chap called Nguyen. He had been stabbed in the chest and was in a critical condition. The doctor said he was conscious. I decided I had better speak with him as soon as possible to obtain a dying declaration that could be used in court later.

I asked a nurse who the two Asian males were standing in the hallway looking sheepish, and she said they had brought the victim in for treatment. I didn't need to dux detective training school to know I would need to chat with them. I told them that if they tried to move they would be arrested and that seemed to do the trick. I told a hospital security guard to watch them just for insurance. I didn't want to be the newest detective in the state to tell the Homicide Squad I had let two star witnesses walk out before they were interviewed. I would have become the only young detective in charge of school-crossing duty.

I took a deep breath, opened the curtain, entered and stood next to the victim. There were wires and tubes all over the place. He was naked from the waist up.

In the right side of his chest was a small cut about two centimetres long. I was standing on his right side. Each time he breathed in, the small cut opened and a large amount of air escaped causing a reddish pink foam to appear. It made a sickly 'Psssshhhhhh' sound. This was not good.

I thought 'Okay, I'm in trouble.' I suffered an immediate flashback to my youth. I remembered 'Show and Tell', when I stood in front of my class in grade three at Oakleigh Primary School. I was explaining to the class how the night before I had seen on TV a man named Rodney Fox get his leg bitten off by a shark. He lay on the deck of the boat with the stump of his leg bleeding profusely. I promptly fainted at the thought of my own words and was taken home to recover.

But that was years before. This time, I thought, I'll be right … I'm a detective for Christ's sake. I attempted to ignore the sight and sound of the escaping air. I said, 'I'm Detective Angus. Who did this?'

I cut to the chase in the chase for the cut.

He mumbled something about an argument and a card game, but I was starting to lose interest. I started to sway. I took hold of the curtain. A nurse asked if I was all right. The next thing I remember was two nurses helping me to a seat in the foyer, right next to the two Asians I had detained. I wanted to vomit but couldn't. This was definitely not in the manual. The hospital security guard helped. I got him to ring my partner. I was crook – real crook.

The Asian male died a short time later. The Homicide Squad took over. It turned out that the one thing that saved me was I had arrested the killer in the hallway. The killer was one of the two blokes I had got the security guard to watch. Ultimately, the autopsy revealed that the killer had stabbed the guy three times without withdrawing the knife. So there was one stab wound through the outer skin but three separate stabs inside. I was told that the killer had made full admissions. I really prayed he didn't mention me being carried out by the two nurses. Over the years I made a conscious effort to toughen up. It didn't always work.

IT was a day shift. I had to drive into the city to obtain a statement from a bank clerk over a deception matter. It was my third day at Carlton as a detective. As I was driving north in Elizabeth Street, a call came over the police radio: 'Any unit clear in the vicinity of The Australian Diamond Company, corner of Swanston Street and Bourke Street, Melbourne – armed robbery alarm.'

This was better than some boring deception matter. This was what I was born for – cops and robbers. I was driving a little blue unmarked Toyota Sedan. It was the smaller of our cars, but it would do the job. Other police units immediately came up on the air and accepted the job. I did a screaming U-turn and accelerated to the scene.

It was 4pm and traffic was everywhere. I needed a siren and blue lights. On the passenger side floor, I saw a blue light. Fantastic. I grabbed the heavy magnetic blue light with the long extendable telephone type cord. I hurriedly wound down my window and slapped the light onto the roof. By this time I was doing Warp Factor Five. I plugged the socket into the cigarette lighter fitting on the dashboard.

I found it hard to drive with the springy cord between me and the steering wheel. I quickly pulled the cord out of the dashboard, passed it under my legs and again plugged it into the lighter fitting.

Now I was free to drive like a lunatic, flat out up the tram tracks along Bourke Street. I timed the whole thing perfectly. All the traffic and pedestrians stopped as they saw me coming.

I skidded sideways across the intersection and came to a screaming halt. Brilliant, I was the first one there. I opened my door and leapt out of my car reaching for my firearm. The cord came up tight and whipped the heavy magnetic blue light off the roof and smashed it onto the back of my head. I fell face first into the roadway. The immense pain closed both my eyes. I wish I was back in St Kilda.

I rolled around holding the back of my head. I got onto my knees. I partially opened one eye and peeped through the pain. More cops started arriving. Two middle-aged women were saying something to me. They appeared concerned about my welfare. I couldn't hear through the pain either. I suddenly remembered why I was there, staggered to my feet and kicked my driver's door closed.

I started to walk toward the front door of the Diamond Company. Something caught my eye, there was the blue light that had nearly taken my head off. It was still flashing away – laughing at me. I was offended that it had hurt me so much and I hadn't even broken it.

I picked it up off the road and stuck it back onto the roof of the car. Carefully holding the back of my head, I started to walk off. Then I stopped and looked at the light and decided I better take it off the roof where it might still be dangerous.

I threw it through the open window of the driver's side door. With one hand feeling the big lump on the back of my head, I paused again. I had forgotten to lock my police car. I realised that someone stealing my car at this time was the last thing I needed. I kept touching the lump on the back of my head and then looking at my hand for signs of brain fluid and blood. There wasn't any, but Christ it hurt.

At last I staggered along the footpath and through the front door of the Australian Diamond Company. To my right was a doorway. I opened it and walked through. It was the stairwell. Sanctuary and privacy – perfect. I leant against the wall and started rubbing the back of my head. I heard through the door, 'Melbourne 307, your last at the Diamond Company is N.O.D.' (No Offence Detected)

I thought 'Thank Christ'. Brain pounding, I left the safety of my stairwell and got back into my car. I had a lump on the back of my head the size of an orange. I slowly and carefully drove back to the office. I knocked off duty and made it home. Stuff the deception matter, I was too sick. I thought if I'm going to be doing this detective stuff for a long time I better slow down to a stop, take a deep breath and think about my actions. But, of course, I never did.

SOMETIMES you have to take a step back to go forward and when a Turkish drug trafficker from St Kilda moved to Carlton I knew it was time to teach a new dog an old trick. I had bought gear from the Turk and locked him up in the old days, but I had done it as Angus.

Now that he was set up in the Carlton Housing Commission flats, it was time to bring Dean Collie out of retirement.

Everybody thought it was hilarious because at Carlton most of the detectives were serious types. I had quite short hair, so I dug out the old fishing bag with the wig and the whole costume. I kept everything together – the shoes, stupid glasses, old woollen beanie – everything. I knew that one day I might just want to be a typical drug-fucked petty criminal again.

So, without any introduction, I knocked on the door. The other detectives had decided there was no way known I was going to buy smack by knocking on this guy's door telling him some bullshit story about how some bloke named John had told me that I could buy heroin and how desperate I was.

They said I would need an introduction from an insider, blah, blah blah. But Dean and I didn't have the time. It worked in St Kilda, so we saw no reason why it wouldn't work here. Anyway, this Turk answers the door. He gave me a real hard time at first. I had my left arm all bandaged up, saying I had crashed my car. I started crying and all this sort of stuff – I should have got an Oscar. So eventually he said 'all right' and agreed to sell me heroin at the phone box at the bottom of the flats. A few minutes later he came down and sold me heroin at the phone box.

My back-ups arrested him immediately and we didn't let on that I was in disguise. Sometimes everything goes according to plan – or so we thought.

As it happened the tape recorder that I wore didn't work and it came up at the contest stage in court 12 months later.

Two days before the court contest date, the Turk's barrister rang me. He asked if I had any tape recordings of his client speaking English. I said, 'No, none whatsoever, no undercover tapes at all.' There were no old tapes of him speaking English from when I charged him in the past as the interviews were just typed and there was no undercover tape. The barrister said, 'That's because my client doesn't speak English.'

I was upset at the fact the tape had failed. The barrister insisted that he had an interpreter throughout the interview because he couldn't speak English.

There were no admissions made by the Turk at all and he had said he was arrested for no reason while he was making a phone call. The lawyer said that when he interviewed his client he needed an interpreter. The brief seemed to believe that his client couldn't speak a word of English. It was obviously going to be an interesting day in court.

The only evidence we had basically boiled down to me giving evidence that he had in fact sold me heroin. We had the small quantity of heroin and photographs but the case was looking pretty thin.

The lawyer was sounding pretty cocky. He said over the phone 'So how could he sell you heroin and how could you have this big conversation that's written in your statement when my client doesn't speak English?'

He then made his offer: 'So my client will meet you half way. He will plead guilty to possess heroin if you drop the traffic heroin charge.' Then he over-played his hand: 'Don't you know what evidence is? You're going to look like a fool. You need evidence to substantiate a charge.' Maybe I would have played 'Let's Make A Deal' if he wasn't a smart arse. I said, 'It's definitely traffic heroin.'

The chances were high that he'd go to jail for some time if he was found guilty, even though it was a small quantity of heroin. So it was an important point.

The Turk had two prior convictions for heroin trafficking. Now, I might have been losing the legal argument but at least I could resort to personal abuse. I said something like: 'He's paying cash is he? I'd wash my hands after touching it if I were you.' It was an oldy but a goody. I slammed the phone down.

He was a smart arse barrister with a bad attitude. But this lawyer had picked the wrong smart arse detective to fuck with. I knew I could be a bigger smart arse than him any day. It was a gift, really.

I immediately started to think of a cunning plan. I needed one to rectify the problem of not having any evidence. So I used the 'buxom blonde' technique, commonly used by crooks and cops alike.

I found a buxom blonde about 22 years old in the Carlton uniform section. I asked her sergeant if she could help me the following morning and he agreed. I sat her down in the mess room and told her the story.

I asked her to dress in something that would appeal to a short, fat, bald Turk. She knew what I meant.

The next morning I handed her a letter which had the Turk's flat number and address written on it. I asked her to go to this Turkish person's flat, knock on the door and ask for this female who was written on the letterhead and try to engage in a conversation speaking in English.

I placed – well, she placed – the microphone between her large breasts.

You get good audio up between the cleavage, although we did get a bit of 'catcho … catcho … catcho … catcho …' type noise with every step that she took as her breasts bounced up and down rubbing on the microphone.

After wiring her for sound, I sent her in. He answered the

door in his pyjamas. He was very keen to speak to her about anything she wanted – or, in fact, didn't want. All in perfect English. She even complimented him on his English. He was so pleased he said he had learnt the language at some English language school. Best of all, he offered the comment that 'I need to speak English for my business.'

So, after a 10-minute conversation, my undercover agent said goodbye, not to the Turk's delight. She came back to me smiling from ear to ear. We had the conversation transcribed. The next day we turned up to court. I slipped the buxom blonde into the prosecutors' office as part of the cunning plan.

When the court case started, I gave the initial evidence. While I was in the witness box the smart-arsed lawyer let rip. He accused me of lying to the court (he was wrong, this time) setting up his client and making the point again and again that the poor Turk couldn't speak the Queen's English, or even Paul Hogan's English.

The barrister said, 'You can see in the court that he is using an interpreter.' I, of course, could not mention to the court that I had charged him in the past. The barrister stated that I was victimising him. I would have liked to victimise the barrister.

I produced photographs of myself dressed as Dean Collie so the magistrate could see that I looked nothing like I did while in his court. The magistrate looked amused to see how I had changed my appearance completely.

I was accused of committing perjury, verballing this Turk, who was a short, fat, ugly bald headed 45-year-old with a bad attitude, not to mention a lot of money for barristers.

The Turk was sitting in court with this interpreter who was talking away, interpreting everything that everybody said and I eventually got out of the witness box after about an hour and a half. I thought I was a good actor. The prosecutor then turned and said, 'I now call Constable Sandra Connors.' Seconds later in came the buxom blonde policewoman dressed in a police uniform. I looked at the Turk. To see his face was hilarious because it went from a look that said, 'Ow, she's all right' through to a puzzled sort of a look that said, 'Don't I know her?' right through to a look that said, 'Fuck'.

The penny dropped and he realised who she was. She stepped into the witness box and described what had happened the morning before.

She then handed tapes and transcripts of the tape to the magistrate, to the defence barrister and to the prosecutor. The magistrate looked at the transcripts and said, 'I take it these transcripts are identical to the tape?'

It was agreed that they were. The magistrate threw a questioning look at the defence barrister. The smart-arsed lawyer was for once stumped for words. He threw a deadly look at the Turk. The barrister then gave me an even worse look, with eyes that would kill because I'd basically embarrassed the hell out of him. He looked at the magistrate and said, 'One moment your Worship, I'd like a moment to speak to my client.'

The barrister then began to whisper in the ear of his client. He then stopped and began to whisper to the interpreter. He then said, 'My client would like to plead guilty your Worship.' The magistrate was not happy.

I was pissed off that my integrity had even been questioned. I sat there and shook my head. The magistrate shook his head and gave him an 18-month minimum inside to polish his language skills. Yummy.

I still bump into that barrister now and then. He has never forgiven me. He knew that I had gone within the letter of the law. He also knew I hadn't lied to him. At the time I spoke to him I did not have any tape. He was absolutely furious that I had not warned him prior to the case, but as I said to him, 'You gave me the idea to do it, you rang me.' I had no idea that he would go ahead and accuse me of perjury (like fun). I could see that he was angry at himself for informing me of his intended defence. He won't do that again. Tough. We played hard ball and convicted a drug dealer. Boo Hoo.

Even an old collie will bite if you push hard enough.

AROUND the same time at Carlton I arrested a crook named Wally. His name suited him. A mate of his told me he had a stolen car parked in Lygon Street and I sat off it until Wally tried to drive off. I was pretty confident he wasn't going anywhere because I had already played with the engine so it couldn't start. Call it insurance.

I knew he bought his heroin from an Asian bloke in the Carlton 'walk up' flats situated in Neil Street. They were called the walk ups because they were Housing Commission flats that were only four storeys high compared to the 20-story high rise nearby.

I managed to persuade Wally to assist me to obtain evidence against the Asian dealer. How I did that is my business. Let's just say he developed a community spirit in a hurry. It made me feel warm inside.

A short time later, Wally met my mate Dean Collie.

They got on well. It was a little like a real life version of Dumb and Dumber. Wally thought I had gone home and Dean had taken over. They were so similar it was scary. Wally thought Dean was the best undercover cop he had ever seen.

Anyway I had six other detectives as back-up. The plan was

for Wally to take Dean to the Asian's flat, I would purchase the heroin. I would then walk away, the arrest crew would then raid the flat, search it and arrest the trafficker. Simple really. Well, that was the plan anyway.

Within the hour I was Dean Collie with Wally walking toward the flats. Wally informed us that you don't have to telephone first, you just rock up for some white rock.

We started to walk over a small grass area toward the concrete staircase. We got about 20 metres from the staircase when Wally grabbed my arm and told me to stand still.

Dean said, 'But you said we go to the flat?' He said, 'No if I bring someone new, we just stand here. One of the dealer's spotters will notify him that we're here.'

We stood there in the dark for about 10 seconds when a kid bouncing a basketball walked past. The kid was about 10 years old. After walking past, he looked back at Wally and held up two fingers. He was giving us the peace sign. I then held two fingers back to him and said, 'Peace brother.' Dean could be cool too, you know.

I said to Wally, 'He's up late.' Wally nodded his head at the kid and said, 'Two, yeah.' Wally said, 'Where's your money?' The kid was the spotter and I hadn't spotted him. I must have been slipping.

I said, 'Hang on, what's this shit?' I was losing control of the situation if I ever had it in the first place. Wally said, 'Quick the money.' I held $180 cash in my hand (two foils of heroin cost $90 each back then before the shit flooded the market).

I then heard a clicking sound. I looked up and there was this arm leaning over the first floor balcony clicking its fingers and waving in an upward direction indicating for us to come up to the flat. This was more like it. I'll go up to the flat with Wally, meet the dealer, so I can identify him when he is arrested during the raid, and search the flea-bitten dump.

We took a couple of steps toward the flat and I handed the cash to Wal. I said, 'Remember I have to be there to see the deal so you don't have to give evidence.' Wally didn't look like a QC, but he seemed to understand. 'Yeah of course you'll see it.' I was reassured by his confidence. I shouldn't have been.

With that Wally stuffed the cash in a small drink bottle he had just finished and threw it up onto the first floor balcony all in one smooth motion. I jumped up to try and stop the bottle but it hit its target. As I was still looking up at the balcony two silver foils started to float down toward us.

Wally said, 'See, our gear, I told you you'll see it.' I pushed my star informer out of the way onto his back and said, 'You fucking idiot, no I'm a fucking idiot, shit, shit.'

I grabbed both foils. I looked at the foils and said out loud 'Great'. My sarcasm was lost on Wally, the master crim catcher. I had two foils of heroin, and no evidence of who took the money or who gave us the heroin.

I had just wasted $180 of our Carlton CIB Social Club fund. Now that was criminal. Wally thought he had done a great job. While he was sitting on his arse he knew he shouldn't ask but he couldn't help it, 'Do you think I could.' I knew he was going to ask for a small amount of heroin for himself as a tip for a job well done. I cut him off short – I would have liked to cut him in half.

'Don't even think about it,' I told him. Wally may not have been that bright but he wasn't totally stupid. He saw my face. I pointed off into the dark. Wally stood up and ran off never to be seen again.

I pulled a police radio out of my old bag. I hid up against the bottom of the flats and told the arrest team, 'I have the gear all okay I'm not sure how many "heads" are in the flat. Confirmed one adult and possibly one child. It's all clear to raid. Over.' They responded, 'One adult, possibly one child, 30 seconds off. Over.'

Seconds later, the arrest crew flowed up the stairs and sledge-hammered the door until it opened. A large amount of scream-ing started to emanate from this flat. These screams drowned out the sound of 'Police, don't move.' In the dark downstairs I was madly removing Dean Collie and placing him back in my bag.

I ran upstairs. I stopped in the doorway as there were bodies lying and screaming out in the Asian language all over the flat. This was a one-bedroom flat. There were nine adults and seven children. This was not good.

When they were all standing up, they could fit, lying down was much more difficult. My sergeant, the boss, walked up to me and said 'Which one sold you the gear?'

I said, 'Um, Um, I'll have to look at them all.' I did believe that the trafficker was male. So that narrowed it down to seven suspects. All seven males had arms and both hands so I could not eliminate any that way.

I heard the boss ask the detectives to find out which of the Asians had the 'marked money.' We were all aware that the Asian in possession of the money used in the 'buy' may not be the trafficker, but it would certainly be of assistance to the investigation.

Unfortunately several of the males were in possession of large sums of money, probably for use at the casino. They were in a dog box of a flat, yet they all had rolls of cash that would have choked a horse – funny that.

Finding the money I had used was going to take time. I realised even if I found it that meant nothing as I saw nothing. I had two foils of heroin and no evidence.

I realised I was in trouble – and if I was in trouble someone else would soon be in the shit too.

I had spent $180 of the Carlton CIB Social Club fund of which the boss was the manager. I needed evidence in a hurry, so I resorted to a method I only used as a last resort.

It might sound ridiculous but over the years I found that when I am struggling or in trouble and the pressure is on, I have to stop, take a few deep breaths and rely on my instincts. I try and shut everything else out.

There were a couple of detectives who asked me to identify the trafficker. I just lifted my right hand without saying a word as an indication for them to wait.

It started to become obvious that all the detectives searching the flat realised that I could not identify the trafficker but no-one was prepared to admit the obvious.

Everyone was searching the flat and finding zip. I slowly started to walk through the three rooms observing each of the seven males one by one and they all seemed to be complaining about something.

I would like to tell you that as a trained detective I knew what I was looking for but it's not true. I was looking for a sign, anything that could give me a lead, help me catch a crook and save face.

I had no idea what I was looking for but I just hoped I could find something. I was looking for something abnormal, something that shouldn't have been there. You can only see that if you know what is normal and what is abnormal. Only then can you see the difference and recognise it. The hard part is knowing when you've seen it, heard it or at times just felt it. Anyway

The boss then called out for everyone to grab their gear as the flat search was over. He was not happy. I was not happy. I wanted to make someone else unhappy so we would be happy again.

I then saw one male being uncuffed by a detective. He had been lying face down on the carpet handcuffed behind his back. After uncuffing the male, the detective lifted the bottom of the bloke's pants, revealing a wooden leg from just below the knee.

The detective asked Hoppy if he was okay because he looked in real pain when the detective touched the leg. I started to walk on, then stopped and walked back.

I reached down and showed concern for his welfare. I then gently touched the male's leg with my right hand and he responded as if I had stabbed him. I asked if this bloke had been properly searched and was told he'd been strip-searched and was clean. The detective said to be careful of his leg as it must hurt like hell. But it didn't make sense, he was reacting like he lost his leg yesterday.

I then put my left leg on his chest and pushed him down to the ground. I then started to try and pull his wooden leg off. Now not being a medical man I didn't know the correct way to do this, so I just grabbed and yanked.

Hoppy started to scream like I was trying to rip off his real one. As I was trying to pull it off, he was pushing as much as he could to keep it on. It must have looked bad but I was not going to stop just because he was sooking-up.

At this moment Detective Inspector Norris arrived at the front door of the flat to inspect the damage. Whenever police damage property like we had by sledge-hammering down the front door an inspector has to view and photograph our handiwork. Apparently Inspector Norris asked the Detective Sergeant what all the screaming was about. I couldn't hear what he was saying because of the screaming. The sergeant informed him that Senior Detective Angus was searching one of the suspects.

The Inspector walked into the room I was in. He looked at me pulling on this male's leg. I could not get it off so I attempted to undo the velcro fasteners. I said to the male, 'For Christ sake anyone would think I'm cutting your leg off.'

The Inspector, standing behind me, said, 'What are you doing?' He was an officer and not that smart. What did he think I was doing, ripping a man's leg off for practice? I said, 'Searching the prisoner, sir.' Just then the leg finally came off. I removed the soft padding that went between the leg stump and the wooden section. The leg was hollowed out to allow for the stump to fit in. There was a small black plastic circle at the base in the middle of the leg. I pulled out a pen knife and dug it out. Nothing. The leg was clean and I was looking like a real idiot. It was going from bad to worse.

I reluctantly handed the leg back to Hoppy and he started to strap it back on. During the search of the leg I had pulled the shoe off the foot. As he was putting it back on I noticed a faint line that ran around the wooden leg just above the ankle.

I grabbed the leg back off him and started to unscrew the whole foot off the leg. There was a steel thread that joined them. When I got the foot off I looked inside the leg. I then pulled a plastic cover surrounding the thread and poured the contents into my right hand. Eighty-seven foils of heroin fell out onto my hand and onto the floor.

That is 87 times $90,which equals a lot of money and a bloody good pinch.

Needless to say the Asian male immediately stopped screaming out in pain. The act was over. The non-English-speaking
male said, 'Shit'. I looked down at him and said, 'That's the
man, I would recognise his hand anywhere.' The Inspector said,
'Well done Angus, keep up the good work.'

He was happy, the Senior Sergeant was happy and I was
happy but Hoppy was unhappy. Who cares?

Good things happen to those who are prepared to get in and
have a go. I call this pro-active policing – others would call it
pure arse. Hoppy was charged and remanded in custody. The
following day the boss came to see me because Hoppy's barrister was screaming blue murder. The boss said to me, 'Angus,
the crook wants his leg back, can you give it to him?' I said
quite gently, 'No boss it's an exhibit.' The boss said, 'It's his
only leg, Christ Angus you're a hard bastard, I'll put his barrister through to you.'

I am always prepared to be reasonable so he got his leg back.
Eighteen months later.

AT Carlton, I arrested a young car thief who told me he bought
his smack from an ethnic character living in the 20-story
Housing Commission block in Neil Street.

The car thief had no idea what flat he lived in. There were 200
flats, containing a large number of ethnic males who looked
like they could be drug dealers. They were probably all called
John.

The young car thief said he had been buying from 'John' for
two months. He also stated that John was missing his right
index finger. Now we were getting somewhere.

I had been told about this dealer by a number of people but I
had never been able to find him. The car thief said that when he

wanted drugs he would just go to the foyer area on the ground floor and John would turn up within 15 minutes.

My thief told me the dealer always had his own spotters to tell him when a customer was waiting. It may not have been as efficient as McDonald's but it worked.

As many local hoons frequented the area at the base of the flats, it was extremely hard for us to keep the place under surveillance. When police attended the area everyone would start whistling out loud. This was their alarm. Crude, but effective as the whistles would echo through the building and all evil activity would cease.

The car thief had $90 in his pocket, just enough to buy heroin. I arranged for him to have bail so he could go to the flats.

You guessed it, this job required a specialist – Dean Collie. I dug out the bag much to the amusement of all my office comrades. Steve and Deb decided to 'cover' me.

I cleared a small area on my desk for the bag to sit on. I placed the bag carefully on my desk, took a deep breath and held it. I turned my head slightly away and began to unzip the bag. At first I thought Dean wasn't too keen to come out. Then I realised it was only the wig caught in the zipper.

I then underwent the metamorphosis from Dr Angus to Mr Collie It was like a caterpillar turning into a butterfly but a lot more smelly. Dean had been in the bag a long time, too long. I mumbled, 'You're going to have to get out more mate.'

I pulled out the old cheap four star jeans. I had worn them out fishing and had wiped my hands down each thigh causing a large amount of blood and fish gut stains.

A long oily wig with a woollen cap on it came out. I then began to fill my cheeks with toilet paper. I filled my top and bottom lips with long thin rolled up piece of paper hand towel.

This made me 'lisp'. I had old cheap zip-up vinyl snow boots which matched the jeans perfectly.

The bag itself was a classic. It was dark green canvas stuck onto thick white plastic. Attached to this was a long adjustable strap. The outside of the bag was covered in blood stains and fish guts. The last thing to complete the change was an old pair of cheap 1960s sunglasses. They were square and only slightly tinted with black plastic frames. I found them in an old cupboard in the first house I bought. After the usual complaints, I was covertly dropped off in the area of the flats. I staggered into the foyer area that was filled with shitheads and appeared to be unnoticed. In fact, I felt quite at home.

I managed to sit down on the floor between what appeared to be puddles of urine. From my position I had full view of the whole foyer area, including the entrance. Hidden under my wig was a radio earpiece. My microphone was under my shirt. I radioed, 'In position, all okay.'

I began to wait for both the car thief and 'No Finger'.

A crook well known as Pud started to organise two of the other shit heads. I knew Pud had been a very close associate of the Walsh Street Crew who had killed two police in cold blood.

Pud had shot people before and was known as a hard bastard. He put one of the shitheads on the door as lookout, and asked the other to take command of the lift.

Pud gave him strict instructions not to allow anyone else to use the lift for the next five minutes. I attempted to ignore this situation and stick to my task of identifying and possibly arresting 'No Finger'.

The car thief then attended and began to wait.

I passed on the information on the radio of sighting Pud, that the car thief was there and that 'No Finger' was expected shortly. No-one took any notice of a vagrant talking to himself. I pulled out an old half-drunk bottle of port that I found in the bottom of my bag. To relieve the stress I opened it and took a sip. To my amazement it had actually improved since I had drunk the top half. It was no vintage rot-gut. I also drank from a large half-filled cordial bottle and rolled a couple of shitty cigarettes from an ancient packet of tobacco.

Pud then appeared from the lift well carrying three hi-tech video recorders and passed them to the next guy. They went straight into a late model Ford station wagon, followed by video cameras, boxes, silverware, china ornaments, paintings, etc.

I was then stuck in a huge dilemma. I had only briefed my back-up crew with the job at hand – No Finger selling heroin to the car thief. I knew that to suddenly change the plan from No Finger to a swoop on a burglary gang of three serious shitheads, two of them unknown, was fraught with danger.

The logistics of attempting to brief my back-up crew in seconds over the radio about what was happening around me was impossible. I made the decision not to attempt to change the whole plan and arrest these offenders. I believed I was making a much more professional decision in not going off on a tangent.

I know that in the past I had often got side-tracked and at times I had been criticised for it by some stick-in-the-mud senior officers. This time I was going to stick to the plan. I was going to be the total professional and nothing would deflect me from The Plan.

As I was watching these activities, I looked like the dero from hell. In the middle of this dilemma, while attempting to look to my left out the door toward the car park I felt a strange warm sensation around my right ear. I looked up to my right and saw that I was being pissed on from a great height. One of the shitheads I had been watching was pissing on me. I screamed and abused the prick. He was laughing, which caused other shitheads to laugh with him. He then got offended at the fact that I had the gall to abuse him. This caused him to kick me twice in the head area. I attempted to deflect the kicks. He walked off quite happy with himself.

I was in shock. I was still sitting on my arse. I looked down at the urine stain in disbelief. I definitely didn't become a member of the thin blue line to be pissed on.

I thought, 'Well Angus you put yourself here'. I looked like shit, acted like shit so they treated me like shit. While all this was happening I looked up and the car thief had gone. The three guys removing the stolen goods all left via the front door, laughing, got into the vehicle with the stolen goods and drove off.

I attempted to use my radio, you guessed it, nothing. The urine shorted the electronics. I got to my feet and walked out with nothing. I walked away and located my cover crew. They were eating fish and chips, chatting, having a great time. I walked past them, they followed me around the corner and picked me up.

I lay down on the rear floor of the vehicle. They asked me what had happened. I said, 'Don't fucking talk about it.' Deb said, 'We updated the boss that you mentioned something about stolen goods, and that Pud was involved.

I said, 'I decided to stick to the original plan.' Deb said, 'Well the boss was excited because he knows Pud from way back, he said he'd be a good pinch.' I said, 'He's gone, they've all gone.'

I got back to the office. I had failed at attempting to identify No Finger, missed a really good pinch, been abused by the boss for making the wrong decision in not having Pud arrested, and to top it all off, been pissed on. I was at the bottom of the learning curve.

Later that afternoon I spoke with an old detective who worked at my office, wanting to get some sort of confirmation that I had done the right thing.

He said, 'Angus, the bottom line is you fucked up. Everyone else sits around waiting to respond to reported crime, at least you get into it. I'll give you that. You did the next best thing to catching Pud, you now know how he operates. It worked for him today so he'll do it again. At least you were there with the chance to fuck up, you saw what no one else saw, so tell em all to get fucked.'

I said, 'Thanks, I feel much better.'

I felt like shit.

I WAS working a Carlton night shift when I got called back to the station to see a victim of an assault. He had been bashed while at a public toilet at 1.30am on Sunday.

I said, 'Were the assailants by any chance homophobic?'

He said, 'No.'

I said, 'So this wasn't a homosexual type bashing?'

He said, 'No, certainly not.'

I said, 'What is your full name?'

He said, 'Naughty Sea Monkey. My first name is Naughty, my middle name is Sea and my surname is Monkey.'

I just looked at him. I thought 'Be nice to the public, he's probably just scared of police and their perceived homophobic attitudes.' Call me a cynic but I wasn't sure he was giving me his real name. I asked for some proof. He gave me his driver's licence. It had his picture and his name. Apparently he had changed it by deed poll. Now I was faced with a dilemma. Should I call him Mr Monkey or be familiar and chat to him as Naughty.

I said, 'Did you tell them your name?'

Naughty said, 'No.' He said 'No' as if I had asked a ridiculous question. I looked at Naughty and the uniform copper, shook my head and left. I was not going to investigate anything reported to me by a Naughty Sea Monkey. If someone thought I was going to write that name on all the forms where the victim's name was supposed to go, not to mention my official diary, they were sadly mistaken. If I had to investigate a crime where this man was bashed, would it be a case of spanking the Monkey? I didn't want to find out.

IT WAS an afternoon shift and we were still three men short for an identification parade. We had eight men and one crook waiting to start the parade. It was a wintry Saturday night and I was very tired and pissed off.

Our crook was quite well dressed so we had to locate a total of 11 other men dressed in a similar way and from a similar class of life. In short we were looking for 30-year-old 'Yuppie' types.

I decided to have one last look down Lygon Street to see who I could find. I very politely asked several men but they were all said they were too busy. I was wearing my suit and my long Country Road cashmere-wool blend overcoat. It was getting late and I was pissed right off with the world.

Ahead of me was a large very scruffy shithead. I had almost walked past him when he held out his hand and stopped me. I stared at him.

He said, 'Give me a dollar for a cup of coffee.'

I said, 'Go away idiot.'

He took offence to that and said, 'Okay, give me all your money or I'll fuck your face.'

With that he stepped forward and held his right fist in the air about to strike.

I said, 'Here you go.'

I reached into my front right trouser pocket. He un-clenched his fist and held out his hand. I then gave him one .38 calibre semi-jacketed, hollow-point bullet. He looked at it carefully while it sat in the middle of his palm. It was as if he didn't like the look of it, but didn't know why. While he was trying to interpret its meaning, I exposed my .38 revolver in my shoulder holster.

I casually said, 'I can give you another one if you want.' He froze. I then whispered, 'Run'.

He ran. Fast.

It was good to be a detective.

CHAPTER 14

It protruded about two
inches out and made a mess
of his expensive disco shirt.

Nailing
the point

CARLTON was certainly different to St Kilda. Lygon Street was the home of the Aussie-Italian Mafia. It was different to St Kilda. In Fitzroy Street most crime was committed by junkies, but in Lygon Street the tough guys were carrying guns.

I was at Carlton CIB for three and half years. In all my time there they only ever shot unarmed men.

I was called to attend at St Vincent's Hospital one day. The call was 'Man with a gunshot wound'. So I attended. There he was. An Italian male of about 50, lying on his back.

He was conscious. Several of his relatives were sitting crying in the foyer. The doctor introduced me to him. The doctor then gently lifted a large pad from his upper thigh. This revealed a large black hole in the meaty part of his thigh. It was reddish in the middle with black sort of crusty edges. It was not a good look.

I could see faint black dots in his skin surrounding the bullet hole. These are known as gunpowder burns and means he was shot at close range. I guessed it was caused by a .45 pistol round. I asked him what had happened. This was his reply, with a very thick southern Italian accent, 'I was sitting in the cafe, drinking my coffee, when I look at my leg and she is leaking, she is a leaking on the floor. Ambulance bringa me here.'

I said, 'Did you hear anything?'

He said, 'No, I hear nothing.'

I said, 'Did you see anyone, maybe with a smoking pistole (I was good at Italian) in their hand?'

He said, 'No, I see nothing.'

The doctors and nurses could not understand why my partner and I were laughing so much.

I knew the cafe was probably full, and no one would have seen a thing. I knew that the only person that would have done it would have been the biggest standover man in Carlton, Alphonse Gangitano.

So I did something to indicate that us 'Skip' detectives, as they called us, knew Lygon Street, and knew what was going on.

I said to my partner, 'Let's go'. We both turned and started to walk out of the casualty area. As we started to walk past his relatives, I turned back to the leaking man and called out, 'Thanks again, sir. We'll protect you. We're going to go and arrest Alphonse, he could have killed you. You won't have to give evidence for a couple of months – leave it to me.'

Well, that caused the old relatives to fall off their seats and run into the room he was in, there was a lot of shouting in Italian.

My partner grabbed my arm and said, 'Are you serious?'

I said, 'Have you ever known me to be serious?'

He thought for a moment, then said, 'Good point.'

I said, 'Let's go to the cafe.'

My partner nodded: 'Good, let's check out the crime scene.'

I said, 'Don't be silly, I just want to keep the chair with the hole in it, for our office. It will be a good talking piece.'

Solving crime is one thing; collecting good souvenirs quite another.

MICK was a bad, mad Italian but a funny bastard. He loved to work in a crowd. It sort of made him more scary, deliberately wanting lots of witnesses to see his work. The more people saw what he did, the bigger his reputation became.

Many people think they are safe in a crowd. Anyway, one night there was a bloke called Gino dancing in a Lygon Street nightclub. He was having a great time jiving away, when across the dance floor came big Mick. The dancers parted, Gino tried to part with them, but there was nowhere to go.

As Mick got close to Gino he removed a six-inch nail from his inside suit pocket, put a 20 cent piece into the palm of his right fist, placed the six-inch nail between the first two fingers of the same fist, resting the head of the nail against it.

Then he punched the nail into Gino's shoulder, into the exact spot where John Wayne was always being shot. The nail embedded itself between bone and flesh, Gino could not pull it out. It protruded about two inches out and made a mess of his expensive disco shirt.

Mick casually spoke to Gino, 'Hang onto that, it will remind you to pay your debts. It's more effective than a piece of string around your finger. Con came to me with his problem, you owe him $500. Con then made it my problem. I make it your problem. You now owe me $2000, and Con nothing. Okay?' It was a rhetorical question.

Gino, contorted in pain, said 'Okay, okay, I'm sorry Mick. Thanks Mick.'

Mick casually walked out. In this instance Mick would probably give Con $100, as we all know it's $100 that Con would never have got anyway. So he is $100 better off.

Underworld logic.

What always makes me laugh is that Mick would never concern himself with the ethical dilemma of whether anyone actually owed anyone any money in the first place. That was never an issue.

I WAS at Carlton CIB and I was backing the CIB car out of the driveway when Felix walked up to the driver's side. I had recently charged him with committing deceptions on the Commonwealth Bank. He had persuaded a young girl bank teller to cash a stolen cheque. He was smooth; she cashed it, and was sacked. I took a statement from her while she was still crying.

Felix said, 'Can I please have my Commonwealth Bank book back? I can't get my dole money without it!'

I said, 'Just hop in the back seat, I'll take you down to the vet and get you put down.' I think I meant it.

My partner said, 'Take it easy, he's still a human being.'

I said, 'Prove it – has he got a certificate?' I thought, 'Christ, I've changed.' Who changed me? Us or them?

TWELVE months after I first became a detective, I got a call via the uniform branch to attended a burglary at a large company that sold nothing but surveying equipment. Very expensive equipment it was, such as theodolites and laser beams that architects and builders use to make straight lines, all missing. Some of the items were worth thousands of dollars.

I called there and spoke to the owner.

He said he'd just finished doing a stocktake and found he was missing about a hundred grand's worth of equipment from the warehouse. He suspected that one or some of 10 employees – six storemen, three sales people and one manager – was responsible for stealing the equipment.

He had no idea how they had been able to steal the gear as none of the storemen had keys or access to the property after lock-up time. This was a warehouse that held well more than a million dollars worth of stock.

I sat down with him and asked him for a list of everyone that worked for his company, including the storemen. That is where my investigation began.

Out of the six, one had a few traffic offences – .05 matters – obviously because he'd had a drinking problem at one stage.

One had a wife that had been arrested for shop stealing. One had a sister that was in a de facto relationship with a drug dealer. The computer tells all, but one thing an investigator must remember is that a computer only knows what you tell it.

One of the workers was Robert King, born 12/11/64, of Humber Road, Coburg. I did the usual checks on driver's licence, gas and electricity records, Telstra, Vodafone and Optus, but nothing came up. I couldn't find anything about him. He was either from Mars or he was up to something. We confirmed his home address, as the owner had dropped him home after work about a week before. Everything at his home address was in his de facto's name. On the computer the de facto came up clean.

I observed King on the day. He was a strong-looking bloke of medium build who was covered in tattoos. He seemed to be quite cheerful and friendly when I first spoke to him the first morning I was there. I had a good look around the warehouse. The owner showed me around the various areas where the items had gone missing. Some of the items were taken from boxes while, in other cases, the thieves had taken the whole crate. The boss said he believed even more things were gone, but he wouldn't know for sure until he completed his final stocktake.

I went back to the office and continued my enquiries. I strongly believed that King was using a false name but I had no idea about his real identity. I considered attempting to get his fingerprints from coffee cups but then decided on something equally sneaky. I decided to conduct surveillance on the company. My partner, Darren, and I decided to sit down the street in a beaten-up old vehicle and keep an eye on what was going on.

I said to Darren, 'If you worked in the warehouse with security everywhere, how would you get the gear out?'

He said, 'Get a copy of the keys, security codes, come back late at night.'

I said, 'It's got to be more simple than that, it's got to be someone in the warehouse area.'

I started thinking aloud … 'Storeman puts more on the truck than is ordered, he arranges that with the truckie, truckie puts it somewhere? That's too complicated for the average idiot. We always give them too much credit. Look for something simple.'

After about 20 minutes surveillance I observed King walk out and throw some paper into the large industrial steel bin, outside the back door.

I said, 'How simple is that?'

Darren said, 'What?'

I had worked out how the thief might have been doing it, and as if to prove my theory, at that moment King walked out of the delivery area again carrying a small box. As he approached the bin he looked back over his shoulder and carefully placed it the bin as though it was quite precious.

I said, 'Shit, I hate daylight saving.'

I started to drive off back to the office and said, 'King's our man. We have to take out a search warrant, get all our equipment ready, organise manpower and plan the raid.'

Darren said, 'Okay, but where does daylight saving come into it?'

I said, 'It's 4.15pm now. It's not going to get dark until nine, so he won't be back to retrieve the gear until after then.'

As we drove I said, 'We know who and how but we don't know where he's hiding all the gear.'

After organising the raid for the next morning we did surveillance on the company. Sure enough, King turned up at about 10pm, removed several boxes from the industrial bin and put them in his car. He drove off and we started to follow him. As we headed towards Coburg, in the distance behind us we could hear a police car with its sirens blasting. As it got closer to our vehicle and King's, he panicked and took off at high speed. He zoomed down several side streets and we lost him. The cop car just kept going past. I was pissed off at King for losing his cool – if he was a better crook all would have gone to plan.

We then drove past King's house but his car wasn't there. We had only attempted to follow him to see if he dropped the stolen goods off somewhere else or simply took them home.

I believed that I'd solved the case and hoped to get a large amount of the equipment back for the company. Darren made the comment that it would be 'a bloody good pinch'.

I really wanted to know who King was and why he had been so secretive about his past. I had a feeling it was more than trying to avoid tax.

As I we were driving home I said, 'Open your mind and try and think how in the hell we're going to find out where the gear was. He couldn't hide it under a bed, he's taken it by the truck load.'

I went home that night having organised six of us to conduct an early morning raid on the house. I had quite a sleepless night as I was very excited and why shouldn't I have been. I was about to crack the big case and be a hero. I woke at 3am, had a bright idea, jumped out of bed, picked up a pen and wrote a note on the inside of my wrist before going back to bed.

Anyway, with the excitement of it all, I got up early and we all met at the office around 4am. We drove out there in three different vehicles and snuck up to the house to find the de facto's car in her driveway. I knocked on the door so quietly you could hardly hear it, then turned and whispered to the sledge-hammer man, 'It looks like they don't want to let us in, you better hit it.'

Sledge-hammer man looked back as if to say 'I was always going to hit the door, you whacker, just get out of the way.'

You see, we are always supposed to knock first, allow them to answer the door, but it's better to just cave it in. Three or four hits later we went running through the house.

The lady-of-the-house was sitting up in bed. We ran through the house screaming 'clear' and other cop things to find that she was, in fact, the only one home.

She started screaming that her boyfriend hadn't come home that night, so I was quite disappointed at not getting our man in the house. We started to conduct a very thorough search of the premises, looking for stolen goods, but we couldn't find any.

One of the search party found some catalogues belonging to the surveying company King worked for, but no stolen goods.

I kept searching the master bedroom, looking for paperwork and looking for all sorts of things that might identify our person and his true name.

We'd been there about 45 minutes when I casually looked under the bed in the master bedroom. It had one of those bed spreads that go down to the floor with only a very narrow gap under the bed. So I knelt down, lifted up the bedspread and peeped under. There looking at me about six inches from my face was Kingy.

In fright I screamed, 'Ahhhhhh,' and so did he at the same time. I fell backwards, jumped into the air, then on top of the bed, ripping my gun out of its holster and screaming at the top of my voice: 'Police don't move!' while pointing my gun at the bed. Now, although I didn't know who he really was or why he was hiding, it didn't stop me dancing on the bed, pointing the gun, screaming for him to put his hands out where I could see them.

I was scared he had a weapon and could have shot me, up through the bed (I don't know why I thought that but I did), so I'm dancing around screaming at him. Every other copper in the house came tearing into the bedroom as well, to see me dancing on this big double bed, pointing a gun at the bed screaming, 'Put your hands out, put your hands out where I can see them.'

They all thought I was mad until the hands came out from under the bed. I jumped off the bed, stood on both of his hands, put my gun away and handcuffed and dragged him out from under the bed.

He had actually shit himself, I mean literally. I almost did, too, so I knew how he felt … almost. We walked him to the bathroom, he walked slowly with his legs wide apart as you would if you had just placed a deposit in them. Anyway, we put him in the shower with his cuffs on.

I spoke to him, he was a hard-arsed, bad-arsed, smelly-arsed bastard who said no comment to every question. He was a general prick. We finished the search, nothing.

King kept saying, 'What is going on? I've done nothing.'

Well, he had. In his pants.

All I had at this time was observations of King placing something into a bin outside his work. I could not prove he had stolen anything, or was guilty of anything other than being in possession of dirty underpants.

There was nothing in his house. I was considering the fact that I might have to let him go when Darren, who had left the academy more recently than I had, told me that we had seen him driving unlicensed the night before.

I then realised that gave me the power to hold him until I was satisfied of his identity. With all the checks that I had done I had grounds to believe that he was not Robert King, born 12/11/1964. I said to Darren, 'I knew that I just hadn't thought of it yet.'

There was nothing more to be done at the house, so we walked him, in handcuffs and a fresh pair of strides, to our car. I informed his de facto that he was only coming back to our station so we could find out who he was. I informed her that the only charge he was facing was unlicensed driving. I knew our power of arrest only existed while we didn't know who he was.

The whole time I was asking him questions about where he had the $100,000 worth of surveying equipment he had stolen. He almost convinced me he was innocent. Or so he thought.

I put the 'kiddie lock' on the back door, and placed King in the back passenger seat. A prisoner never sits behind the driver for obvious reasons. The other detectives all started leaving. I put King's seat belt on and closed the door so he couldn't hear what I had to say.

In a last desperate effort to nail this prick, I looked at Darren in and said, 'We need to find the gear, mate, or he walks.'

Darren said, 'I've checked everywhere. His roof is clear, nothing under the house, the secondhand dealers haven't got any of it, we've got nothing.'

We jumped in the car and headed off as the de facto farewelled us with a mouthful of abuse. We got about a kilometre from the house when, all of a sudden, I had a flashback. I looked at the inside of my forearm and my mind flashed back to what had come to me at 3am.

I told Darren to do a U-bolt back to the house. Darren and King thought that I must have forgotten something. I wouldn't tell them exactly why I wanted to go back, mainly because I didn't want the crook to know the game was on again. When we got back, I said to the de facto that I had forgotten something and walked in before she could think.

In the middle of the hallway was a telephone on a little table. Next to it were two Yellow Pages, A-K and L-Z. I picked them up, and headed back to the car. No, I wasn't going to beat a confession out of him. That was Plan B.

King's arms were still handcuffed behind his back. I sat next to him and placed the A-K on his lap. Smiling from ear to ear, I said, 'Where should we look – S for surveying or E for equipment, B for building – where should we start?' He tried to kill me with a look, but it didn't work. He looked at the roof and closed his eyes. He didn't say a word. He didn't need to.

I then looked under B – nothing, then I looked under S for surveying and 'Bingo' – two pages covered with hand-written notes such as 'Ian the manager' and notes on when and where to meet various people, and what they were interested in buying.

He'd quoted theodolites at $1200 each.' The pages were covered with incriminating writing. The names of each person at each company with ticks and crosses next to them. There were notes on who wanted to buy what, when and where.

I couldn't help but smile from ear to ear as I realised we had all the evidence we needed to account for all the missing equipment stolen over the past 12 months. I said, 'Are you still innocent? I'll just ring, umm, Phil of Coburg Engineering … Is Phil there … G'day, Phil, it's Robert King's brother Jim, I wondered how the theodolite Rob sold you is going … great … do you need any more …' I mimed hanging up on the call and said to Darren, 'Best we pay Phil a visit.'

We were elated but there was one loose end. 'You would be that stupid. I'll let my fingers do the walking – where could you hide a heap of stolen gear?'

I opened the book at the 'Storage' section. Only two storage companies were marked with a blue pen, one was crossed out, the second had prices and names written next to it.

We turned right and headed to his storage hideout and I said to him, 'Now all we need is to find out who you are.'

King sat there and growled.

We drove to the long term storage centre and located a large storage container in the name of Robert King. Sure enough, it was half full of the stolen surveying equipment. It was a great pinch. We were able to identify him via his fingerprints. Just as I thought, the King was really a knave – he was wanted in Perth for a vicious abduction rape. No wonder he wanted to be anonymous.

Later, while we were having a coffee, one of the crew asked, 'What the hell made you think of that?'

I said, 'Well, I thought of it about 3am and I wrote it on my arm but, when I had a shower it washed off and I'd forgotten about it until after we left the house, then it came back to me.'

Which means the crook almost got away with it because I like to be clean.

CHAPTER 15

You could have knocked him over
with a feather. I would have rather
knocked him over with a baton.

If I were
a rich man

I HAD been stationed at Carlton CIB for almost 12 months when a fellow detective told me I had a phone call on line one. It was Clive, a local solicitor, who was also a good friend.

We were often on opposite sides, but found we had similar interests. At the time we were both attempting to carve careers in the criminal industry. This carving was hard work and it required a large amount of lubrication. Clive's end-of-financial year office parties every June 30 were legendary. Anyway, back to the story.

When I picked up the phone this particular day it was a very worried Clive on the other end. He asked me to come to his office as soon as possible. He said he was missing one of his titles. I asked, 'Which one? The solicitor or the barrister bit?' He didn't laugh so I hung up. As his office was about 50 metres away, I was there within seconds.

Clive introduced me to a Mrs Lorraine Cornell. He told me he was responsible for looking after the title to her home. This lady was on the verge of tears. She told me how she had received a letter addressed to a Mr Samuel Wise of her address. As she had never heard of him she opened the letter. It said, 'Dear Mr Wise, congratulations on the purchase of your new home situated at 13 South Crescent, Northcote.'

She sobbed, 'That's my home and has been since July, 1971. Now Clive tells me that my duplicate title is missing from his safe and that is not my signature.' She pointed to an entry in a large ledger.

I looked at Clive. He was clearly in shock. Clive explained that whenever he takes possession of a title he signs it in through the ledger. I asked whether he believed someone had broken into his safe and signed out a title.

At that moment he was not the fearless defender of innocent criminals, he was a very real victim. Most of all, he was a nice bloke. I felt proud that he asked me for help. It would not have been easy for him to call. He knew he had become a victim of the very people he was sworn to defend. I knew that we would laugh about it at some stage, but now was not the time.

It turned out that Clive was not insured for this type of theft, and it was ultimately to cost him many thousands of dollars.

I shot back to my office and rang the author of the letter, a Patricia somebody of the Commonwealth Bank. She confirmed she had provided a Mr Wise with a substantial loan to buy the Northcote house.

I told her the loan was fake and the property was owned by Mrs Cornell. She said the loan was in order and she had the title to prove it.

The loans officer looked in the file to find the amount was $175,725. I asked her to keep quiet about the matter while we got on with trying to catch the mysterious Mr Wise. At this stage I was at my desk in my office on the first floor above the Carlton uniform police station. While everyone else involved in the case was shattered, I was rapt. It was incredibly exciting for me because it seemed like the biggest investigation ever.

It was a burglary, a theft of $175,000, and, best of all, a safe breaking. And it was all mine. I was in charge of the crime, which meant that I got the crooks. I would get to interview them, charge them and run the prosecution. The better the crime the better the crooks and the more difficult the trial. This challenge was huge. I turned to the other three detectives in the office and couldn't resist bragging. 'I've got a good one.'

It soon dawned on me that I had problems. I was by far the most junior officer at Carlton CIB. I was a detective constable by name only. Every time I picked up the phone and said, 'Carlton CIB, Detective Constable Angus speaking,' I was stealing the title 'detective' as I had not completed the three months intensive training at detective training school. This meant that my new investigation was open to being poached. I knew I should play this one close to my chest. but, of course, I couldn't. That was not in my nature and it was all too exciting.

I must now mention my next problem – detective sergeants. Real detectives, let alone new plastic ones like myself, have to report to them non-stop. Sergeants are supervisors and can only supervise properly when fully apprised of all the facts. Therefore it was a detective's duty to keep them in the dark as much as possible so that when we stuffed up it was never their fault.

Our office had three sergeants. One had transferred, one was on a day off and the third was a worry. Let's call him Rinse. He was the sort of sergeant who never let you forget that he was a sergeant. He thought he was God's gift to women and had a much higher opinion of himself than we did. He was never wrong, happy or nice and friendly. He would never listen to anyone. I tolerated him until one morning when it all went pear–shaped.

He walked in and sat at his desk. He had permed his hair and dyed it a reddish strawberry-blond colour. The hair alone was making a fashion statement without equal, but he had added bright-red suede shoes.

A CIB office was supposed to be full of tough detectives. Rinse was seriously assaulting that theory. He looked as if he could have had his own float at the Mardi Gras in Sydney.

Rinse was not around so I walked into the boss's office, followed by several sticky beaks. The boss stopped writing, looked up with trepidation and said, 'Angus, just give me the cake – not the recipe.'

I told him of the safe break in a solicitor's office and the theft of $175,000. I added that they were obviously bloody good crooks.

The boss reluctantly said, 'I suppose I need the recipe.' I knew he would. I told him and the others the story as it stood. As the boss dismissed me he finished with the mandatory, 'Keep me up to date.'

My mate, Johnno, somewhat reluctantly followed me down to the car park. I noticed that he had hesitated in the boss's office behind me. This indicated to me that the boss gave him the nod after I left. That nod said, 'Johnno, keep an eye on him for Christ's sake.' I didn't have to go to detective training school to work that out.

After several almost green traffic lights we arrived at the bank. A flashed badge or two later I was speaking to Patricia. I again informed her that a Mrs Cornell had had her title stolen from her solicitor's office and the bank had sent a letter to a Mr Samuel Wise congratulating him on the purchase of his new house.

Patricia stood firm, saying she had given a housing loan to a Mr Samuel Wise and the loan was in order. The bank manager, a Mr Scott, then joined her. They were prepared for my visit. They had the file in their possession and informed me the loan was in order and that there was no need for concern. I informed them that the owner of the house was very concerned as she has not sold or bought her house in the past 20 years. Her duplicate title had been stolen from her solicitor's office and she had never heard of Samuel Wise.

Patricia didn't get it, or perhaps she didn't want to. She said, 'We, the bank, hold the title. As I have said, the loan is secure.'

I asked her if she could identify this Mr Wise. She said, 'Of course, I interviewed him for the loan.'

She said she had requested identification, but he said he had lost his driver's licence for drink driving. He assured her that his licence was to be re-issued in a fortnight.

Then she said something that shocked me. It was not bank policy to request identification during a loan application.

I asked, 'How much did you give him?'

She got her nose out of joint. 'It is not a matter of give. The loan was secure, all the documentation was in order and a loan for $175,725 was approved.

'On the 19th of July I was assigned to conduct settlement of the purchase of the property. It was conducted at the Law Institute of Victoria.

'At the Law Institute I gave a woman who said she represented the vendor's solicitor the bank cheque. I checked and it was cashed the following day.'

I said, 'You gave a bank cheque for $175,000 to an unknown woman for a person that said his name was Samuel Wise to buy a house and land that belongs to someone else and it was cashed the next day.'

Patricia started to see the problem. Then Mr Scott tried to take over. He said the bank would conduct an investigation.

Now it was time for me to pull rank. I told him, 'This is now a criminal investigation. We have no idea who Wise is or how many times he has done this, so I must ask you to keep this to yourself and please do not speak to anyone. It looks like the title has been stolen from a solicitor's safe and there may well be more. I will speak to you soon so please don't talk to anyone.'

They agreed without hesitation and we left.

When obtaining the loan Samuel Wise said he was employed by an engineering firm. The letterhead on his documentation gave the address of a suite in Clarendon Street, East Melbourne. I decided to drive there, as it was only two minutes away. As I pulled up out front I realised that this address was directly across the road from the Victoria Police Internal Investigations Department, as it was called then. I commented to Johnno that they might be able to assist the investigation. He did not agree. He didn't want to go anywhere near the toe cutters. We walked upstairs, slowly and quietly looking for the engineering firm. There was none.

I stopped outside a door. There was a big sign on it, that said:
Girl Friday Secretariat.
A Division of Woods and Woods Pty Ltd.
We are a Secretarial Agency providing Telephone Answering Telex, Facsimile messages and typing services.

I opened the door. Inside was slim, young woman working flat out. She was standing in a semi-circle consisting of 16 telephones. Each phone had a bright yellow sign on it. She would answer the phone by stating the name of each company and finishing with 'Can I help you?' She politely held up one finger indicating that she would only be a minute. I held up my police badge to her and walked forward.

On one of the phones in the middle was the name of the engineering firm and the names of six of its supposed 'staff members'. One was the mysterious Mr Wise.

The phones finally stopped for a second and we introduced ourselves. She was not surprised by our visit at all. Obviously, many of her clients were the type that interested the police. She showed me a list of messages. As we were talking the phone rang. She picked it up and said, 'Douglas Mitchell Engineering – can I help you?'

On a message pad in front of me she wrote,

To Douglas Mitchell, August, 89

Mr Scott – Commonwealth Bank

Re Samuel Wise loan

I took the phone from her ear. I heard Mr Scott pleading: 'I really need to talk to him.' I interrupted, as I really had to growl at the bank manager. 'Mr Scott, I warned you. I told you not to contact anyone.' Within a second I went from extreme anger to real pity. Mr Scott was responsible for approving the loan and he felt his job was in jeopardy.

I felt sorry for him, but there was nothing I could do. I said I would charge him with attempting to pervert the course of justice if he made any more calls which could stuff up my case. He promised me that he had not rung anyone else. Once I had made him a lot more upset I let him hang up.

It was obvious to me that the house of cards was falling and we had to catch a crook ASAP or he would go to ground, never to be seen again. With a shit load of someone else's money, of course.

On returning to our office, I found Rinse and Inspector Peters being updated by the boss. I immediately informed them that the crooks had cashed at least one bank cheque for $175,000 at the Bank of Melbourne in Bourke Street .

Sergeant Roberts walked into the room. They were more coppers there than at the police picnic. The boss had called her at home and she came in to assist. She was fantastic.

She had done heaps of very large investigations and I knew that if she were involved this job would be done professionally. She was the daughter of the well-known Judge Roberts.

As I spoke with her, Clive attended downstairs. He informed me that 10 titles to properties had been stolen from his safe and they had all been signed out in his Deeds Register.

He went on to say the signatures appeared to be written in the same pen and handwriting.

The boss called for a briefing involving the whole office. Sergeant Roberts was quite a bit senior to Rinse (thank Christ) so she took charge.

The briefing started with Inspector Peters stating, 'I want you all to know that crimes committed in Carlton's area for the next four days will be handled by Russell Street CIB. You will all be able to work on this operation together without worrying about anything else.'

Inspector Peters asked the boss what code name he had given the operation. I called out, 'Operation Sting, sir.' I made it up. I was good at that stuff. So Operation Sting it was.

Four extra detectives were seconded from nearby CIB offices to assist.

Sergeant Roberts had a full-time log keeper placed on the

door of our office to note down the date, time, name and the designated job of each investigator as they left our office.

The investigation grew with every inquiry. The Bank of Melbourne revealed it had actually cashed well over a million dollars worth of bank cheques in the previous two months.

This cash was given to a Mr John Champion of John Champion Conveyancing.

We had everyone compiling face images of John Champion, Samuel Wise and a Robert Freeman. All the images were different – but they still could have been the same person.

I don't recall how that first day ended, but it did. I didn't sleep that first night thinking of how we could get ahead of the crooks.

Every time we tried to trace them it led nowhere. Paperwork we had seized had been analysed for fingerprints. The print expert stated that there were glove prints on the paperwork consistent with common dishwashing gloves. It became clear that the longer this investigation went the less likely it was that we would catch the crooks.

Another thing that became clear was that these crooks were good. Too bloody good.

Halfway through the second day of the investigation our office was pumping. Two members of the Major Crime Squad turned up. I briefed them. The safe breaking made the job fall within their parameters. They didn't really like the part where I explained how the crooks had broken into the safe, stolen the titles and then locked it again without leaving a trace.

I got the feeling they needed it to be blown up with dynamite or similar. This job had too much of a paperwork, deception, statement-taking nightmare attached to it to interest them.

The majors officially designated the job to us. (In other

words, if I had told them the full truth they would have taken it in a second.) The bottom line was the crooks had stolen titles to houses from a solicitor's safe, and then organised a crook to attend at a bank to obtain a loan to purchase the property connected to the title.

It was obvious to me the crooks were very professional. The documentation in support of the loan was often completed before the loan was sought.

What amazed me was that the crooks could obtain a loan for $200,000 within four days! I had recently bought my first home and it took over a month for all the checks and authorisations – and I was a cop.

The crooks had officially registered five businesses, specialising in property, engineering, financing and conveyancing. They had the lot covered.

On top of this there was at least one courier picking up documents and messages. One thing that gave me hope was that they had completed re-direction orders on each of the properties sold which allowed the scam to keep going.

Several of the fake loans had their monthly payments made in advance. It was obvious the crooks still had loans pending. The problem we had was that we could not telephone each and every bank in Victoria. We had no idea what names they were going to use – only names they had used in the past.

I left my name and number at every place I visited. The crooks were using a secretarial services to receive all their messages and mail. They would telephone the service up to six times a day to obtain their messages. This was 1989 and we had no way of quickly putting a telephone intercept in place. So we were stuck with pure old fashion investigation techniques. Spooky, eh?

I arrived home at about 12.15am after completing 17 reports and making hundreds of inquiries. We had no idea who the crooks were or where we could find them.

By this stage the investigation was worth over $2 million and involved 17 homes. I drifted away for an hour or two. Then I lay on my back looking at the ceiling for another two hours and went to work early.

I decided the courier was our best bet. There were only three places that he could turn up. They were the two secretarial services offices and the suite in Drummond Place, Carlton, which was the business address of John Champion Residential Conveyancing Specialists.

At 3.42pm I answered the phone in our office. It was Maria, the manager of Drummond Place (John Champion's office). She told me there was a courier waiting and I asked her to try to hold him up.

I put the phone down and screamed that I needed a car, but the boss said they were all out. Funny, when you want a police car you can never find one.

Drummond Place was about 500 metres south from our office so I took off. While running full bore down the street I realised I hadn't put my jacket on so my shoulder holster, revolver and handcuffs were exposed.

I felt like Mel Gibson in a *Lethal Weapon* movie, but without being run over by cars or being shot at by machine guns. As I ran into Drummond Place I saw a bloke in his early 20s leaning next to a green Commodore in the car park of the office block. As I gasped for air I said, 'Detective Angus, Carlton CIB, there's been an armed robbery around the corner. Hold your hands away from your body.' He politely obliged. I patted him down. Nothing.

I said, 'What is your name and address?'

He said, 'Andrew Smythe, Station Street, Port Melbourne.'

He did not appear the professional type at all – just an average guy.

I asked him a few basic questions and he told me he was 24 and worked for Mr John Champion of Residential Conveyancing Specialists.

He answered freely and innocently. If he was a crook, he was a cool one. I reached into his vehicle and removed several large envelopes from the front passenger seat. The first envelope was addressed to: The Manager, State Bank, cnr Bourke and Elizabeth Streets, Melbourne.

Smythe told me he had been told to deliver the document. I asked if he could ring Champion, but he said it was the boss who rang him.

As my partner drove up next to us and stopped I decided it was time to be a Dirty Harry type of copper. 'I don't have time for polite fucking around. Do you understand?'

Young Andrew nodded. I knew he looked like a smart fellow.

I said, 'This is important, where can I find John Champion?'

He said, 'I've only met him once, when he interviewed me in his office over there. At the interview he gave me a key to a box at Spencer Street Railway Station.' He then pointed to an A4 size piece of paper that was in between the envelopes I was holding. I looked at the document. The instructions began with the words strictly confidential.

That was a good sign.

He said, 'Mr Champion rang me this morning and told me to go to the box and get this. That's how I know what to do for the day. He also gave me a car phone, but it's not working yet.'

The document instructed Andrew to attend at both secretarial agencies and pick up mail and messages. It then told him to go to Drummond Place. It then read, 'Must deliver yellow envelope to the manager, State Bank, Melb, by 4pm.'

I told Andrew we needed him to come back to the station. I asked him to drive me back in his car while my partner followed. Andrew was happy to assist. He was no rocket scientist, but he obviously knew he had been doing something shifty for a long while.

On the way back in the car he told me that one of his jobs was to pick up security bags full of heavy documents from the Bank of Melbourne. He told me how he would place these documents into the box at the station.

He had no idea that these documents were in fact cash, bags full of folding cash.

I know this because he went on to tell me how proud he was to be paid his wage in cash. He said that he always got an envelope in the box with his instructions that contained $120 in cash. In new, crisp notes!

He was rapt. He went on to say that he was highly paid so he did a good job. No doubt if he'd known what was really going on, there soon would have been one missing courier.

Back at the station I placed him in an interview room. I updated Sergeant Roberts in the presence of the whole office. When I got to the letter of instructions I stopped and thought. There is always a first time for everything.

I looked at my watch. It was 4.06pm. I quickly picked up the phone and dialled directory assistance. I then rang the State Bank, Melbourne. I introduced myself to the receptionist and asked to be patched through the manager.

She said Mr Tilson was far too busy in an interview to be disturbed. 'Is it a loan application?' I asked.

'Yes, and he cannot be disturbed,' was the stern reply. She was good at her job, but I wasn't half bad either.

I started to get stern and told her to round up the assistant manager.

I heard her call out, 'I've got a detective on the phone. It sounds important.' It was in the days before they had intercoms, but still had staff in banks.

A bloke named Timothy Rodan jumped on the blower. It was not the time for a long chat.

'I am Detective Angus from Carlton CIB, and this is important. I need you to tell me who your manager is talking to right now,' I blurted out.

He said, 'He is in an interview and I cannot disturb him. I will get him to ... '

No wonder half of them ended up getting retrenched.

I cut him short and said, 'I believe the person he is talking to right now is responsible for stealing more than $1 million. I don't give a flying fuck what his name is today, but I need you to look at the documentation and tell me what company he represents. But please don't mention anything about police at all.'

There was a silence at the end of the phone. I turned to the other detectives in my office and whispered, 'he's checking who the manager is with right now.'

Moments later a voice said, 'Are you there? I don't know his name but he is employed by Douglas Mitchell Engineering.'

I said, 'Right. Now, listen to what I have to say: surround the interview room, hit the armed robbery alarm button, and for Christ's sake don't let that bloke out of the bank. We will be there in one minute. Have you got that?'

He understood. Finally he had got with the program.

I hung up the phone and yelled to the boss, 'We've got one of them now in an interview with the State Bank manager, Bourke and Elizabeth.'

Grabbing equipment, we ran in all directions. Ross called, 'I've got keys.' So I followed him and after a short argument he tossed me the keys.

From there on it's all a bit of a blur. I can sort of recall my partner sticking the magnetic blue flashing light onto the roof. It came off during one of my turns. The magnet must have been weak or something. The cord and light became jammed under the front driver's-side wheel arch and was making a crunching grinding noise. Not good for the duco.

The next thing I recall is driving south down Elizabeth Street up to the intersection with Bourke. I saw the State Bank and aimed for it. I can't remember why, but my partner was scream-ing. I entered the intersection sideways. Luckily the uniform policewoman on duty was able to stop all the traffic. She then ran and dived out of the way and lived to tell the tale.

It was at that moment that I realised I was not driving a high performance pursuit vehicle. It was, in fact, a four cylinder Toyota Corona with wheels as thin as pizza cutters, and they weren't slowing me down much at all.

Luckily we hit the gutter almost sideways, leapt into the air and stopped on the footpath. It worked out quite well, as I don't think we hit any cars or pedestrians at all. It would have been hard to explain wiping out a crossing full of office workers in a high-speed fraud investigation.

We ran down the escalator to the main banking area. Flashing my badge, I made my way through the crowd of bank security guards and uniformed police. I met with assistant manager Rodan.

I pointed to a closed door. 'Is he is still in there?'

Rodan said, 'Yes, he is still with the manager, the manager has no idea what is going on so … '

I cut him off for a second time, making a mental note not to go to him for a house loan.

I flashed my badge at the guards on the door and they walked out of the way. I stood still for a moment. It's moments like these that you never forget. If they were all like that I would still be a copper.

I looked at my partner. There was nothing to say. I can recall the next few moments vividly. I remember taking a couple of big deep breaths in an attempt to calm down.

It didn't work so I opened the door anyway and casually walked into the small room. It contained two men seated at a table. The table was covered in our target's letterheads.

The person who was obviously the bank manager had just finished asking a question. Our target was in the middle of answering him as I walked in.

The first thing I noticed was that he was an Orthodox Jew. The second was that he had a very strong Canadian or American accent. He stopped talking and looked up at me.

I dropped my badge onto the table and said, 'I'm Detective Angus and you're under arrest for the theft of about a million dollars.' I stepped forward and grabbed both his sleeves lifting him to a standing position.

'You are not obliged to say or do anything, but anything you say may be taken down and given in evidence against you. Do you understand that?'

He said nothing. He just looked at me.

I said, 'Do you understand what I just said?'

He still remained mute.

I held both of his arms in the air as I began to search him. The first thing I found was a small spiral bound notebook. As I flicked through it I asked him his name and address.

He just looked at me. He didn't look sad, angry or upset in any way. He did everything I asked except speak. He had the Jewish hat, the long London Fog overcoat, a grey two-piece suit, brown silk tie and brown shoes.

His notebook looked damning. It contained pages of notes detailing seven different identities with dates of birth, addresses from NSW and current addresses in Melbourne.

It contained questions he was likely to face during bank loans and appropriate answers. I said, 'Well, who's a naughty boy then?'

This was by far my best arrest ever and I was enjoying the moment. You can go a lifetime without catching anyone red-handed, but this one was right on the money.

The best bit was that no-one could wish for more evidence than this. I thought it couldn't get any better than this. I was wrong. I lifted his hat off. I noticed there was a skin-coloured substance smeared in the inside rim of the hat.

I looked at his head; I then wiped his bonce near the hairline. It was make-up. At the risk of stating the obvious I said, 'Your head is covered in make-up. Why?'

No answer.

I said, 'Everything is false – your past, your clothing, the lot. What a classic. Let me guess, you're about as Jewish as the Pope, aren't you?'

Later, we were to find the make-up was Revlon Foundation natural beige, commonly used for covering skin blemishes. He used it to colour the freshly shaved head, which was designed to give him the Orthodox Jewish look.

The office filled with cops. When Sergeant Roberts walked in, I updated her, without the unknown male hearing. I showed her all of his personal belongings.

Amongst the items was a small plastic RACV tag with Drummond Street, North Carlton, written on it. But no vehicle registration number.

Sergeant Roberts said, 'I'll have someone check it out and we'll get a warrant.' She told me to find out what car he was driving, his associates and a million other things.

I informed her he wasn't 'assisting me with my inquiries.'

She told me to find out if he had prior convictions, whether he was on bail and all that other copper-type stuff.

She was smart, but this time she wasn't with it. I said gently, 'No, when I say he's not saying anything I mean nothing. Not a yes or a no. Not his name – absolutely nothing.'

I went on to tell her that he was speaking English when I walked in and that he spoke with what I thought was either an American or Canadian accent. He stopped talking, looked at me and turned into Marcel Marceau. She said she'd have a go. She tried everything short of using the phone-book. He just gave her that same blank look.

Detectives stayed at the bank to find out as much as they could. Three of us drove him back to the station. On the way back I began to think how good these crooks were. Again, this whole job stank of top-quality crooks with good legal advice.

I thought the idea of saying nothing was a pretty good way of telling your criminal associates that you were not talking. It had never happened to me before (or since, for that matter) and by Christ it was annoying. I've had heaps of no-comment types but never one who wouldn't say a word.

I know some suspects left the interview room not remembering their names, but I didn't know of any who would refuse to identify themselves from the start.

I knew that we now had to catch the co-offenders as soon as possible or they would destroy evidence and do a runner. We were desperate to find out everything from our man, but he gave us nothing.

I wondered if anyone had seen me do that low-profile entry into the bank. I imagined one of his associates seated in a vehicle nearby, with the engine running, watching us arrive the way we did.

I was worried my loutish entrance might have spooked them off. As it turned out I was to find out days later that we hadn't.

There was no co-offender nearby. Unknown male drove himself there and his vehicle was parked around the corner, although we didn't identify it for two days.

We hoped this meant none of his criminal associates knew he had been arrested and were still going about their criminal ways. You can't catch a fish if they won't bite.

We arrived back at the station. I tried every interview technique I knew. Then I tried a few others that I just sort of made up as I went along.

At one stage I went and got a cup of coffee. On my return I found a much more experienced detective than me, applying, I mean trying, another technique that I hadn't thought of. Still nothing.

At first we were trying to get him to say something incriminating, even name his associates etc. But after a while I would have been happy with 'Hello'. In the end I tried, 'Sorry, I forgot. Was that sugar or no sugar in your coffee?' Nothing, not even an ouch.

I'd heard of Alaskan malemutes. They're a breed of dog, like big huskies. But this was a Canadian male mute – and he was no dog, at least as far as his fellow crooks were concerned. He soon became known officially known as the Unknown Male. I asked Sergeant Roberts what was found at the address he had in his pocket.

She said she hadn't heard from Sergeant Rinse for a while and he was in charge of that side of the investigation. Right on cue the man of the moment came in and went straight into a deep conversation with Sergeant Roberts.

I couldn't wait to be brought up to speed as I needed something new to put to my pet mute. The two started to have serious words. It did not sound good. Rinse looked washed out as he stormed out of the room.

Sergeant Roberts told me the wonder-boy went to the address – a huge, expensive terrace house in North Carlton. He sat off it for a while then walked up to the front door and knocked. No-one answered so he entered with the keys we found on the crook.

Sergeant Roberts continued with the story, but I sensed there would be no happy ending. Apparently, he was in the middle of the house when a man walked in the back door and found him. Rinse identified himself as a detective sergeant and said he wanted to know who lived there.

'Good,' I thought. A bit of tough talking from a straight ahead copper with a warrant and the law on his side.

Err, wrong. No warrant. To make it worse the man who walked in was a solicitor. And he didn't answer any questions. He ordered Rinse out of there.

I was speechless. I could not believe it. This was to reverberate through this investigation for the next three years. More about that later.

I knew the crooks would be destroying every bit of evidence they had. As soon as we learned any addresses connected with the scam we would get warrants and head out to carry out raids.

We went to John Champion's office in Drummond Place, All Property Transfers in Bouverie Street, Carlton, and the secretarial agencies. At these locations full crime scenes, fingerprints and photographs were done.

The acting mute kept acting and we kept on asking him questions. After two hours he began to smile a bit. All of us could only be serious for so long. I charged him with conspiracy to steal $2.4 million and the actual theft of $1,256,850.76. It took me 10 minutes to write out the amount.

I emerged from the interview room after interviewing myself in the presence of the acting mute. Sergeant Roberts informed me that Sergeant Rinse was out executing the warrant on the solicitor's home with several other detectives. Even if it was too late.

Moments later Rinse arrived back at the station. He walked in and informed us all that he could not execute the warrant, as it was a warrant to search for evidence. This type of warrant could only be executed during daylight hours. From sun rise to sunset. He informed us that sunset was officially 6.32pm and he was not ready to execute the warrant until 6.38pm. He told everyone that it was too late.

I could no longer contain myself. 'Officially? Who officially gives a flying fuck. Let that be argued in court – evidence first, and the six-minute-late argument later,' I said.

'Whose side are you on?' I asked, rather lamely.

Sergeant Roberts stopped me. I didn't like Rinse, but he outranked me. How anyone with dyed, strawberry-blond permed hair and red suede shoes could outrank me was beyond me. At least I had my mute. I escaped back into the interview room and continued to interview myself in his presence.

It took a while, but eventually I got sick of answering my own questions. Anyone who knows me would know that would take some doing.

The acting mute appeared relieved when he was charged and remanded in custody to appear next morning at the Melbourne Magistrates' Court.

We had fingerprinted our man and had him checked against our records. Nothing. I then requested his prints be checked via Interpol, in particular America and Canada. I was told that would take some time.

At 10am the next day we took him to court. With us were several detectives and Inspector Peter Harvey, a good bloke for an officer.

The irrepressible and most entertaining Chief Magistrate, Darcy Dugan, was presiding over the courtroom where the action happened. He wore his bright bow tie and a big smile. He was a great entertainer and a bloody good magistrate. This case was made for him.

If they had been serving drinks inside the court it would have been as good as Vegas. He must have read about the Unknown Male and brought it to the front of the list. As soon as Darce sat down he had the case of the Unknown Male called before him.

When the case was called a young blonde woman stood up in the court and said, 'I am Diana Cotter from Pat Dwyer's office. I represent the Unknown Male.' As this happened our Unknown Male was brought into the dock from the holding cells.

The prosecutor, Senior Constable Mick Berkley, then called me to the witness box. I then told the court about the arrest of this Unknown Male and the evidence against him. I informed

Mr Dugan that in excess of $1 million in cash was still missing. Magistrate Dugan was not impressed at our silent friend. Mr Dugan asked Ms Cotter, 'Have you spoken to your client?' She said, 'Yes, yes, I have.' Mr Dugan asked the obvious. 'Did he give you his name?' She shook her head and said, 'No.'

Mr Dugan looked at the Unknown Male and told him to stand. He did what he was told – for once. The larrikin magistrate said, 'Are you going to tell us who you are?' The answer was no.

Mr Dugan said, 'You're not doing yourself any good. If you want to apply for bail you are going to have to give us your name. Why don't you be sensible about it?' He remained silent.

Darce then said, 'Do you want to speak to your solicitor?'

He replied, 'No.' He was then remanded in custody. This was perfect for our silent friend.

It was going to be all over the media soon and everyone in Australia would know our man was not talking. All his criminal associates would have had time to hide and destroy incriminating evidence.

He was not going to get bail anyway, so not talking did not disadvantage him at this stage of the legal game.

I walked up to Diana and introduced myself as she left the court. I wanted to know how she came to represent our man in the first place. She politely refused to comment. A lot of people were telling me nothing. I was not happy.

At this point her boss, Pat Dwyer, walked in. I knew Pat well from other cases and felt I could be frank. I told him what I thought about what was going on.

Inspector Harvey also knew Pat well. The two of them had a huge disagreement. Harvey said Pat had to know the name of his client, but Dwyer said that an envelope with $2000 in cash turned up at his office with instructions to represent the Unknown Male.

At this time we still had about a dozen detectives working flat out on all aspects of the thefts and deceptions, as well as trying to identify our man.

Word then came in that Interpol had matched the fingerprints of our man to a George Eugene Papp, born 03/06/1958. Papp had one prior conviction in Ontario, Canada, in 1980, for theft and deception.

I went with Harvey to the City Watch House to say, 'Hello George.' He sort of grimaced. You could say it was a bit of a Papp sneer.

George then spoke about the weather, his cell, us, his family – everything but his co-offenders or his crimes. He went so far as to inform us that he was innocent. I responded, 'Well sorrrreeeey … Guards, let this man go free. We got the wrong bloke.'

George laughed.

We now had someone to investigate. It turned out George Papp was a top chef. He had worked at some of Melbourne's best restaurants. He had come to Australia nine years before with his parents.

By all accounts he was a friendly, likeable bloke with a smiley, happy disposition. One of his friends did say, however, that he had a lack of respect for authority.

Later that day the legal section of the Fraud Squad arrived. I didn't even know we had one and I certainly didn't know what they did. I was to find they specialised in investigating and prosecuting bent solicitors. I didn't fully understand how good these guys needed to be to do that job until later.

We gave them a full briefing. They looked over the whole job and decided they would take it on. Inspector Harvey asked me if I would like to be seconded to the legal section of the fraud squad to complete the brief. I wanted to hang on to the best case had seen – so I went.

Detective Sergeant Greg Payne, Detective Senior Constable David McInnes and I worked on the case. I was under the impression that the Fraud Squad worked from 8.30am to 4.30pm weekdays only. That they stopped at 10am precisely for morning tea and took the full lunch hour. The legal section was the opposite of this theory. We worked huge hours finding out all sorts of good shit.

A lawyer named Edward owned the address on the keys found in George's pocket. Edward worked as criminal lawyer, but also specialised in conveyancing. He ran his conveyancing business in Brunswick with his next-door neighbour and business partner, Fat Joe.

Joe was a very well-known and serious criminal. He and his two brothers specialised in blowing up safes. They often blew up most of the building around each safe as well. They were best-known for posting large amounts of dynamite through the posthole in night safes in banks, thus blowing up the safe and everything else around.

They found that most of the money was being burnt in the explosion. So they then set about posting in several balloons full of water through the letter slot of the night safe and then the dynamite. The theory sounded fine, but in reality it made large amounts of paper mache.

Joe's most famous crime by far (up until this one) was when he tunnelled under a bank in Coburg. Somehow the major crime squad got onto it. They watched for two weeks as Joe and two mates started digging a large tunnel right under the bank. They did the digging in the middle of the night. They concealed the entrance to the hole with a large steel plate, then covered the plate with a metre of gravel.

It was like something out of an old prisoner-of-war movie. When they were observed carrying several sticks of dynamite into the hole it was finally time for the 'majors' to move and the team was arrested.

The only appropriate charge was attempted burglary. Joe defended himself and beat it. The other two were found guilty. Joe did a great job in the court but he did get two years' jail for possession of several sticks of dynamite, luckily located in his office filing cabinet across the road from the bank. Just bad luck I suppose. Sometimes I miss the major crime squad

After we worked on affidavits in support of several search warrants a magistrate authorised them. These affidavits had to be rock solid and watertight, as they included the home address of the solicitor Edward and his wife and the next-door neighbour, Joe.

Joe was living with a barrister – no wonder he was a good jail-house lawyer.

After a month of warrant and affidavit preparation it came to the crunch. We needed 38 detectives to execute six warrants.

My job was to assist with the search of Joe's house. It was about 7.15am when we knocked on the door of his palatial home. It was very similar to Edward's house next door, but a lot bigger.

Fat Joe had done well. His house was a beautiful, fully-renovated, two-storey Victorian home with a servants' entrance. We stood at the front door and knocked a bit louder. I had to remind myself that we were with the fraud squad and therefore we should knock politely. We didn't smash restored Victorian doors down with sledge hammers and run in like lunatics. The door opened. Fat Joe looked very surprised. He could not believe we hadn't smashed his door down. I felt like the Avon Lady.

He actually asked to see our badges again because he couldn't believe real detectives would knock. Neither could I.

Joe said, 'I don't know what to say. I'm normally bashed and handcuffed by now.' He said you could have knocked him over with a feather. I would have rather knocked him over with a baton.

Joe was a large bloke and his purple dressing gown didn't suit him. He has one of those 'I know everything and you're a dickhead,' sort of smiles. This time he was right; the search was about a month late.

We entered. Then down the stairs came what appeared to be a very angry fire-spitting dragon. I later found out she was not angry or upset or even a dragon. It was Joe's bedmate, and she was apparently always like that. She was dressed in a long black court gown and carrying her white horse hair wig in one hand and a brief with a purple ribbon around it in the other. She also had a handbag over her right shoulder.

She didn't look great, but she scrubbed up better than Fat Joe. She ever so politely spewed vile verbal abuse at us while trying to push past me. I stopped her. She went right off the planet.

I explained to her that we had a warrant to search the premises and that included what she was carrying. I took her brief and removed the purple ribbon. My actions would later become the subject of much debate.

The lady barrister and the neighbour-come-solicitor, Edward, claimed privilege in regard to numerous documents we had seized.

So only hours later I found myself under cross-examination. I was also examined during various investigations after she and, of course, Joe, complained to the Internal Investigations Department.

The world is a spooky place. Coppers could bash Fat Joe and he accepted it as part of the game. I grab a brief and they want to put me in the Star Chamber.

I had to choose my words carefully. I scanned the documents for evidence. After being satisfied that they were not evidence pursuant to the said warrant, I handed them back. No, I certainly did not read the documents, I scanned and searched them for evidence. The English language is a wonderful thing. It turned out that Dragon-Lady was in the middle of a rape trial and the brief contained her notes and clients' instructions. Or so I heard later.

I never did find out what sort offence I had committed, but, as a detective, I knew that whenever you feel as if you've done something naughty, you should avoid, deflect and flat out deny anything the defence wants you to admit.

Joe's home was thoroughly searched. During this search we found something that made me feel sick. You know how you feel when you look down over the side of the Spirit of Tasmania as it steams through Port Philip Heads and your favourite sexy-looking sunglasses fall off your face into the drink, or when you walk out your front door and your driveway's empty because your car has been stolen.

Well, that is how I felt when I looked out Joe's back door and into his backyard.

The side fence dividing Edward's and Joe's properties had been removed. At the rear of Joe's yard was a large portable office. It had big glass front windows. It was complete with tables, chairs and a couple of broken typewriters. It even had its own small kitchen and toilet. It was the same type of office that can be found most large construction sites.

I walked forward and smiled as I saw two pairs of pink dish washing gloves on the ground outside the office door. I paused for a moment and easily imagined what it would have been like when it was running red-hot.

This was where several months of hard criminal activity had taken place. It was also where Edward had been just before he walked in through his back door and found Sergeant Rinse. But we won't go there. He didn't.

It turned out the raiding, I mean searching, party next door had missed Edward. He had left for work earlier than they had. We arrested him as he entered the Melbourne Magistrates' Court later that morning. He became most upset as he was searched and handcuffed.

We then found a beautifully polished, hand-crafted, push button flick knife (made in the USA) in his inside suit coat pocket. It was like something out of *West Side Story*. We went back to his house and found several firearms. This was one serious solicitor.

We seized mountains of paperwork from both addresses. The Dragon Lady and Edward claimed privilege regarding all of the documents. We had to deliver all of the boxes of documents to the Melbourne Magistrates' Court.

The defence argued that we were not allowed to read the documents. We argued that we had to scan and search the documents to see if they were relevant to our search warrant. Once we promised that we would not read the documents they were handed back to us.

No matter how often we scanned the documents we couldn't

find enough evidence to pin Fat Joe, so we had to let him go. Months later we were still taking statements from witnesses and victims. It turned out the crooks had stolen a total of 16 titles to houses from three separate solicitors' offices.

All of these offices had alarms and safes; all were broken into without leaving a trace. At the crime scenes we had hundreds of fingerprints unidentified. They were all eliminated one at a time as they were found to belong to bank staff and others who had legitimate access.

I received three letters from the fingerprint branch asking me to explain why my prints were on documents.

Anyway, there was one unexplained, unidentified print left. Fingerprint expert Gary William Bell developed a latent fingerprint on the handset of a telephone. This print was found on the underside of the handset of a phone located in John Champion's office at 21 Drummond Place. Now, the only time we could ever find that Champion was in this office was when he interviewed the courier Andrew Smythe.

What was interesting was that no phone call was ever made from that phone at the time. So the crook must have picked up the phone, then realised that he better not call out from it as the number would be recorded, then put it down.

That slight lapse in concentration was to prove costly.

I kept myself busy finding photographs of tall professional criminals who could be the mysterious John Champion. But it was Gary Bell who struck the blow, identifying the man through fingerprints as one Paul Rancic.

Two days later we raided Rancic's home and arrested him. He was a real cool professional criminal. He was about 190cm tall, of medium build and carried himself as though he was superior to all of us. No wonder so many witnesses thought he was a solicitor. But then we strip-searched him. He was covered in tattoos and scars. He dropped his shoulders a bit and turned back into what we call in the trade, a scumbag. But definitely not your average one.

In January, 1992, the trial in the County Court began. All but one of the 238 witnesses were ready.

Several months into the investigation I realised we had not seized the courier's uniform that Andrew Smythe had been issued by the crooks. So I drove around to his Port Melbourne home. A young woman greeted me at the door. I introduced myself and said, 'May I speak to Andrew Smythe?'

She said, 'No, I'm sorry. You had better speak to the Homicide Squad.' That didn't sound good. I said, 'Why should I do that?'

She said, 'Because he went missing, believed murdered. You better speak to them.' I almost fell over. It turned out that Andrew had been at home one minute, and was gone the next. His house had been all smashed up and he has never been seen again.

When I returned to my office I walked down three flights of stairs and into the Homicide Squad. They informed me that he was missing, believed murdered, over a domestic dispute involving him bashing his girlfriend.

We all believed our crooks were great murder suspects. It turned out they were right and we were wrong.

Years later they found what was left of Andrew in the foundations of a bayside house. The woman who owned the joint didn't know she had been walking on a murder victim for more than 10 years.

Anyway, the trial started and was expected to run for two to three weeks. Ten weeks later we were still going. After three full days the jury was almost about to start when one of the women selected opened her hand bag and handed the tipstaff a summons.

She said, 'You better hold onto this until I get called.' She was a teller with the Commonwealth Bank and one of the witnesses in this same trial. Not only was she extracted from the jury but every person that had been in the jury pool with her over the previous three days had to be discharged and sent home.

Eventually Paul Rancic pleaded not guilty. George Papp put his hand up at the last minute and pleaded guilty. The court decided to hear George's plea first.

The jury was stood down until the plea was over. So for two days George's barrister told the court how guilty and sorry poor George felt. Then right at the end of the plea George jumped the box.

This time there was no barrister talking for him; the words were coming out of his mouth. George explained to the court how he had no idea at all that what he was doing was wrong.

He explained how he was just doing his job. He was employed by his friend and solicitor Edward to conduct some secret surveys on banks and that he thought everything was above board.

Until then I didn't know you could lose a plea of guilty. The judge then explained to George that when you plead guilty you actually have to say you did it. That was not in George so off to trial we went.

I found the trial was great fun in the beginning, but the fun certainly didn't last. If anything in the case was done, should have been done or wasn't done it was my fault.

At one stage I was accused of planting the only real evidence against Rancic. The defence actually accused me of placing

Rancic's fingerprint on the telephone in the office of 21 Drummond Place. They said I found one of his fingerprints then picked it up using sticky tape and placed the print on the phone handset.

If I wanted to plant evidence it would have been against one of the main players, not against someone like Rancic.

Rancic's defence was full-on. They attacked me, my credibility, my professionalism, my parentage, my dress sense – the lot. If they weren't attacking me for what I had done they would turn on me what I hadn't done.

No-one at the trial, especially the jury, ever entertained the notion that George was innocent. The first exhibit the jury received was an unsigned personal copy of George's greatest photos. If his guilt was ever questioned the prosecutor would just ask them to examine the photographs taken of George on the day of his arrest. They were trial-winning photos. I loved them.

Photos and photo identification boards played a large part in this trial. In the five months leading up to the fingerprint identi-fication of Rancic, I prepared 14 separate identification boards. Every time a new suspect was identified I would get his photo, cut his head out and stick it in a folder with 15 similar heads.

After so many suspects I decided to burn a couple of witnesses by showing them a single photograph of one of my suspects. It didn't work, so I went back to compiling folders. Like all serious trials they tend to find the truth.

Two witnesses gave evidence that I had shown them a single photo of a male. So the defence called me back into the box and grilled me like a chump chop.

They forced me to admit that I should not have showed them a single photo, as that was not what I was taught at detective training school (I had been to the course since the investigation began in 1989). It was a stupid thing for me to do. I told the jury that at the time I was desperate to find out the identity of John Champion.

The defence tried (and succeeded) in making me look foolish. When the jury finally left the court to deliberate they only came back to ask one question.

That was, 'What dates did that idiot Detective Angus show the single photographs to the witnesses?' I then realised the jury would now know there was no way known I could have planted the fingerprint and then spent five desperate months pretending to look for its owner.

After a few weeks of being called back into the witness box and being grilled about conversations and things I had done three years before, I recall thinking that if we won the case I would scream out 'Yes' and high five myself in the middle of the court.

On 13 April, 1992, the jury finally entered the court and found them both guilty.

It was an anti-climax. All I felt was relief. The judge then asked the jury to remain in court while Paul Rancic's prior convictions were read out. This action by the judge was quite rare. The jury appeared to be relieved when they heard he had a lengthy criminal record.

Just as Rancic was being led out of the court, he stopped, looked at me and nodded his head. I took his nod to be a handshake, and a gesture that it was nothing personal. My nod said the same. George just slunk away. He had not earned my respect at all.

Some time later Joe met with and asked investment advice from a close friend of mine. Joe had lost his share of the money in a failed attempt to develop a large portion of land near Melton. That's karma for you. Or for him, anyway.

Edward left Australia and flew to Poland just after we searched his house. Warrants of apprehension were filed at the Victoria Police Criminal Records Section with his name on them.

Rancic came out jail after serving a six-year sentence with a four-year minimum. He had well and truly earned his portion of the cash pie.

I had arrested George in the middle of his first attempted bank loan. He had made nothing so the crooks gave him nothing. So for his extremely offensive haircut and crimes against the state he received four years jail with a two-year minimum. Not to mention, of course, his photo in this book.

Mind you, he was unlucky to be tied into the whole scam. The only proof that he was connected with the entire dastardly plan, rather than just part of it, was a single fingerprint.

You'd never guess where we found it ... or maybe you would. George, it seems, was a well-brought up little Canadian. So, when he'd used the toilet in the temporary office set up in Fat Joe's backyard, he lifted the seat first. We found a partial print of his right index finger on the bottom of the seat. He hadn't left a print anywhere else, but some habits are hard to break.

At the conclusion of the trial a barrister representing all of the defrauded banks prepared to make good the acquisition of the properties.

The banks argued that the owners of the houses that had their titles stolen were responsible for the safe keeping of them and should suffer the loss of their properties as a result.

I informed the barrister that I was contacting Channel Nine's *Current Affair* and 3AW's fearless fighter for freedom, Sly of the Underworld, and I was sure that they would be interested to hear about this claim.

A short time later they dropped off and removed the caveat they had placed on the properties almost two and a half years earlier. They were all heart.

Paul and George went to jail. Fat Joe kept his purple robe and no doubt went back to crooking. I went back to Carlton CIB. I had learnt heaps about how to, and how not to, collect evidence but, most of all, I learnt why trials are called trials.

To think it all started with a postman delivering a letter that he shouldn't have and a woman who opened that same letter when she shouldn't have.

ONE of the many boxes of documents found in Joe's home contained old stained blue paper. On this paper were hand-written notes which outlined a cunning sting that involved stealing titles from solicitors' safes.

These safes apparently stored unencumbered titles. These notes bore the fingerprints of two well-known criminals. One was Joe and the other was Gregory John Middap, also known as Gregory Chase. I researched Joe's history and found they just happened to have shared a prison cell for over two years.

What a coincidence.

CHAPTER 16

My heart will always
be with The Job.

Looking back

ONE of the most dramatic changes in policing I saw in the past 16 years was the introduction of audio-tapes to record police interviews. In the formative years when I first joined the job when you caught a crook you spent about four hours typing a police interview.

This was due to the fact that we were mostly two-finger typists. During this time you could get to know them, build up a rapport. We had the old-fashioned massive manual typewriters. I recall often having the crook leaning over the interview room table trying to work out where I was up to.

Often the crook would speak so fast that you would have to tell them to slow down and at times, 'Do I look like your secretary? Shut up a second.'

I recall saying, 'You said something good a minute ago what was it again?' Often I would be typing something the crook said five minutes earlier. I would have to type out my question, ask it and then type the answer. It took hours. We would stop for a smoke and a coffee. At these times I found that you could get a glimpse at the real person inside the tough bullshit exterior.

If they trusted or feared you – or best of all trusted and feared you – they would inform on their criminal associates. Informers made the whole legal system go round. It was that simple – the best cops had the best informers. The more criminal the informer, the more up to date and relevant his information. In all my years the best informers were the crooks that gave you information because it was fun. They enjoyed the exciting, covert, secrecy of it all.

I often thought they felt like undercover cops while they snuck around spying on their mates, making sure they would not be identified as the 'leak'. It somehow made them important and clever in what was actually an uninteresting often stupid world.

In the late eighties the typed interview was abolished. All interviews were taped. This, in conjunction with computer technology, meant that you could arrest, convey back to the station, process, bail or remand well within an hour. All conversations must be taped, or it cannot be used in evidence.

All this made sure that no professional bond was ever made, no-one got to know or understand each other. My view is that this lack of communication has caused a massive breakdown in police training. The most important type – on-the-job training.

If a crook looks at a cop and sees nothing but authority, a robot in uniform, how can either learn anything? The greatest loser is the cop. He or she must learn to understand why, what, when, who, where and how crooks think. To become a good crook catcher, you have to understand all these things.

One of the greatest lessons I learnt was to always underestimate your target. I've not come across Lex Luther yet. In the main, crooks are stupid, lazy, alcohol or drug dependent, idiots. That is why they are crooks. They can't survive in mainstream society so they fall to the fringes. But we coppers will always over-calculate their mental capacity just in case our unemployed drug addicted loser of a target is streets ahead of us. They are playing draughts while we are playing chess.

To become a good detective or a copper of any sort, you have to have extensive experience. The more crooks you catch and process, the more you learn. Learning how to collect admissible evidence is paramount. The only way to learn that is to live through hundreds of court cases. Cops learn heaps from crooks, barristers and the whole court system.

The better the barrister, the better the cop. I used to love hearing a criminal say that they had a top barrister. I took it as a challenge.

Every time I was cross-examined by the likes of Brian Rolfe or Robert Galbally, I learnt heaps.

A good barrister always attacked you on all your weak points. I would make sure no barrister ever caught me out again in that way.

After years and years of this, I found that I could put together a brief of evidence that would stand up in court – at least most times.

I enjoyed giving evidence. Sometimes I didn't want the perfect case because the bastard would plead guilty and what would be the fun in that?

I SPENT almost seven years as a senior detective in the Drug Squad. I was both an active undercover operative and an investigator. All our targets were high-level drug suppliers and traffickers. They always had heaps of cash. This assured great (meaning expensive) legal representation.

Like all police everywhere, the Drug Squad hunted in packs, using all methods – undercover operatives, audio tapes, telephone intercepts, cameras, videos, telescopes etc. All witnessed by numerous police witnesses.

Our evidence was on the main very compelling. This meant that the barristers only really fought long and hard at bail applications and to minimise jail time during sentencing.

Committal hearings were often designed to attack police witnesses and minimalise their client's criminality. The committal was held at the Magistrates' Court to test the evidence. The full trial would be held later at the County Court.

If the defence barrister ever touched upon any evidence it was by coincidence. Barristers always found it impossible to argue against extensive audiovisual evidence.

The evidence was often far too embarrassing to mention in open court. Thus pleas of guilty often followed later at the County Court.

ON retiring from the force after 16 years I've had cause to reflect. I feel privileged to have been allowed to be part of an incredibly professional organisation.

I became passionate about catching criminals, this helped me work undercover and become a detective. I first began working undercover in Fitzroy Street, St Kilda. In early 1986 I was a uniform constable. I was chosen to work plain clothes in special duties and at the local district support group. I immediately started purchasing small amounts of heroin around the St Kilda Cafe area. I continued to purchase heroin and other drugs as an undercover operative right up until April, 1999.

I was issued Covert Operative Number 004. I may not have

been James Bond and I didn't officially have a licence to kill, but at the time I felt my job was very important. I felt invincible. I was getting paid to live in another world. To live for a little while in my own real live action movie.

To lie about everything. The only truth I could not forget was that I was in fact a cop. But of course I had to lie about that but inside, I would never forget. If I did I would be no good as an undercover or as a copper. You had to remember which side you were on.

Being an 'Undercover Cop' was the ultimate in adrenalin pumping action.

But it was not a movie, it was real. It took me from my first job, buying $90 heroin, to my last job, buying the same amount for a $20 heroin deal in April 1999 to realise I was nothing more than a tool. A tool to collect and present evidence at court. The detective investigator used me to collect evidence just as he would use a listening device hidden in a criminal's home or a telephone intercept or an informer. It was all about the next case and the next pinch.

To me, pulling off an undercover job against difficult career criminals was the best rush you could get. No person knows what a cop goes through unless they're a cop and nobody knows what an undercover goes through unless he or she has done it. And that includes cops.

So many people think that a cop that grows a bit of a beard and wears scruffy clothes is undercover. They are not; they are cops in plain clothes.

A real undercover is different. They are trained and registered. They're real people working a real job in a totally bullshit world and at the end of the day they just so happen to be cops. They play a role that might last weeks, months or years. They infiltrate to betray. They become liked by their targets.

They drink and laugh together. But the undercover knows he is there to betray them. If he makes a slip the case could be dead and so could he.

Always the police investigators want more, want him in deeper. One more buy, one more tape before the big bust. You are an actor with no audience. You go home sometimes and don't know who you are.

Are you a policeman? Are you a family man? When you socialise with real people and they ask you what you did during the week you do what has become second nature. You lie. You can hardly say, 'Oh, I bought half a kilo of smack while pretending to be a drug buyer from interstate.

No wonder you go half mad in the end. There is no danger money, no extra pay of any sort. When I was undercover on the Pettingill family I got paid the same as some fat arse senior detective in an outer suburban station.

That stinks and it should be addressed.

On one occasion I was in the witness box at the Melbourne County Court. I was giving evidence against a large-scale drug trafficker. The defence barrister commenced his cross examination with, 'So you're Undercover Operative 004, using the assumed name of Lenny Rogers correct?'

I said, 'Yes.'

He said, 'It's not Lenny Rogers is it, so you lied to my client about your name?'

I said, 'Yes that is correct.'

He said, 'You lied to my client about what job you did?'

I said, 'Yes.'

He said, 'About where you were from?'

I said, 'Yes.'

He said, 'Why you were there?'

I said, 'Yes.'

He said, 'You lied about where you were going and where you had been.'

I said, 'Yes I did.'

He said, 'But you expect this court and in particular this jury to believe you, a professional liar, you are a professional liar aren't you?'

I said, 'Well.'

He said, 'You lie and get paid to do it don't you?'

I said, 'Yes.'

He said, 'Let's say you tell us a lie right now, now to the court, do you think the jury could tell that it was a lie.'

I said, 'I would not lie to this court.'

He said, 'Spare me Mr Rogers or who ever you are, you have been a professional liar for years, that's right isn't it?'

I said, 'Professional liar is a bit harsh, I have been an active undercover operative for many years, yes.'

I LOVED giving evidence, it was always fun. It was fun living and working in the grey areas of life. I found that time often blended truth and lies together. It was often very hard mentally coming to terms with being an undercover operative working within the legal system and the police force.

The ramifications it had on my personal life were far greater. I found it a constant battle, trying to work out what my personality was, what my true feelings were, true morals and to remember who I was. For a time I think I lost me. I spent so much time being other people, all of whom were not very nice. It took me many years to find the answer. I finally found out that all of the people I played as an undercover were me. Their personalities and thoughts were me, it was all me. I wasn't ever lost at all. They were all different parts of the one person that we all carefully keep apart.

Only when I realised that then did I truly become what I believed to be a good undercover operative.

Lenny Rogers was me, no acting required.

The best part about being undercover is being in a safe place afterwards.

Just after a good job I would think, 'Am I as good as I think I am?' If I weren't the most egotistical bastard that ever walked, I wouldn't do it. I felt like a zebra walking into a lion's den commencing to convince the lion that I was not a zebra at all but in fact another striped lion. If I didn't believe – believe is not strong enough – if I didn't know I could walk the walk and talk the talk, I wouldn't be there and I wouldn't be here.

If I couldn't convince myself, how could I convince them?

In the undercover world, 'Money talks, bullshit walks.' These words are often used but in my shadowy world they were very true.

Undercover cops sell the most valuable product in the world, themselves.

Being an undercover cop was often a delicate balance between being sane enough to convince the police shrink you can continue and mad enough to actually continue. I never let sanity get in the way of a good undercover job.

If I was asked now, 'What was the best part about being a cop?' I would say, 'Catching crooks, covertly, overtly, in uniform, a suit whatever.

Driving fast cars and catching crooks. And getting paid to do it is good as well.'

Now I have left the force I realise I have been injured by what I have done. By coincidence I recently met another undercover cop at a hotel in Prahran.

We ignored each other for about an hour just in case one of us was on a job. Finally we signalled the fact that we were off duty. He was a very successful U/C who had done some very large protracted undercover jobs.

After a few beers he said to me, 'Are there some jobs you shouldn't have done?' I said, 'Yeah mate, a couple.' He said, 'Me too.' I was on the verge of tears. I felt somewhat relieved at the fact that I was not alone.

We were both injured in similar ways. I told him that I had left large chunks of my chest at several undercover meetings. I will never get those bits back. The wounds are internal and permanent. Hopefully time may help. I don't know.

Now that I have resigned, I am one of them not one of us. I have left the Brotherhood. So often the Brotherhood has been spoken of as a bad thing.

It is not. I was one of a band of brothers working to protect and serve the public. That will never change. My heart will always be with The Job.

What's left of it.

FRAGILE

Bangkok Airways